Zabel

WESTFIELD MEMORIAL LIBRARY
WESTFIELD, NEW JERSEY

O9-BUA-130

CELEBRATIONS

🌲 OF 🌲

CHRISTMAS

Have Better Homes & Gardens® magazine delivered to your door.
For information, write to:
ROBERT AUSTIN, P.O. BOX 4536, DES MOINES, IA. 50336.

WESTFIELD MEMORIAL LIBRARY
WESTFIELD, NEW JERSEY

CELEBRATIONS ♠ OF ♠ CHRISTMAS

A Family Workshop Book
By Ed & Stevie Baldwin

Chilton Book Company
Radnor, Pennsylvania

745.5941
Bal

863764

Copyright © 1985 by The Family Workshop, Inc.
All Rights Reserved
Published in Radnor, Pennsylvania 19089 by Chilton Book Company

No part of this book may be reproduced, transmitted or stored in any form or by any means, electronic or mechanical, without prior written permission from the publisher.

Library of Congress Catalog Card Number 85-47831
ISBN 0-8019-7447-x
ISBN 0-8019-7448-8 (pbk.)
Manufactured in the United States of America

Created by The Family Workshop, Inc.
Executive Editor: Janet Weberling
Editors: Suzi West, Mike McUsic, Robert R. Hill
Art Director: Wanda Young
Production Artists: Janice Harris Burstall, Roberta Taff, Rhonda Wells
Typography: Kathy Dolbow
Project Designs: April Bail, D.J. Olin, Ed and Stevie Baldwin, Jan McKinney (Caftan), Jolinda Brattin
            (Rainbow Wreath & Stocking), Julie Stefani (Dress-Me Bears), Mary Seigfreid (Super
            Crepe Creche), Suzi West (Pinata)
Photography: Bill Welch
Photographic Stylist: April Bail

The information in this book is correct and complete to the best of our knowledge. All recommendations are made without guarantees on the part of the authors or publishers, who disclaim all liability in connection with its use.

The Family Workshop's catalog of project plans is available for $2.95 from: The Family Workshop, P.O. Box 1000, Bixby, OK 74008

1 2 3 4 5 6 7 8 9   4 3 2 1 0 9 8 7 6 5

WESTFIELD MEMORIAL LIBRARY.
WESTFIELD, NEW JERSEY

Preface

A good idea is hard to suppress. If you've ever been cajoled into holiday festivities by friends chanting, "Where's your Christmas spirit?" you know exactly what we mean. Since ancient times, people have found midwinter cheer a good idea.

In our modern technological world, both high-tech and handmade contribute to a rich diversity of the celebration. Old and new customs from different cultures are mixing as never before. All this can sometimes lead to a bewildering, even conflicting, mish-mash of activity that becomes just so much noise.

To bring some order out of this Christmas chaos, a little focusing is required. You don't have to be an expert in world cultures to find a sense of direction for Christmas celebrations; you just have to make a few delightful choices — and stick to them.

Whatever the custom, you get out of Christmas what you put into it (plus a few extra pounds). That's where this book comes in...by choosing a holiday theme, you can make your own Christmas a little more personal. By giving the gifts and decorations and foods you've prepared, you can make your Christmas less commercial. By reading something of the essence of the customs you're practicing, you can sense the irrepressible age-old urge to splurge — a very good idea.

Come travel the celebrations of Christmas with us as you explore the histories, music, menus and handmade projects described in this book. We'll trace the character of celebrations of years gone by, and you can fill in the outlines. In each of the six sections, we've tried to capture the feeling of a particular Christmas spirit. Besides a brief description of the chief ways of celebrating, we've included a special menu and recipes for preparing a unique feast in each section. You will also find a discography of currently available recorded music. And at the bottom of each of these Christmas stockings, the most special present of all — instructions for preparing some of our most treasured Christmas toys and decorations.

Christmas celebration is our idea of a wonderful do-it-yourself project because it's something no one else can do for you. We hope to help get you started...and what better time than the present!

WESTFIELD MEMORIAL LIBRARY
WESTFIELD, NEW JERSEY

Contents

Tips & Techniques

If you are as crafty as Santa's elves, you may already know all you need to about sewing, soft-sculpting, and woodworking techniques. We have included this section just in case you run into an unfamiliar procedure, or decide to try your hand at something new.

ENLARGING SCALE DRAWINGS

A scale drawing appears on a background grid of small squares, and includes a legend at the top that specifies the scale: 1 square = 1 inch. There are several ways to enlarge the drawing to full size:

Pantograph: A pantograph is a tool containing several joined rods and two styli (pencil leads). As you trace the scale drawing, using the guide stylus, the secondary stylus draws the full-size pattern.

Opaque Projector: Place the scale drawing in the projector and aim it at a flat wall. Move the unit forward or backward until the projected squares of the grid measure exactly 1 inch square. Tape paper to the wall and trace the outlines of the patterns.

Grid Paper: For this method you'll need paper containing a grid of 1-inch squares (drafting paper or dressmaker's pattern paper). To make the full-size pattern (**Figure A**), work one square at a time as you reproduce onto the full-size grid the lines that appear on the scale drawing.

SEWING & FABRIC TIPS

The Basics

Fabric: We specify the types and colors of fabric that we used for each project. Feel free to substitute, but choose similar weights and finishes. Launder and press the fabrics to prevent shrinkage problems later.

Half-Patterns: Most symmetrical patterns are provided as half-patterns, and the words "Place on Fold" appear along one edge. Double the fabric and place the designated edge of the pattern along the fold line. Do not cut along the fold.

Seam Allowance: On all patterns a solid line indicates the outer edge (cutting line), and a broken line indicates the seam line. The area between the two is the seam allowance.

Figure A

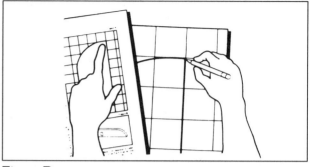

Figure B

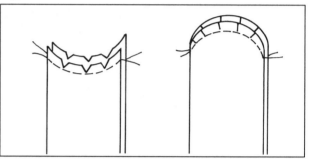

Clipping Curves and Corners: Some seam allowances must be clipped so the fabric will lie flat when it is turned right side out. Take care not to cut the seam. Clip curves as shown in **Figure B**. Clip corners by cutting off the corner of the allowance.

Circular Patterns: To draw a large circle, place your tape measure on the fabric and insert a pin through it and into the fabric, where the center of the circle will be. Measure from the pin a distance equal to the radius of the circle, and make a small hole in the tape. Insert the tip of a pen, and draw the circle as you rotate the pen and tape measure around the pinned center point.

Piecing Strips: To make a long fabric strip, you may have to piece together several shorter ones. Place two strips right sides together and stitch the seam (**Figure C**). Press the seam open. Continue adding strips in this manner until the desired length is achieved.

Bias Strips: Use bias strips to bind curved edges and to make piping, because they are stretchy and will not wrinkle. To cut bias strips, first cut a fabric square along the grain. Fold the square in half diagonally and cut through both layers (**Figure D**), to the desired width.

Blindstitch or Slipstitch: This hand stitch produces an almost invisible seam (**Figure E**). Slide the needle

Figure C

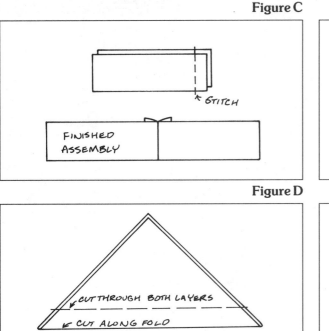

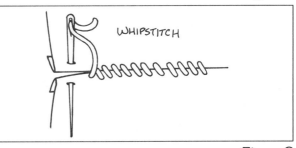

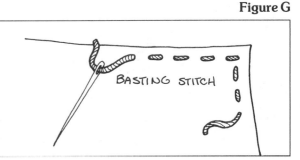

through the top fabric, then pick up a small stitch on the bottom fabric. Keep the stitches evenly spaced.

Whipstitch: Use the whipstitch when fast-and-easy is more important than neatness, because it will show (**Figure F**).

Basting: Basting stitches are used to secure an assembly temporarily, and also in gathering. To hand baste (**Figure G**), make running stitches about ½ inch long. To machine baste, set your stitch selector to the longest straight stitch. Use a contrasting thread color that is easy to see.

Topstitch: This is a final stitch on the right side of the fabric. It should be as straight as possible, and a uniform distance from the edge or seam (**Figure H**).

Glueing: Glue can often be used in place of stitches. If you use white glue, pin or clothespin the assembly while the glue dries. Hot-melt adhesive is used with a glue gun. It sets up very fast and forms a strong water-proof bond.

Embroidery

Cotton embroidery floss is composed of six twisted strands, which can be separated. The fewer strands you use, the finer the finished work will look. Use an em-

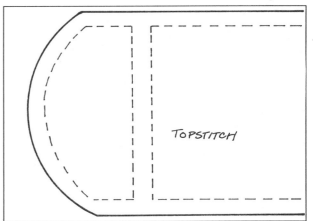

Figure I

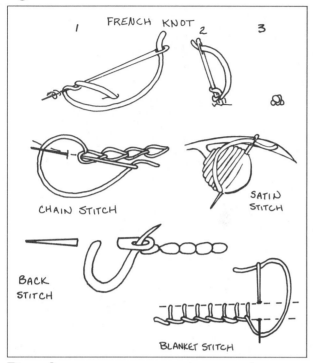

FRENCH KNOT 1 2 3

CHAIN STITCH

SATIN STITCH

BACK STITCH

BLANKET STITCH

Figure J

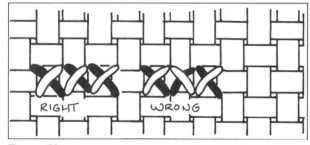

RIGHT WRONG

Figure K

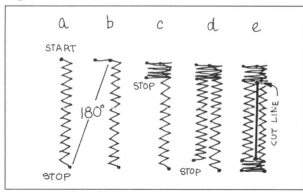

a b c d e

START

STOP

180°

STOP

STOP

STOP

CUT LINE

broidery hoop to hold the fabric flat. Several embroidery stitches are shown in **Figure I**.

Counted Cross-Stitch looks best on an even-weave fabric such as linen or aida cloth. Two rows of cross-stitches are shown in **Figure J**. The blunt-tipped tapestry needle is inserted through the holes between the fabric threads. Each cross-stitch consists of two straight stitches, one crossed over the other. Be sure to cross each stitch in the same direction, as indicated by the "right" and "wrong" diagrams. To follow a cross-stitch graph, start in the center so your design will be centered on the fabric. Legs of adjacent stitches should share the same holes, unless a space is indicated on the graph. Count the stitches shown on the graph, and work the same number of cross-stitches on the fabric.

Buttonholes

Buttonholes can be worked by hand or machine, but the latter is fastest and easiest. You'll need a machine with a buttonhole attachment or zigzag capabilities; otherwise, bind the edges of the buttonhole by working closely spaced hand blanket stitches.

Placement of the buttonhole should be marked on the fabric. The length should be ¼ inch longer than the diameter of the button, to allow for the bartack at each end (see **Figure K**). If your machine has a buttonhole attachment, follow the instructions provided with it. If not, follow the steps listed here.

1. Set stitch selectors for closely spaced, medium-width zigzag. Work one edge of buttonhole (**Figure K**, step a).

2. Rotate fabric 180 degrees and take one stitch to move needle to left (step b, **Figure K**).

3. Reset stitch selector to widest zigzag and stitch bartack (step c), ⅛ inch long.

4. Reset to medium zigzag and stitch second edge of buttonhole (step d), stopping ⅛ inch from end.

5. Reset to widest zigzag and stitch bartack (step e).

6. Use small sharp scissors or blade to cut open (step e). Don't cut through bartack stitches.

Zippers

When working with delicate or stretchy fabrics, or those with thick pile, it's best to hand stitch the zipper in place. Use a tiny prickstitch (**Figure L**). To shorten a zipper, first baste it into the zipper opening. Whipstitch across the zipper teeth ¼ inch below the end of the fabric opening (**Figure M**). Sew a metal eye-bar above the whipstitches, as shown. Cut off the excess zipper ½ inch below.

Applique

An applique is a decorative fabric piece that is attached to a larger background piece or garment. Here are a couple of methods of attaching appliques:

Method 1: Cut applique with a ⅜-inch seam allowance. Pin or baste to the larger fabric, placing fiberfill underneath for a puffy look. Run closely spaced machine zigzag stitches around seam line (**Figure N**). Trim seam allowance close to stitches, being careful not to cut stitches.

Method 2: Cut applique with no seam allowance. Zigzag around edge, making sure the needle penetrates both applique and background fabric.

Method 3: Cut applique with a ¼-inch seam allowance, and press allowance to wrong side. Hand stitch, using closely spaced blanket stitch.

Method 4: Cut applique with no seam allowance. Adhere to larger fabric using glue or fusible interfacing. Stitch around edge by hand or machine.

Patchwork and Quilting

When cutting fabric pieces for patchwork, cut straight along the grain of the fabric. This will help produce smooth patchwork that does not pucker and wrinkle.

Finish quilting secures the patchwork to batting and fabric backing layers; three methods are shown in **Figure O**. For bed quilts, make a yarn tie at each patchwork intersection (diagram 1). More common techniques are shown in diagrams 2 and 3. The quilting can be worked by hand or machine. For normal finish quilt-

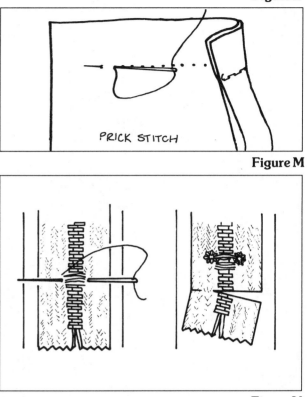

Figure L

Figure M

Figure N

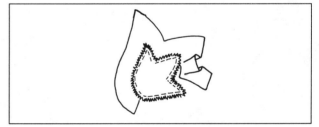

Figure O

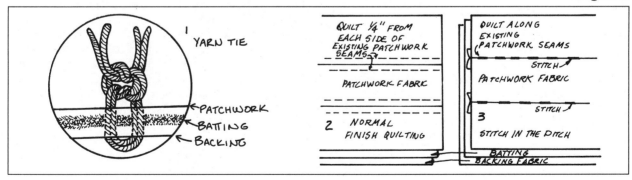

Figure P

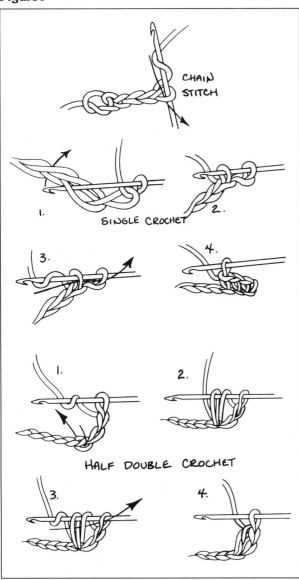

CHAIN STITCH

SINGLE CROCHET

1. 2.

3. 4.

HALF DOUBLE CROCHET

1. 2.

3. 4.

basic stitches are illustrated in **Figure P**. Most crochet projects begin with a row of chain stitches. The illustrated single crochet and half double crochet stitches are shown starting from a row of chain stitches.

Here is an explanation of the abbreviations and terms used in the crochet instructions:

beg – begin or beginning
ch – chain stitch
sc – single crochet
dc – double crochet
hdc – half double crochet
tr – triple crochet
sl st – slip stitch
sp – space (the next available stitch in the work)
rnd – round (one complete row of work)
* – repeat the steps between the asterisks
() – indicates further explanation

Fabric Painting

Acrylic paint straight from the tube is a good thickness for most fabrics. Thin paint will bleed into the fabric; thick paint will not penetrate. Test on a piece of scrap fabric. Acrylic paints are water-soluble, but once dry, they are permanent.

HOSE & SOFT-SCULPTING

Unless otherwise specified, use normal-weight hose. "Flesh-tone" means any normal skin color, dark to light. Queen-size hose are specified for large projects, but you can substitute regular-size hose if you reduce the size of the project.

Only a portion of one leg is required for many projects, so you can use throw-away hose that have runs. Use sandal-foot hose for projects in which an entire leg is stuffed to form an arm, so the fingers won't be darker than the hand.

Pantyhose seams can be machine stitched, using a straight or narrow zigzag setting. Stretch the hose gently as you go, so the thread will not break when the assembly is stuffed and stretched later. White or hot-melt glue can be used to adhere hose to fabric or hose to hose.

When attaching a stuffed pantyhose head to the body of a doll, begin whipstitching at the center back – otherwise, the head will swivel. Finished projects should be sprayed with a light coat of clear acrylic to help protect from runs and dirt.

ing, stitch ¼ or ⅛ inch from each patchwork seam. For "stitch-in-the-ditch," run the stitching directly along the patchwork seams.

Crochet

If you have never done crochet, you may wish to consult a more complete text on the subject. Three

Stuffing and Shaping

Stuffed hose are very pliable and moldable, as long as they are not stuffed too tightly. If a shape is over-stuffed, there is no room for the fiberfill to give when you wish to manipulate or sculpt a feature.

When forming the head for a doll, insert your fist inside the hose and stuff around it, so there is a small cavity in the center of the stuffing. Manipulate the shape to resemble a real head, not just a round sphere. The facial features are created by soft-sculpting, but you want to start with a realistic-looking shape.

Sculpting

A type of needle called a "sharp" is best for sculpting. Use a long one, so it won't get lost inside large stuffed forms. The best sculpting thread is heavy-duty 100% nylon with a bonded finish.

A single 18-inch strand of thread is sufficient to sculpt the facial features on most dolls. Diagrams provided with the instructions show numbered points at which you enter and exit the needle. Mark the points on the stuffed head before you start sculpting.

When the instructions read, "reenter at the same point," insert the needle as close as possible to the last exit point. When you pull the thread to define a sculpted area, be careful not to rip the hose. To secure the defined area, take a couple of small stitches at the exit point; this is called "lock the stitch."

If you see a run begin to develop, apply clear fingernail polish. If you run out of thread, lock the stitch and cut the thread. Rethread your needle, reenter at point 1, exit where you locked off, and continue sculpting from there. The most important thing to remember is that you don't have to settle for what you get the first time. You can remove sculpting stitches, and you can even turn a head around and use the back if you don't like what you did on the front.

WOODWORKING TIPS

The Basics

Selecting Wood: When purchasing lumber, look at the end grain of each board. Heartwood (**Figure Q**) is cut from the center of the tree. It may become

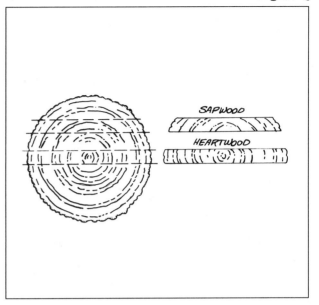

thinner as it dries, but it is less likely to warp, crack, swell, and fall prey to insect damage than sapwood.

Lumber is graded according to quality (amount of knotholes, knots, other imperfections, strength, and general appearance). You need not use the highest grade for every project – the grade should fit the style. If you're in doubt, talk it over with your lumber dealer.

Adhesives: Permanent joints should be secured with both glue and fasteners. Aliphatic resin (carpenter's wood glue) is good for indoor projects, but waterproof marine glue or two-part epoxies should be used for outdoor projects.

Finishes: If you use hardwood you won't want to cover up that gorgeous grain with paint. We recommend Danish oil, which is a combination stain and penetrating sealer. For children's projects, we recommend non-toxic finishes. Plain vegetable oil gives a nice, clear finish and brings out the wood grain.

Fasteners and Hardware: Common "mild steel" hardware is fine to use on indoor projects, but will eventually rust outdoors. To eliminate this problem, use hardware that is galvanized or made of brass, bronze, or stainless steel.

Cutting and Joining

Butt Joints: A butt joint connects one piece to

Figure R

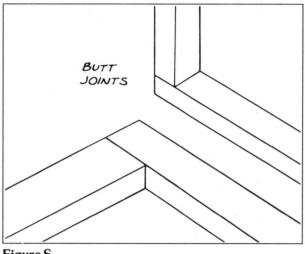

Figure S

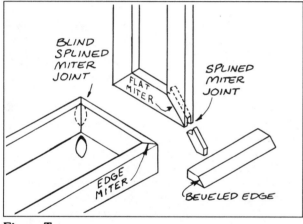

Figure T

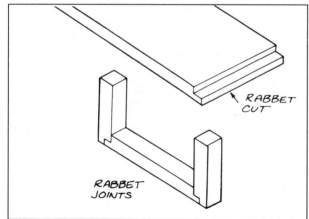

Figure U

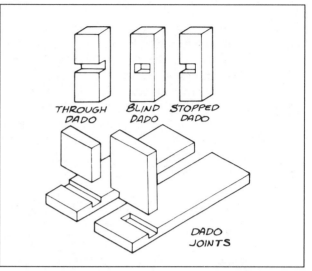

another with no interlocking edges (**Figure R**). This joint should be reinforced with glue blocks, splines, nails, screws, or dowels.

Miters and Bevels: A miter joint connects two angle-cut ends (**Figure S**). It can be reinforced with splines, dowels, or fasteners. A flat miter is cut across the width of the board; an on-edge miter is cut across the thickness. A bevel cut is made along an edge or surface.

Rabbets: A rabbet is an L-shaped groove (**Figure T**). Matched rabbets make a strong joint, providing more surface area to be glued.

Dadoes: A dado is a groove (**Figure U**). The most accurate way to make this cut is to use a table saw with a dado blade. Otherwise, use a router with a straight bit, or chisel out the dado using a hand chisel.

Mortise and Tenon Joints: The most common mortise and tenon joints are shown in **Figure V**. A pegged mortise and tenon joint is one in which the tenon extends out beyond the mortise, and is itself mortised to accommodate a peg. The pegged mortise and tenon is a handy joint to use in furniture that you wish to be able to disassemble for storage or transport. The easiest way to cut a mortise is to use a mortise-chisel attachment on your drill press. Otherwise, drill a pilot hole and insert a saber saw blade to cut the outlines; or use a hand mortise chisel.

Splines: A spline is a thin strip of wood used as a connecting member between two boards (**Figure W**). It fits into grooves cut into the edges to be joined. If you are working with standard 1-inch lumber, the grooves should be ¼ inch wide and just over ⅜ inch deep. The spline should be ¼ inch thick, ¾ inch wide, and the same length as the grooves.

Securing Joints

To prevent splitting the wood, drill a pilot hole for each screw, using a bit slightly smaller than the screw shank. For a nice finish, countersink the screws and cover the heads with wooden plugs or wood filler. Plugs cut from matching stock are almost invisible – plug-cutter attachments for your power drill make this a very easy job.

If you are working with hardwood that is nearly impossible to drill or drive a nail into, try coating the nails, screws, and drill bits with a little lard. Be sure your drill bits and nails are good and sharp.

Joints should be clamped while the glue dries, but not so tightly as to force out most of the glue. Thirty minutes is sufficient for most, but joints that will be under a great deal of stress should be clamped overnight. Joints secured with power-driven screws need not be clamped.

Figure V

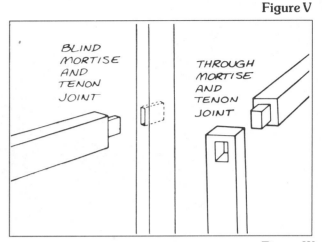

BLIND MORTISE AND TENON JOINT

THROUGH MORTISE AND TENON JOINT

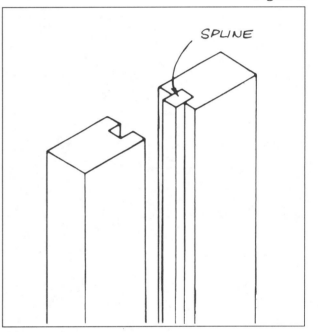

SPLINE

An Old World Christmas

C hristmas, now one of the most widely celebrated festivals in the world, had its not-so-humble beginnings in the antiquity of the Roman empire. The sun never set on the empire, but the cold mid-winter darkness was still hard to ignore. The original revelers centered their celebrations around the shortest day of the year, the winter soltice. This month-long festival, called Saturnalia, included feasting, drinking, gift-giving...all to celebrate the return of the sun.

The peoples of northern Europe brought their winter festival into the picture. They saw natural rebirth and survival through the winter in Yule-log fires and evergreens, which they used to decorate their houses for the festival. Their giver-of-presents, Woden, swept out of the north bearing gifts. Through the centuries, there has been a subtle and unifying shift in the character of these "holy days" or holidays. Elements of both religious and secular festivals have grown into the traditions we know today as Christmas.

In this section, you'll find projects as traditional as the wooden sheep and shepherd, and the Christmas carolers; and as timeless as the straw wreath & bird. The patchwork lap quilt and country rocking horse are projects that echo a time rich in the values of handmade craftsmanship.

Old World Christmas

Wooden Sheep & Shepherd

Bird's Nest Wreath

Antique Miss

Country Rocking Horse

Patchwork Lap Quilt

Menus and Melodies

A Medieval Menu

A medieval holiday menu certainly would have included roast boar, borne into the dining hall in a grand procession accompanied by the singing of "The Boar's Head in Hand Bring I." The boar would have been followed by roast goose, capon, or a special treat, peacock; and platters laden with cakes, breads, pastries, plum puddings, and mince pies. All this good food would have been washed down with the customary holiday drink, wassail.

Wassail, a combination of ale, apples, sugar, eggs, nutmeg, cloves, and ginger, was served piping hot to help shoo the winter chill from body and spirit.

Medieval mince pies contained finely chopped venison or veal combined with suet, sugar or honey, apples, raisins, currants, nutmeg, cloves, cinnamon, salt, brandy or hard cider, and (if available) citrus or citron. These fruits and spices symbolized the exotic treasures brought by the Wise Men from their eastern homeland. The pie was baked in an oblong shape with a sunken lid to represent the manger.

The "plum" in plum pudding refers to the way raisins plump up during cooking – neither old-world nor modern recipes contain any plums! Burning brandy symbolized the rebirth of the sun, and a sprig of holly or evergreen placed on top symbolized everlasting life. Early plum pudding recipes included more suet than modern tastes prefer, but other ingredients are much the same now as then.

Plum Pudding
(1-pound mold)

1 cup all purpose flour	1 tsp. baking soda
1 tsp. cinnamon	½ cup sweet
½ tsp. each cloves,	cracker crumbs
nutmeg, and salt	1 cup raisins
½ cup chopped walnuts	½ cup honey
1 beaten egg	½ cup fruit juice
¼ cup brandy	½ cup finely ground suet

Sift dry ingredients. Add cracker crumbs, suet, raisins, and nuts. Combine honey, egg, and fruit juice, add to dry mixture, beat until smooth. Pour into 1-lb. mold, cover. Pour two cups water in cooker, place mold on rack. Steam 30 minutes without pressure, then at 3¾ lbs. pressure for 1¾ hours, or 15 lbs. for 1 hour. Remove from mold, pour brandy over pudding, light, and carry flaming to table.

The following holiday recipes are of old English and German descent.

Charlotte Russe
(German dessert – makes one 15-inch loaf pan)

6 eggs, separated	1 cup milk
1 cup sugar	2 Tbsp. gelatin
1 qt. heavy cream	4 doz. ladyfingers,
1 tsp. vanilla	split lengthwise

Line loaf pan with ladyfinger halves (bottom and sides). Dissolve gelatin in small amount of warm milk. Combine egg yolks, milk, sugar, and gelatin in sauce pan. Bring to boil and simmer a few seconds, stirring constantly. Let cool. Whip the cream. Beat egg whites until stiff. Fold together yolk mixture, whipped cream, egg whites, and vanilla. Pour into lined pan and chill until set.

Cinnamon Stars

(German Christmas cookies – makes several dozen)

6 egg whites	1 lb. powdered sugar
1 tsp. cinnamon	1 lb. ground almonds

Beat egg whites stiff. Combine with sugar and cinnamon, and beat 15 minutes. Remove 6 Tbsp. of this mixture and refrigerate (to be used later for icing). Add the ground almonds to remaining mixture, combine well, and refrigerate overnight.

Preheat oven to 300°. Roll out almond dough about ¼ inch thick. Cut in star-shapes. Spread each cookie with reserved icing mixture. Bake about 10 minutes – do not brown! The less they are cooked, the chewier they'll be. Should not be crunchy.

Lemon Curd

(English jelly-type condiment – makes 1 cup)

4 Tbsp. unsalted butter	½ cup sugar
½ cup fresh lemon juice	4 egg yolks
1 Tbsp. grated lemon peel	

Combine butter, sugar, lemon juice and yolks in 2-qt. saucepan. Cook over lowest possible heat, stirring constantly, until thick enough to coat back of spoon heavily. (This takes a while, so pull up a stool and read a book.) Do not allow to boil, or yolks will curdle. Pour into small bowl, stir in lemon peel. Refrigerate. Use as topping on toast, ice cream, etc.

Treacle Pie

(Traditional British recipe)

9-inch pastry shell	1½ cups English
1½ cups fresh soft bread, shredded	golden syrup (or 1½ cups light corn syrup
½ tsp. ground ginger	combined with 1 tsp.
1 egg lightly beaten	molasses)
1 Tbsp. fresh lemon juice	

Combine syrup, crumbs, lemon juice, ginger and egg in large bowl. Stir well. Pour into pastry shell and smooth out. Shell should be about two-thirds full. Bake in medium oven 20 minutes or until firm to touch. Serve with custard sauce.

Music to Enjoy

Old-world musical celebrations of Christmas were decreed to be somber and reverent, in keeping with the atmosphere of the church. Many popular carols were considered improper for religious ceremonies, and so were sung in the streets by the common folk. Some of these popular carols originated as folk songs and lullabies, and often emphasized the secular pleasures of the season. The recorded albums listed here include both somber and secular expressions of the season.

Christmas in Cambridge
Clare College Singers and Orchestra
Capitol Records #SM-10567
Includes traditional carols such as "The Twelve Days of Christmas" and "I Saw Three Ships."

Medieval Christmas
Boston Camerata
Nonesuch Records #71315
Contains eighteen medieval carols.

Holly and the Ivy
Mormon Tabernacle Choir
Columbia Records #XMS-6192
Offers such traditional carols as "Angels We Have Heard on High," "While Shepherds Watch Their Flocks," "The First Noel," and "What Child Is This."

O Tannenbaum
Hermann Prey and the Tolz Boy's Choir of Bavaria
Capitol Records #SM-10568
Traditional German carols such as "O Tannenbaum" and "Lo, How a Rose E'er Blooming."

Lots of folks have trouble remembering the order of gifts "my true love gave to me," when singing "The Twelve Days of Christmas." The lords a'leaping often wind up where the swans should be a'swimming, or worse! Here's a list in the proper order:

Partridge in a pear tree
Two turtledoves
Three French hens
Four calling birds
Five gold rings
Six geese a'laying
Seven swans a'swimming
Eight maids a'milking
Nine ladies waiting
Ten lords a'leaping
Eleven pipers piping
Twelve drummers drumming

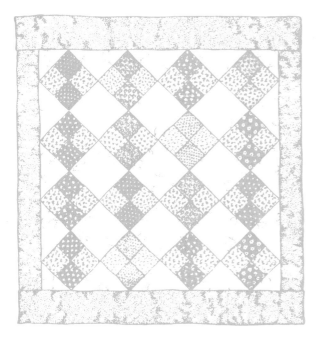

Patchwork Lap Quilt

This thickly stuffed patchwork lap quilt is just the right size for a baby or one person's lap. The machine-sewn patches are simple combinations of calico and muslin squares joined in a diamond pattern. The layers are secured using yarn ties at the corners and center of each patch.

Materials

1½ yards of 45-inch-wide calico for backing piece
Small amounts of various calico prints for the patches (We used eleven different prints, for a total of ½ yard of 36-inch-wide fabric.)
1 yard of unbleached muslin
34 x 38-inch piece of quilt batting
Yarn or embroidery floss for the quilt ties
Heavy paper or cardboard (not corrugated) for the pattern template

Cutting the Pieces

1. Scale Drawings for the Muslin Full Square, Half Square, Quarter Square, and Calico Small Square are provided on page 49. Enlarge the scale drawings to full-size paper patterns. (See Tips & Techniques section on enlarging scale drawings.) To save wear and tear on the paper patterns, cut pattern templates from cardboard. A template will be especially helpful for the Calico Small Squares, because you will be cutting sixty-four of them. You will not be cutting as many muslin squares, but if you want to protect and save all of the patterns, make a cardboard template of each one.

2. Cut the pieces listed in this step from the specified fabrics. If you use the template, then use the fabric marking pen to trace the pattern onto the fabric. If you prefer to use the paper pattern, simply pin the pattern to the fabric. You can fold the fabric in half and cut two squares at a time. However, if you are using the template we don't suggest that you cut more than two fabric pieces at one time, because the fabrics might slip during cutting, resulting in uneven edges. Pinning the layers of fabric together really doesn't help, because the scissors cannot make straight and even cuts through many layers at one time.

Calico: Small Square – cut sixty-four
        Backing – cut one, 40 x 50 inches
Muslin: Full Square – cut nine
        Half Square – cut twelve
        Quarter Square – cut four
Quilt batting: Cut one, 34 x 38 inches

Establishing the Pattern

The quilt top consists of sixteen calico patches. Each patch is made up of four Calico Small Squares. Each calico patch alternates with a Muslin Full Square, sewn into strips. The longest strip is joined on both edges to progressively shorter strips, resulting in a diamond pattern. The triangular-shaped areas around the perimeter of the quilt top are filled in with Muslin Half Squares and Quarter Squares so the top ends up being square.

Figure A

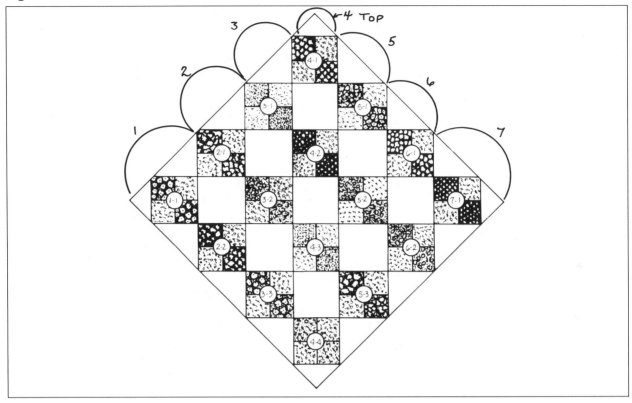

1. Refer to **Figure A** for placement notations. The double numbers within the patches correspond to the strip placement numbers; for example, strip 3 contains patches 3-1, 3-2, and 3-3. Cut sixteen small pieces of paper, and write one placement notation on each (1-1, 2-1, 2-2, etc.). Set these aside for the moment.

2. Arrange the Calico Small Squares and Muslin Full Squares on a large flat surface until you find the color and pattern combinations that you like, using **Figure A** as a guide to what the finished quilt should look like. (We used two different calicos for each patch, but you may prefer a different combination.)

3. When you find an arrangement that pleases you, stack together the squares for each patch, and pin the appropriate placement notation to each stack.

Assembling the Patches

Note: All seam allowances are ¼ inch unless other-

wise specified in the instructions.

1. To make the first calico patch (1-1), place two of the Calico Small Squares right sides together and stitch the seam along one edge. Trim the seam allowance to about ⅛ inch, and press the seam open. Repeat for the remaining two Squares.

2. Place the two patchwork assemblies right sides together. (If you are using the same arrangement that we did, the squares of the same fabric should be diagonal to each other.) Stitch the seam along one long edge, trim the seam allowance, and press the seam open. Reattach the placement notation.

3. Repeat steps 1 and 2 to assemble the remaining fifteen calico patches.

Assembling the Strips

Note: Throughout the assembly, remember to place right sides together, to trim the seam allowances, and to press the seams open.

Figure B

Figure C

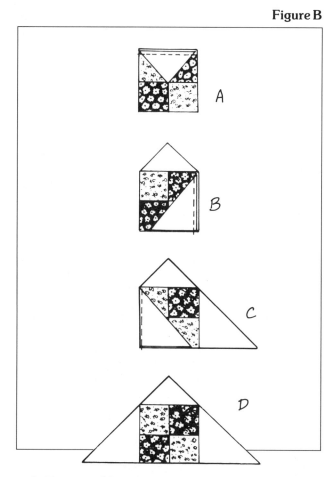

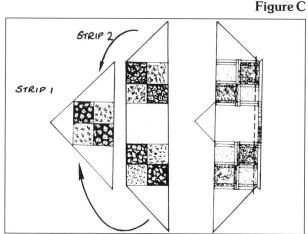

Key to abbreviations: FS: Muslin Full Square
HS: Muslin Half Square
QS: Muslin Quarter Square

a. Strip 2: HS, 2-1, FS, 2-2, HS
b. Strip 3: HS, 3-1, FS, 3-2, FS, 3-3, HS
c. Strip 4: QS, 4-1, FS, 4-2, FS, 4-3, FS, 4-4, QS
d. Strip 5: HS, 5-1, FS, 5-2, FS, 5-3, HS
e. Strip 6: HS, 6-1, FS, 6-2, HS
f. Strip 7: (Reverse the assembly as for strip 1.)

Assembling the Top

Note: Stitch the strips together beginning at the left corner (**Figure A**), and working toward the right corner of the quilt top. This will keep the bulk of the fabric on the left side of the sewing machine, and out of the way.

1. Refer to **Figure C**. Place strip 2 on top of strip 1, aligning the strip-1 calico patch with the strip-2 Muslin Full Square. Align the edges as shown, stitch the seam, and open out the strip assembly.

2. Place strip 3 on top of the assembled strip 1 and 2, aligning the edges. The calico patches should be opposite the Muslin Squares. Stitch the seam, and open the assembly.

3. Add strips 4, 5, 6, and 7 in the same manner.

4. Lightly press the assembled quilt top.

Finishing

The layers (backing, batting, and top) are tie-quilted together, and the excess backing folds over the front of the quilt to form borders.

1. To assemble strip 1 (**Figure B**), place the long edge of one Muslin Quarter Square on top of the left-hand edge of patch 1-1, and stitch the seam (step a).

2. Place the short edge of one Muslin Half Square on top of the upper edge of patch 1-1, and stitch the seam, as shown in step b.

3. Place the short edge of one Muslin Half Square on top of the lower edge of patch 1-1, and stitch the seam, as shown in step c.

4. Patch 1-1 should look like step d when it is finished and the fabric is opened out. Reattach placement notation 1-1 to the completed strip. This is now strip 1.

5. Refer again to the placement diagram in **Figure A**, and to the following list to assemble the remaining strips. Be sure to turn the Half Squares the right way, so that when they are opened out, they face the direction shown in **Figure A**. Pin the appropriate placement notation to each finished strip.

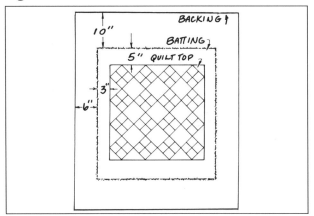

Figure E

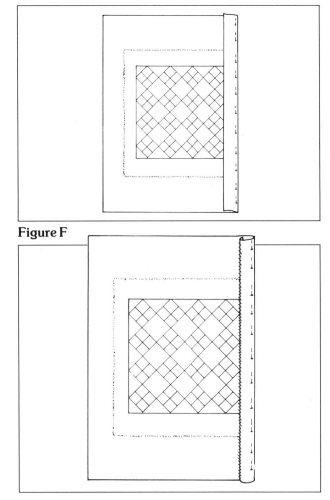

Figure F

1. Refer to **Figure D** for this step. Place the backing piece right side down on a flat surface. Place the quilt batting on top, allowing the backing to extend about 10 inches at the upper and lower edges and 6 inches on each side, for the borders. Place the patchwork quilt top right side up on top of the batting, allowing the batting to extend about 5 inches at the upper and lower edges and 3 inches on each side. Baste the layers together securely, working from the center to each corner, and from the center to the center of each edge, to keep them from shifting.

2. Fold one side border evenly over the batting all the way up one side, as shown in **Figure E**. Insert pins in a few places to keep the fold even.

3. Fold the seam allowance under (**Figure F**), so that it lies about ¼ inch inside the side edge of the patch-work quilt top. Pin it in place, and then blind stitch the border to the quilt top.

4. Repeat step 2 for the opposite side border.

5. Fold, pin, and then blind stitch the upper border in the same manner. You will also have to blind stitch along each side where the lower edge of the top border overlaps the side borders.

6. Repeat step 5 for the lower border.

7. To tie-quilt the layers together, thread a needle with yarn (or six strands of embroidery floss). Take a stitch through all three layers at each corner and at the center of each patch, as shown in **Figure G**. Tie the yarn in a square knot on the front side of the quilt.

Figure G

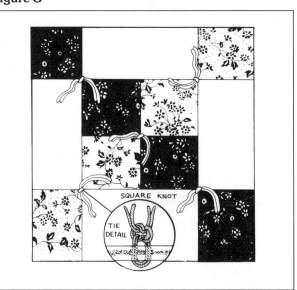

Country Rocking Horse

This high-stepping wooden steed will be a handsome addition to the playroom or the corral. He'll give the toddlers an exciting ride, but he won't buck or kick, and he's guaranteed not to eat too much.

Materials

3-foot length of pine 1 x 4
8-foot length of pine 2 x 8
10-foot length of pine 2 x 10 (**Note:** If your lumber dealer carries or can get pine 2 x 16, purchase a 2-foot length of 2 x 16 and a 6-foot length of 2 x 10, instead of the 10-foot 2 x 10.)

Wooden Dowel Rod:

3-foot length of ¼-inch
2-foot length of ½-inch
2-foot length of ¾-inch
3-foot length of 1-inch

White string-mop head
Flathead wood screws, 1½ inches long
Carpenter's wood glue; wood filler; and plain vegetable
    oil or other finishing materials of your choice

Optional Materials

When we built this rocking horse, we had some odds and ends of ½-inch-thick walnut lumber left over from another project we had just finished. We cut the horse's hooves from this stock, which made a nice contrast to the light-colored pine. For the horse's half-moon-shaped eyes, we planed another small piece of walnut to a thickness of ¼ inch. You can achieve the same effect by cutting these parts from pine and using a dark stain on them, but if you have in your "leftovers" pile a few pieces of dark-colored hardwood, consider using them for the hooves and eyes.

Preparing the Patterns

Scale drawings are provided on page 242 for the Ear Front, Ear Side, Eye, Saddle Edge, Saddle Top, Rocker, Body, Foreleg, and Hind Leg. Enlarge the drawings to make full-size paper patterns. (Refer to Tips & Techniques section on enlarging scale drawings.) Transfer any cutting directions or instructions to the paper patterns.

Cutting the Parts

1. Cut two 11¾-inch lengths of pine 1 x 4, and label them as the Leg Supports.

2. Cut two Ears from the remaining pine 1 x 4, using the full-size Ear Side pattern. Cut a curved groove across one side of each Ear, at the lower end, using the Ear Edge pattern as a guide.

3. We used a wood gouge to shape a small hollow on the outer side of each Ear at the front, as shown in **Figure A**. The shaded areas in the diagrams indicate the area we chiseled out. Remember that the Ears will be attached to opposite sides of the horse's head, so make them mirror images of each other.

4. The Hooves and Eyes are cut from the remaining 1 x 4, but the stock must be reduced in thickness first. (Or, you can cut these parts from dark-colored hardwood, as we said in the "Optional Materials" section.) Rip or plane to a thickness of ⅜ or ½ inch, a sufficient amount of 1 x 4 to cut two Hooves, each 2¼ x 3½ inches. Round off all four edges of each Hoof. To cut the

Figure A

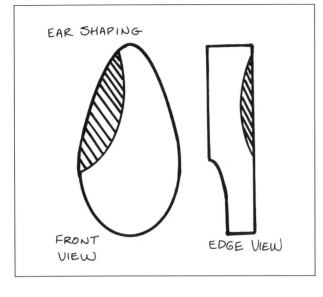

EAR SHAPING

FRONT VIEW

EDGE VIEW

Figure B

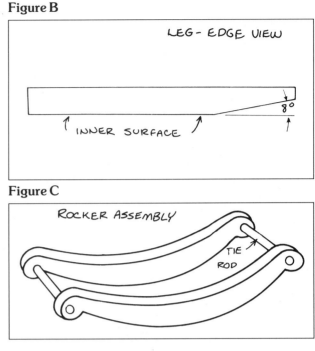

LEG - EDGE VIEW

INNER SURFACE

8°

Figure C

ROCKER ASSEMBLY

TIE ROD

Eyes, you'll need a 2 x 2-inch piece of 1 x 4 ripped or planed to a thickness of ¼ inch. Cut two Eyes, using the full-size pattern provided. If you are using pine, use a dark stain (or food coloring) to darken the edges of each Hoof, and the edges and one side of each Eye.

5. Cut from pine 2 x 8 two Rockers. Temporarily clamp the two Rockers together, and drill the 1-inch-diameter holes simultaneously.

6. Cut from the remaining 2 x 8 two Saddles, using the Saddle Top pattern. Use a wood rasp or sander to contour the upper and lower surfaces of each Saddle, using the Saddle Edge pattern as a guide.

7. Cut from the pine 2 x 10 two Forelegs and two Hind Legs.

8. (Skip this step if you were not able to find 2 x 16 pine stock.) Cut one Body from 2 x 16 pine.

9. (Skip this step if you cut the Body in step 8.) If you could not purchase 2 x 16 pine, you'll have to spline together narrower boards in order to cut the Body piece. Cut two 20-inch lengths of the remaining pine 2· x 10; each one should be the full width of the stock. Edge-join the two boards, using a spline joint, so that you have one large piece that measures about 1½ x 18½ x 20 inches. (The exact thickness and width will depend on the thickness and width of your 2 x 10.) If you're not sure how to go about making a spline joint, please refer to the Tips & Techniques section. To spline-join 2-inch lumber, the basic procedures are the

same but the dimensions will differ. In this case, the spline should measure ½ x 2 x 20 inches; it can be cut from a length of leftover 2 x 10 that has been ripped or planed to a thickness of ½ inch. The dadoes that will house the spline should be cut ½ inch wide by 1⅛ inch deep. They can be cut using a router with a ½-inch straight bit, or a table saw with a dado blade. Be sure to set your guides so that the dado is centered along the edge of the board. Glue and assemble the joint, and clamp until the glue has dried. Cut one Body from the splined stock.

10. The Forelegs and Hind Legs must be beveled, so that they will slant outward from the Body. We'll begin with the Forelegs. Temporarily place the two Forelegs against the two sides of the Body piece, making sure that each one is turned so that the front edge indeed faces front. Make a small pencil mark on the inner surface of each Leg (the surface that is against the Body piece), so you'll know which side is which when you cut the bevels. To make the Forelegs slant outward from the Body, bevel the inner surface of each one at an 8-degree angle, beginning 5½ inches from the rounded upper end, as shown in the edge-view diagram, **Figure B**. For the Hind Legs, repeat these procedures to determine which will be the inner surface of each one, and

CELEBRATIONS OF CHRISTMAS

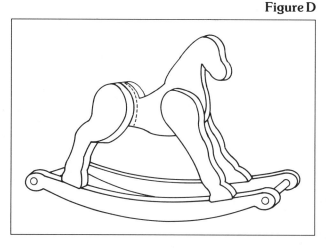

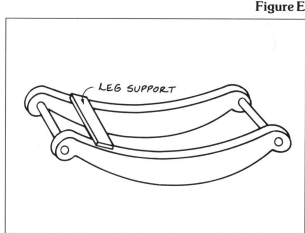

LEG SUPPORT

bevel them in the same manner.

11. Each Leg is compound-mitered at the lower end, so the hooves will sit flat on the rocker assembly. A compound miter is not cause for panic — you'll just be cutting across the lower end from corner to corner, instead of straight across from edge to edge as you would for a normal miter. This is not difficult to do, but you'll need to think carefully before cutting, so each Leg is mitered in the proper direction. We'll begin with one Foreleg — remember that the bevel determines which is the inner surface, and the contour at the hoof end determines which is the front edge and which is the back. Cut an 8-degree compound miter across the lower end of the Foreleg, so that the miter is widest at the inside back corner and narrowest at the outside front corner. Miter the other Foreleg in the same manner. For each Hind Leg, the 8-degree compound miter should be widest at the inside front corner and narrowest at the outside back corner.

12. Each Foreleg is drilled to accommodate a footrest dowel. Drill a ¾-inch-diameter socket, about 1 inch deep, into the outer surface of each Foreleg at the marked location.

13. The neck portion of the Body is drilled through to accommodate a handle dowel. Drill a ¾-inch-diameter hole through the Body at the marked location.

14. Cut from ¾-inch dowel rod one 8-inch Handle, and two 5-inch Footrests. Round off the circular edge at both ends of the Handle, and at one end of each Footrest. Cut from 1-inch dowel two Tie Rods, each 13¼ inches long. The remaining dowel parts will be cut during assembly.

Assembly

1. The base consists of the Rockers, Leg Supports, and Tie Rods. Glue the Tie Rods into the holes in the Rockers, so that the ends of the Rods are flush with the outer surfaces of the Rockers (**Figure C**).

2. The Leg Supports are mortised into the Rockers (see **Figures F** and **I**), but in order to be sure of a proper fit you'll need to perform a temporary assembly of the horse. Use a temporary holding nail to attach each Foreleg and each Hind Leg to the Body, as shown in **Figure D**. (Approximate placement lines for the Legs are provided on the Body pattern.) Place the horse on the rocker assembly, as shown, and swivel the Legs forward or backward until the bottom of each Leg is level with the Rocker. (The leg spread is not as wide as the rocker spread, because the legs will sit on the Leg Supports between the Rockers, as shown in **Figure I**. But you can move the horse from Rocker to Rocker to test the angles.) It may be necessary to sand the mitered lower ends of the Legs slightly, because it's difficult to get a perfect miter the first time. When you have a good match on all four Legs, mark the upper edge of each Rocker at the front and back edge of each hoof.

3. Remove the horse, and place a Leg Support across the Rocker assembly, as shown in **Figure E**. Adjust it so that it lies between the front and back markings for one set of legs, and overlaps the Rockers evenly. Trace a pencil line around the end of the Support on the upper edge of each Rocker. Remove the Support, and chisel out a ¾-inch-deep mortise at the inner

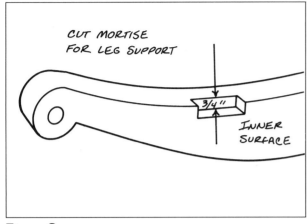

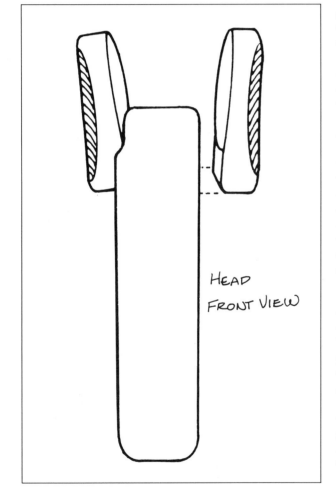

corner of each Rocker, using the pencil line as a guide (**Figure F**). Repeat these procedures to mark and chisel out the mortises for the second Leg Support, near the opposite ends of the Rockers.

4. Glue the Leg Supports into the mortises, and clamp until the glue dries. We reinforced these joints using dowel pegs. Drill two ½-inch-diameter sockets into each Support-to-Rocker joint, making them about 1¼ inches deep and drilling at a slight angle, so your drill bit does not break through the inner surface of the Rocker. Cut eight 1¼-inch lengths of ½-inch dowel rod for the pegs, and glue a peg into each socket. Trim the pegs flush with the Supports.

5. Replace the horse on the rocker assembly, to be sure the Legs still line up properly and sit flat on the Leg Supports. If not, adjust the Legs and/or sand the mitered lower ends. Mark the Body piece on each side, so you'll know where to reposition the Legs. Remove the holding nails from the Legs, and glue the Legs to the Body. We reinforced these joints using dowel pegs. Drill two ¼-inch-diameter sockets, about 2 inches deep, through each Leg and into the Body. (If you drill one of the sockets at the point where the holding nail was, you won't have to fill in the nail hole.) Cut from ¼-inch dowel eight pegs, each 1⅞ inches long. Glue a peg into each socket.

6. Glue an Ear to each side of the horse's head (**Figure G**), along the placement lines indicated on the pattern. The side of each Ear containing the curved groove goes against the head, and the shaped area on the outer surface should face front. To peg the Ear joints, drill a ¼-inch-diameter hole straight through one Ear, the head, and the other Ear. Cut a length of ¼-inch dowel for the peg, glue it into the hole, and trim the ends flush with the Ears.

7. Glue a Saddle to each side of the Body (**Figure H**), just in front of the Hind Legs and flush with the upper edge. Be sure that the two Saddles are even at the front and back ends. Drill two ¼-inch-diameter sockets straight through each Saddle, from the outer edge into the Body. Cut pegs from ¼-inch dowel and glue them into the sockets. Trim the dowels flush with the outer edge of each Saddle.

8. Glue the unrounded end of a Footrest dowel into the socket in one of the Forelegs (**Figure I**). Glue the second Footrest into the other Foreleg. Glue the Handle dowel into the hole in the Body, leaving equal extensions on each side. Glue an Eye to each side of the head, as shown.

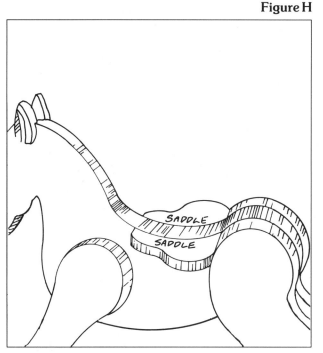

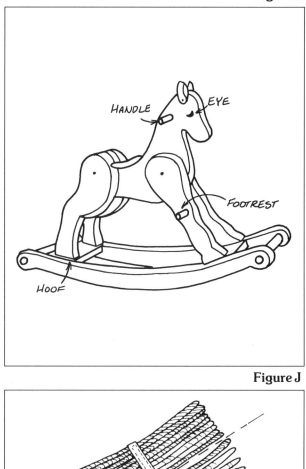

9. Center and glue a Hoof to the bottom of each Leg. Place the horse on the rocker assembly (**Figure I**), and glue the Hooves in place. To secure, insert two screws up through the bottom of the Leg Support, through the Hoof, and into each Leg. Countersink the screws.

Finishing Up

1. Use a wood rasp or power sander to round off the upper curved edge on the outside of each leg (the "haunch" portion). Carefully sand the entire horse, using a wood rasp where necessary and eliminating all sharp corners and edges.

2. To finish the horse, we rubbed plain vegetable oil into the wood, as it is non-toxic and brings out the wood grain nicely, but you may wish to paint or stain and seal.

3. Cut the mop head in half across the binding strip, as shown in **Figure J**. To prevent the strings from coming loose, glue together the cut ends of the binding strips on each half. Fold the strings in half over the strip on each section.

4. One mop-head section will serve as the horse's tail. Spread glue on the exposed side of the binding strip, and attach it to the back of the horse at an appropriate spot.

5. The remaining mop-head section will serve as the mane. Spread glue along the exposed side of the binding strip. Glue it to the upper edge of the head, extending from just in front of the ears to just behind the ears. To create the forelock, pull several strands of the mane forward, and trim them to about 3 inches long. Secure the mane using a few tacks.

Wooden Shepherd and Sheep

Carry the old-world style all the way to your lawn decor with this wood-and-fabric tableau. Unlike the modern, plastic, glow-and-glitter outdoor decorations, this grouping evokes the spiritual joy of the season in a subtle and attractive way. It can be lighted by a single flood lamp.

Materials

For the shepherd:

One 8-foot length and one 6-foot length of pine 1 x 12
6-inch length of pine 2 x 6
4½-foot length of 1¼-inch wooden closet rod
¼-inch-diameter machine bolts: four 2½ inches long, one 3½ inches long, and one 4½ inches long, each with a wing nut to fit
16 x 36-inch piece of fabric for the headband

2½ yards of 50-inch-wide fabric for the burnoose
4¾ yards of 40-inch-wide fabric for the robe
Heavy-duty thread to match the fabrics
3 yards of thick cotton cord for the waist tie and head-band wrap

For one sheep:

1-foot length of pine 2 x 12
5-foot length of pine 2 x 6
2-foot length of pine 2 x 2
8-foot length of 1¼-inch-diameter wooden closet rod
16 x 44-inch piece of ½-inch hardware cloth
Two 5 x 8-inch pieces of black vinyl fabric
45 x 54-inch piece of white or off-white sheep-fur fabric
2-yard length of grosgrain ribbon, at least 1 inch wide
A large bell to hang around the sheep's neck
Heavy-duty white thread

Miscellaneous:

Waterproof glue; dark wood stain for the sheep's face and legs; light wood stain for the shepherd's body; waterproofing wood sealer; staples or tacks; and four 1½-inch-long flathead wood screws

THE SHEPHERD

The shepherd's body consists of twelve separate wooden parts joined by bolts (**Figure E**), so you can pose him many different ways. The fabric pieces that form the clothing are draped over the wooden body.

Cutting the Parts

1. Scale drawings for the shepherd's Head, Lower Arm, Leg, Foot and Crook (for his staff) are provided on pages 47-48. Enlarge the drawings to make full-size patterns. Transfer to the full-size patterns any placement markings that appear on the scale drawings.

2. Cut from the 8-foot pine 1 x 12 the parts listed in this step, using the specified dimensions or patterns. Label each part for reference during assembly.

Part	Dimensions	Quantity
Body	11¼ x 40 inches	1
Leg	use pattern	2
Upper Arm	5 x 15¾ inches	2
Lower Arm	use pattern	2
Spacer	4 x 6 inches	1

3. Cut from the 6-foot pine 1 x 12 the parts listed in this step, and label each one.

Part	Dimensions	Quantity
Body	11¼ x 40 inches	1
Head	use pattern	1
Foot	use pattern	2

4. The two Body pieces are modified as shown in **Figure A**. Temporarily nail or clamp them together, so you can drill and contour them simultaneously. Drill three ¼-inch-diameter holes through the two Bodies and round off the ends, as shown.

5. Drill a ¼-inch-diameter hole through each Leg, each Lower Arm, and the Head, where indicated on the patterns.

6. The Upper Arms are modified very much like the Body pieces were, as shown in **Figure B**. Temporarily nail or clamp together the two Upper Arms, so you can drill and contour them simultaneously. Mark a drilling point 2 inches from each end and centered between the long edges. Drill a ¼-inch-diameter hole through both Upper Arms at each marked point. Round off the ends as shown.

7. Drill a ¼-inch hole through the center of the Spacer, and round off the ends.

8. Cut from pine 2 x 6 one Crook, using the full-size pattern that you made in step 1. Drill a 1¼-inch-diameter socket, about 1½ inches deep, into one end of the Crook. Round off all sharp edges and corners.

9. Sand all of the parts lightly.

Body Assembly

1. Begin by bolting an Upper Arm to one Body piece, as shown in **Figure C**. Insert a 2½-inch bolt through the Body first, and then through the Upper Arm. Secure on the outside of the Upper Arm with a wing nut. Bolt together the remaining Upper Arm and Body.

2. Bolt a Lower Arm to each Upper Arm (**Figure E**), placing the Lower Arm on the outside and using a 2½-inch bolt inserted from the inside of the Upper Arm. Secure on the outside of the Lower Arm with a wing nut. Be sure that the Lower Arms are attached so that the thumbs point in the same direction when the Bodies are turned with the inside surfaces facing each other.

3. A Foot is attached to each Leg using glue and screws, as shown in **Figure D**. You should already have transferred the Leg placement lines to the Foot pattern. Glue a Leg to a Foot inside the placement lines – be sure that the toe end of the Foot faces the same direc-

Figure A

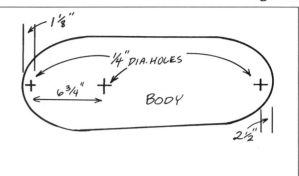

Figure B

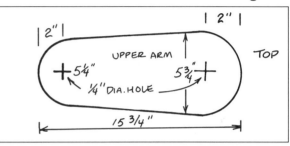

Figure C

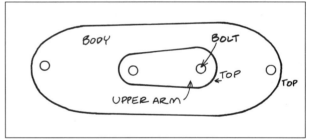

Figure D

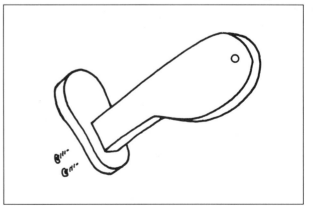

Figure E

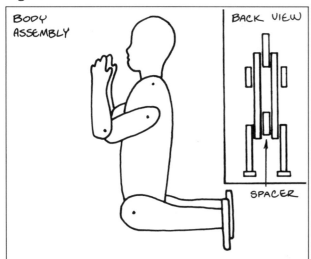

BODY ASSEMBLY

BACK VIEW

SPACER

Figure F

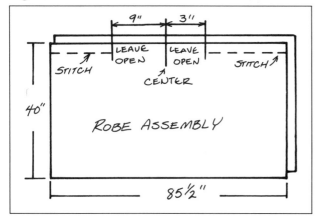

9" 3"

STITCH

LEAVE OPEN

LEAVE OPEN

CENTER

STITCH

40"

ROBE ASSEMBLY

85½"

Figure G

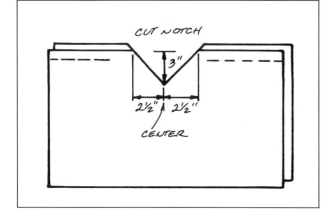

CUT NOTCH

3"

2½" 2½"

CENTER

tion as the front edge of the Leg. Drill two screw pilot holes up through the Foot and into the Leg, and insert the screws, as shown. Assemble the second Leg and Foot in the same manner; be sure that the Foot is turned so that the assemblies are mirror images.

4. Place a Leg-and-Foot against the outside of one Body (**Figure E**), aligning the bolt holes. The longer edge of the Foot is meant to be the inside edge, so make sure you have the correct Leg-and-Foot. The toe end of the Foot should point in the same direction as the thumb. Insert the 4½-inch bolt through the Leg from the outside, and push it on through the Body. Place the Spacer against the inside of the Body, aligning the holes, and push the bolt on through the Spacer. Place the second Body against the opposite side of the Spacer, making sure it is turned correctly, and push the bolt on through the Body. Place the remaining Leg-and-Foot against the outside of the Body, push the bolt on through it, and secure with a wing nut.

5. Place the neck edge of the Head between the upper ends of the two Bodies (**Figure E**), with the face pointing forward. Align the bolt holes and insert the 3½-inch bolt. Secure with a wing nut.

6. Arrange the body parts as you like by loosening and then retightening the wing nuts. The position we settled on is shown in **Figure E**.

7. To assemble the staff, insert and glue the 4½-foot length of closet rod into the socket in the Crook.

8. Apply a coat of light-colored stain to the shepherd's Head, Lower Arms, Legs, and Feet. Apply waterproofing sealer to all parts, and to the staff.

Making the Clothing

1. To prepare the 16 x 36-inch piece of fabric for the headband, stitch a narrow hem along each edge.

2. To prepare the 2½-yard length of fabric for the burnoose, stitch a narrow hem along each edge.

3. The 4¾-yard length of 40-inch-wide fabric will be made into the robe. First, fold the fabric in half widthwise, placing right sides together. You should now have a double layer of fabric that measures 40 x 85½ inches. Cut the fabric in half along the fold, and leave the two layers stacked evenly with right sides together.

4. The two fabric layers are now stitched together as shown in **Figure F**. Mark the center point along one long edge. Measure 3 inches from the center point in one direction and 9 inches in the other direction, and mark these points. Stitch a ½-inch-wide seam through both layers of fabric, from each end up to the marked outer point, as shown. This should leave a 12-inch-long off-center opening between the marked points.

5. Now cut a triangular notch into the open portion of the seam, as shown in **Figure G**. To do this, first measure along the seamed edge 2½ inches from the center point in each direction, and mark these points. Measure 3 inches straight downward from the center of the seamed edge. Cut the notch, using the marked points as the corners of the triangle, as shown. Press the seams open, and turn the robe right side out.

6. Fold the robe wrong sides together along the seamed edge, and then fold in half again, as shown in **Figure H**. (It should now be folded in quarters.) Mark and cut the outer edges in a curved contour, as shown. Open the robe, and stitch a narrow hem around the entire outer edge.

7. Place the robe on the wooden body, slipping the head through the center opening. Adjust the robe so that the longer slit is at the back. Drape the robe evenly around the body.

8. Cut the length of cotton cord in half, and tie a knot at each end of each length to keep the cord from raveling. Wrap one of the lengths around the robe and body at waist level, and tie at the side (**Figure I**).

9. Fold the hemmed headband fabric lengthwise several times, so that it is about 1½ inches wide (**Figure J**). Wrap the remaining length of cotton cord around the headband, and secure the ends with glue.

10. The burnoose is held on the shepherd's head by means of the headband, as shown in **Figure K**. Fold the burnoose fabric to find the widthwise center line. Open the fabric, and place it right side up over the shepherd's head; align the center of the fabric along the forehead edge of the head, as shown, and allow the bulk of the fabric to hang evenly over the shoulders. Wrap the headband around the head and burnoose, and secure the ends together at the back using glue, tacking stitches, or a knot. Tuck the sides of the burnoose up underneath the headband.

11. We posed the shepherd as shown in **Figure E**, and placed the staff between his hands. If the arm bolts are sufficiently tightened, the staff should stay in place. You may wish to pose the shepherd differently, and to glue or otherwise secure the staff to his hands.

THE SHEEP

The frame for the sheep consists of wooden fore- and hindquarters joined by lengths of closet rod (**Figure**

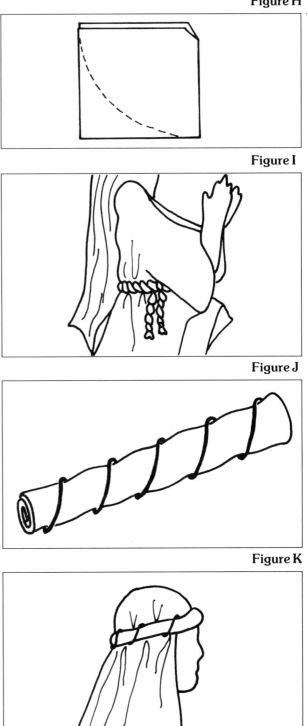

Figure H

Figure I

Figure J

Figure K

Figure L

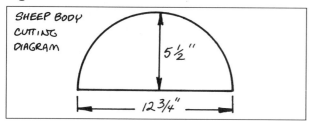

SHEEP BODY CUTTING DIAGRAM

5½"

12 ¾"

Figure M

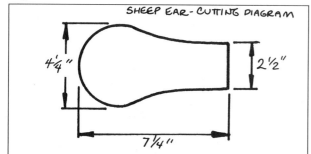

SHEEP EAR - CUTTING DIAGRAM

4¼"

2½"

7¼"

Figure N

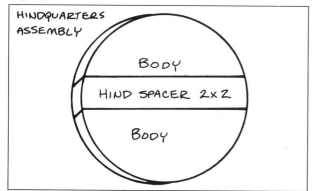

HINDQUARTERS ASSEMBLY

BODY

HIND SPACER 2 x 2

BODY

Figure O

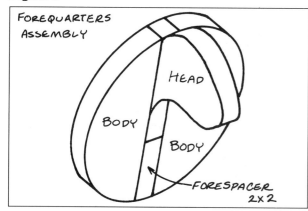

FOREQUARTERS ASSEMBLY

HEAD

BODY

BODY

FORESPACER 2 x 2

Q). Hardware cloth is wrapped around the frame and covered with sheep-fur fabric. Black vinyl ears and closet-rod legs complete the picture (**Figure T**).

Cutting the Parts

1. A scale drawing for the Sheep Head is provided on page 47. Enlarge the drawing to make a full-size pattern. Cut one Sheep Head from pine 2 x 12.

2. A cutting diagram for the basic Body piece is provided in **Figure L**. As you can see, it is a 12¾-inch-diameter half circle that has been shortened slightly. Make a full-size paper pattern for the Body. Cut four Body pieces from pine 2 x 6.

3. Cut from pine 2 x 2 one 4½-inch length and one 12¾-inch length. Label the shorter one as the Fore Spacer, and the longer one as the Hind Spacer.

4. Cut from closet rod four 11-inch lengths for the Legs, and three 14-inch lengths for the Body Spacers.

5. A cutting diagram for the Ear is provided in **Figure M**. Make a full-size pattern, and cut one Ear from each vinyl rectangle.

Assembly

1. The hindquarters are assembled as shown in **Figure N**. Glue the 2 x 2 Hind Spacer between the straight edges of two Body pieces, as shown, and clamp while the glue dries.

2. The forequarters are assembled as shown in **Figure O**. Glue the 2 x 2 Fore Spacer and the Head between the straight edges of the two remaining Body pieces, as shown. The back edge of the Head should be flush with the back surfaces of the three other parts. Clamp while the glue dries.

3. The hindquarters are drilled as shown in **Figure P**, to accommodate the body and leg rods. The 1¼-inch-diameter sockets for the Body Spacer rods should be ½ inch deep and centered about 1½ inches from the circular edge of the hindquarters. The 1¼-inch-diameter sockets for the Leg rods should be drilled up into the lower edge of the hindquarters, one on either side of the lower Spacer socket, as shown. These should be about 1 inch deep.

4. The forequarters are drilled in the same manner as the hindquarters. Be sure to drill the Spacer sockets into the back surface of the forequarters (opposite the sheep's face). **Note** that the Spacer sockets must be aligned precisely with those in the hindquarters.

5. The body assembly is shown in **Figure P**. Use the

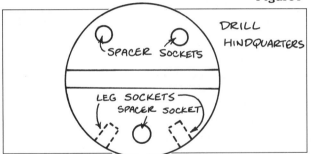

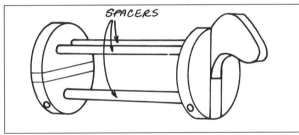

Figure R

Figure S

Figure T

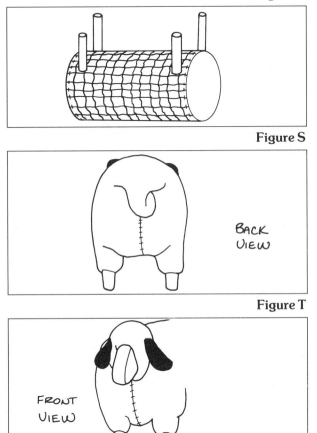

three Body Spacer rods to connect the fore- and hindquarters, glueing them into the sockets. Glue a Leg rod into each leg socket; trim the lower ends of the Legs at an angle, so they sit flat on the floor.

6. Sand and stain the head and legs, and allow to dry before proceeding.

7. Wrap the hardware cloth around the sheep form (**Figure R**), stapling or tacking it to the edges of the fore- and hindquarters.

8. The sheep-fur fabric is tucked and folded around the form as shown in **Figures S** and **T**. Lay the fabric over the hardware cloth, placing the widthwise center line of the fabric lengthwise along the top of the sheep's back. Adjust it so that it extends over the sheep's head at the front. Pull together the fabric edges underneath the sheep, fold under the raw edges, and whipstitch them together along the underside.

9. To finish the tail end, pull together and whipstitch the fabric edges along the center back (**Figure S**), tucking and folding the upper corner so it resembles a short sheep's tail. Fold the excess fabric around the two hind legs, as shown, and whipstitch where necessary.

10. At the front end (**Figure T**), fold under the top front edge of the fabric two or three times to fill out the head shape. Glue the fabric to the top and sides of the wooden head. Below the head, pull together and whipstitch the fabric edges along the center front line, as shown. Wrap the excess fabric around the two front legs, as you did for the hind legs, and stitch together any remaining loose edges underneath the sheep.

11. To attach one vinyl Ear, first fold the Ear in half lengthwise, and glue together the short straight edge in this position. Allow the rest of the Ear to unfold; the glued edge should create an overall ear-like curve. Glue or staple the short folded edge of the ear to one side of the sheep's head, as shown in **Figure T**. The inside of the curve should face forward. Prepare and at-

tach the second Ear in the same manner.

12. The bell will hang from the grosgrain ribbon, around the sheep's neck. Cut the ends of the ribbon at an angle. Thread the ribbon through the bell hanger-loop, and wrap the ribbon around the sheep's neck. Adjust it to an attractive length, and tie in a bow.

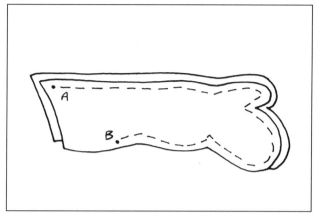

Antique Miss

This beautiful antique miss doll will delight your little miss. She is simple to make, and features a lace trimmed dress and bloomers, yarn-star eyes, brown coiled braids, and a crown of dried flowers in her hair.

Materials

2 yards of 45-inch-wide ivory or cream-colored cotton fabric for the body and clothes

8-inch-square piece of black cotton fabric for the shoes

1 yard of 2-inch-wide lace trim

2 yards of ¼-inch-wide grosgrain ribbon

10-inch length of bias fold-over tape in a color to match the dress fabric

One skein of brown yarn for the hair

Brown embroidery floss for the eyes

1 yard of ¼-inch-wide elastic

Six ⅜-inch buttons for the shoes and dress

One bag of polyester fiberfill

Regular sewing thread

A selection of dried flowers (such as baby's breath) for the crown

Florist's wire

Cutting the Pieces

1. Scale drawings are provided on pages 50-51 for the Yoke Back, Yoke Front, Arm, Leg, Shoe, Torso, Sleeve, Dress Front/Back, and Bloomers. Enlarge the drawings to make full-size paper patterns. (Refer to the Tips & Techniques section on enlarging scale drawings, if necessary.)

2. Cut the pieces listed here from the specified fabrics. Fold the fabric to cut matching pieces.

Cotton: Dress Front - cut one
       Dress Back - cut two
       Yoke Front - cut one
       Yoke Back - cut two
       Sleeve - cut two
       Bloomers - cut two
       Torso - cut two
       Arm - cut four
       Leg - cut four

Black cotton: Shoe - cut four

Making the Arms, Legs, and Torso

Note: All seam allowances are ⅜ inch unless otherwise specified in the instructions.

1. Place two Arm pieces right sides together. Begin at point A and stitch around the contoured edge to point B, as shown in **Figure A**. Clip the curves, and turn the arm right side out. Press the seam allowances to the inside along the open edges.

2. Assemble another arm in the same manner, using the remaining two Arm pieces.

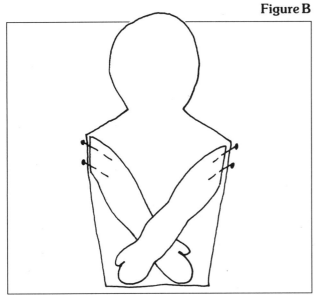

Figure B

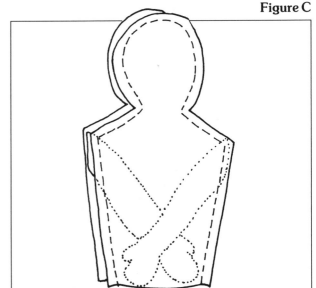

Figure C

3. To assemble the Torso (**Figure B**), first place one Torso piece right side up on a flat surface. Pin one arm along the shoulder edge, making sure the thumb points upward. Pin the remaining arm along the opposite shoulder edge in the same manner.

4. Place the second Torso piece right side down on top of the stack (**Figure C**), sandwiching the arms between the pieces. Stitch around the contoured edges, leaving the straight edge open and unstitched. (Make sure that you don't stitch any of the lower arm material in this seam.) Remove the pins, clip the curves, and turn the torso right side out.

5. Stuff the arms tightly with fiberfill through the short openings in the seams. Whipstitch the opening edges.

6. Stuff the torso and head firmly with fiberfill, right up to the seam allowance along the lower straight edge.

7. To make the leg/shoe assemblies, place one Shoe piece and the lower straight edge of one Leg piece right sides together, and stitch the seam, as shown in **Figure D**. Press the seam allowances toward the shoe. Repeat the procedures for the remaining leg/shoe assemblies, using the remaining six Leg and Shoe pieces.

8. Place two leg/shoe assemblies right sides together and stitch around the contoured edge, leaving the top edge open and unstitched (**Figure E**). Clip the curves, turn right side out, and stuff tightly with fiberfill right up to the seam allowances.

9. Place the two legs on top of the torso, as shown

Figure D

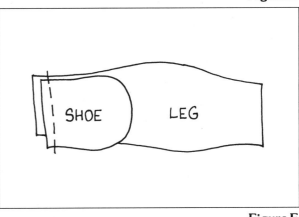

SHOE LEG

Figure E

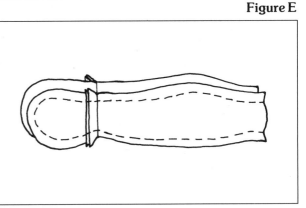

Figure F

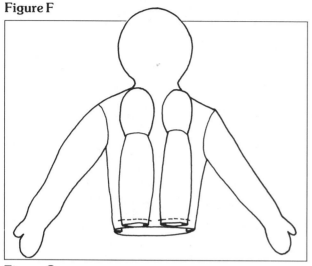

Figure G

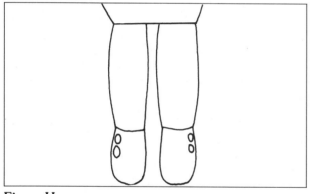

Figure H

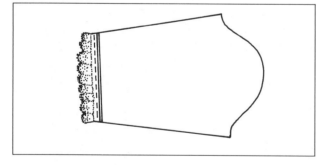

in **Figure F**. Stitch across the top of each leg to attach it to the front layer of the torso only. Turn the legs downward, and press the torso seam allowance to the inside around the lower edge. Whipstitch the pressed front and back lower edges of the torso together

Figure I

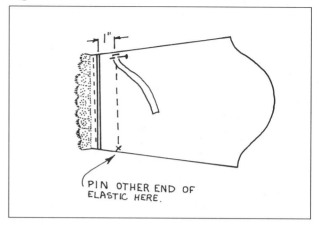

PIN OTHER END OF ELASTIC HERE.

10. Glue two small buttons to the side of the shoes, as shown in **Figure G**. Repeat for the remaining shoe.

Making the Dress

1. Turn and press a ¼-inch hem to the inside along the wrist edge of one sleeve. Turn under the hem again, making a double hem, and press. Place the edge of the lace along the pressed hem, and stitch, securing both the lace and hem at the same time (**Figure H**).

2. Cut a 5-inch length of elastic. Pin one end of the elastic strip to one side edge of the sleeve (**Figure I**), placing it about 1 inch from the hemmed edge. Pin the other end of the elastic to the opposite sleeve edge in the same manner. Stretch the elastic until it is flat against the fabric. (If the elastic won't stretch completely across the fabric, run a line of basting stitches across the sleeve width, and then gather the fabric until it fits the stretched elastic. Adjust the gathers evenly.) Hold both ends of the elastic and stretch it as you stitch the elastic in place. Do not let the sewing machine needle take any of the pressure or it might break.

3. Repeat steps 1 and 2 to assemble the second sleeve in the same manner.

4. Place the Yoke Front right side up on a flat surface. Place one Yoke Back on top, matching the shoulder and armhole edges (**Figure J**). Stitch the shoulder seam. Attach the remaining Yoke Back to the opposite shoulder edge in the same manner. Press the seams.

5. Stitch lace down the front of the Yoke, as shown in **Figure K**.

6. Run a line of basting stitches across the top edge of the Dress Front piece (**Figure L**). Pull the basting

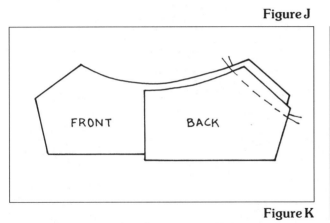
Figure J

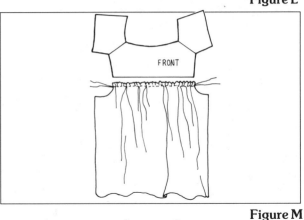
Figure L

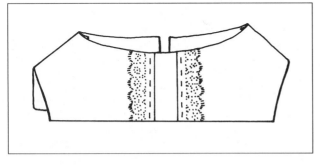
Figure K

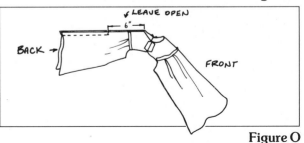
Figure M

threads to gather the Dress Front until it matches the width of the yoke. Pin the gathered Dress Front to the yoke, placing right sides together. Stitch the seam, remove the basting thread, and press the seam allowances toward the dress.

7. Gather and stitch the Dress Back pieces in the same manner as you did the dress front, matching the armhole and back neck opening edges, as shown in **Figure M**.

8. Fold the dress back assemblies right sides together (**Figure N**), and stitch the back seam, leaving the top 6 inches unstitched. Press the seam open, and press the seam allowances to the inside.

9. To attach one sleeve (**Figure O**), run a line of basting stitches along the curved shoulder edge of the sleeve. Pull the basting threads to gather the sleeve to fit the armhole opening, adjusting the gathers evenly across the sleeve. Pin the sleeve to the armhole edge, placing right sides together. Stitch the seam, remove the pins and basting threads, and press the seam allowances toward the sleeve. Stitch the remaining sleeve in the same manner.

10. Fold the dress so the front and back are right

Figure N

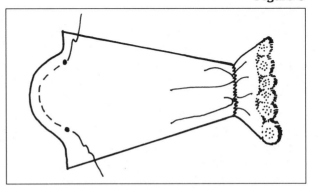
Figure O

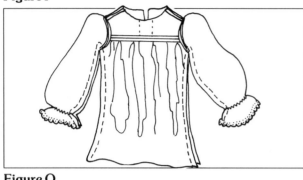

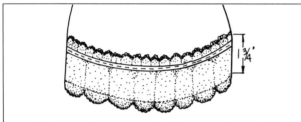

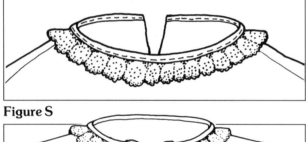

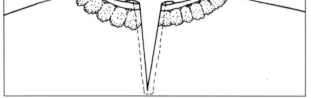

Figure T

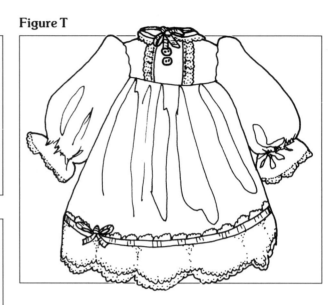

as you did the wrist edge on the sleeve, omitting the lace. Stitch the 2-inch-wide lace on the right side and along the lower edge of the dress (**Figure Q**). Place the lace about 1¾ inches above the hem, so a little of the lace extends below the hem. Stitch a length of grosgrain ribbon near the top edge of the lace, as shown.

12. To finish the neck edge (**Figure R**), first baste a length of lace around the neck about ¼-inch from the edge. Encase the raw neck edges in bias fold-over tape, making sure the upper edge of the lace is underneath the tape.

13. Turn under, press, and then topstitch the neck edges and seam allowances along both edges of the back opening, as shown in **Figure S**.

14. Figure T shows the finished dress. Tie a length of the grosgrain ribbon in a small bow, and tack it to the front of the dress, on top of the lace. Tie another length in a small bow, and tack it to the front center of the neck edge. Sew two small buttons down the center front of the yoke.

Making the Bloomers

1. Turn under and press a ¼-inch double hem along the lower edge of one Bloomer piece. Stitch a length of lace along the pressed hem, securing the lace and hem at the same time, in the same manner as you did for the sleeves.

2. Stitch elastic across the leg 2 inches from the hem, in the same manner as you did the sleeve.

sides together, matching the underarm seams, wrist edges, and lower dress edge (**Figure P**). Begin at the wrist edge and stitch the underarm and side seam, as shown. Clip the curves, and press the seam open. Repeat the procedures for the remaining underarm and side seam. Turn the dress right side out.

11. Turn under and stitch a ¼-inch double hem along the lower edge of the dress in the same manner

Figure V

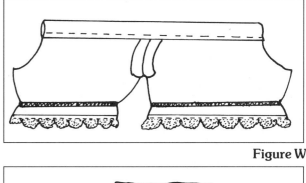

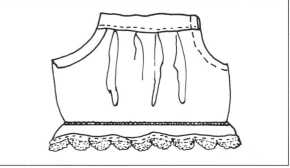

Figure X

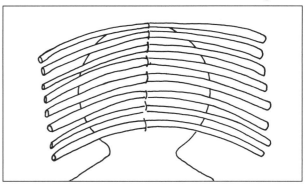

3. Repeat the procedures in steps 1 and 2 for the remaining Bloomer piece.

4. Place the Bloomer pieces right sides together, as shown in (**Figure U**), and stitch the center front seam. Clip the curve, and press the seam open.

5. To form the casing at the waist (**Figure V**), open the bloomers and press a ¼-inch hem allowance to the wrong side of the waist edge. Turn the waist edge down again about ½ inch, and stitch through all layers to form the elastic casing.

6. Measure and cut a piece of elastic slightly longer than the doll's waist measurement. Tack one end of the elastic to one edge of the casing. Thread the elastic through the casing, and tack the opposite end of the elastic to the casing.

7. Fold the bloomers right sides together and stitch the center back seam, catching the ends of the elastic in the seam, as shown in **Figure W**. Clip the curve, and press the seam open.

8. Refold the bloomers (still with right sides together), matching the center front and back seams, and stitch the inner leg seam from one lower edge to the other (**Figure X**).

Making the Hair and Eyes

1. To make the hair (**Figure Y**), first cut about one hundred 30-inch lengths of yarn. Place the center of the

Figure Z

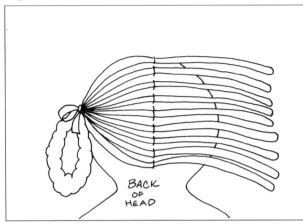

BACK
OF
HEAD

Figure AA

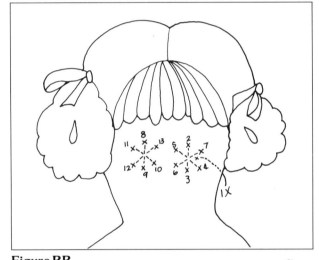

Figure BB

yarn strands across the head, and evenly distribute the strands from front to back. Stitch the yarn in place down the center of the head. This will also create the center "part" to divide the braids.

2. Pull about twenty lengths to the front for the bangs. These will be trimmed later, but for now, use a rubber band or string to hold the yarn out of the way.

3. Smooth half of the yarn to one side of the head, and tack it in place about where the ear would be (**Figure Z**). Braid the yarn, securing the end with a 12-inch length of grosgrain ribbon tied around it. Bend the end of the braid back toward the head, and tack it in place, as shown. Finish the yarn-hair on the opposite side in the same manner.

4. To make the yarn-star eyes, thread a long embroidery needle with all six strands of the brown embroidery floss (don't separate the strands as you normally would). Tie a knot in one end of the floss. Follow the entry and exit points illustrated in **Figure AA**.

    a. Enter at point 1 on the back of the head underneath the hair (so the knot won't show), push the needle through the head, and exit at 2 on the front.

    b. Pull the floss across the surface, and enter at 3. To prevent the dark floss from showing through the light fabric, take a deep stitch between 3 and 4, and then exit at 4.

    c. Pull the floss across the surface, enter at 5, take a deep stitch between 5 and 6, and exit at 6.

    d. Pull the floss across the surface, enter at 7, push the needle through the head, and exit at 1 on the back. Tie a knot, and then cut the floss.

    e. Repeat sub-steps **a** through **d** for the remaining eye, using points 8 through 13.

5. To make the bangs, first remove the rubber band or string. Smooth the front yarn over the head, and trim the bangs.

Making the Crown

Begin with two or three dried flowers and a long length of florist's wire. Stagger the flowers so each flower head is a little below the other, as shown in **Figure BB**. Wrap the wire a few times around the stems. Place the next flower a little lower, and wrap the wire around it. Continue adding flowers and wrapping wire until it measures approximately 12 inches long. Carefully bend the flowers into a circle, and secure the ends by wrapping wire around the stems.

Figure A

Bird's Nest Wreath

This simple straw wreath will add a touch of natural charm to your entryway or living room, and it also makes an inexpensive and original Christmas gift! No matter how chilly the holiday winter, the comfortably nesting bird will put your family and friends in touch with the warm springtime ahead.

Materials

12-inch-diameter straw wreath (If you prefer a vine wreath, gather some long flexible vines such as wisteria or grape.)

One artificial bird, about 4 inches long from beak to tail

A small woven basket or artificial bird's nest, about 4 inches wide and 2½ inches deep

3½ yards of 1¼-inch-wide calico ribbon, in colors that coordinate with the bird you purchased

A handful of nesting material such as Spanish moss, grass clippings, or tiny twigs

You may wish to use additional decorations such as small Christmas bells, red berries, dried flowers, etc.

Decorating the Wreath

Note: If you opted for a vine wreath follow the instructions in the next section, "Making a Vine Wreath," before beginning this section.

1. Cut a 2¼-yard length of calico ribbon and wrap it around the wreath at about 2-inch intervals, as shown in **Figure A**. Pull the ribbon tight enough to smooth out all the wrinkles. Twist together the ribbon ends at the point where they meet, and tie securely in a square knot on what will be the front of the wreath. We trimmed the ribbon ends in a V-shape.

2. Use the remaining 1¼ yards of ribbon to make a

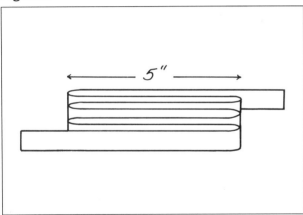

Figure C

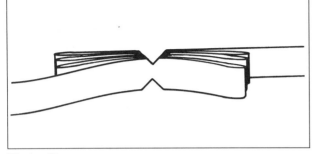

Figure D

Figure E

bow, as shown in **Figure B**. This is quite simple – just fold the ribbon into successive loops, about 5 inches across, leaving 4 or 5 inches at each end for a tail. Clip a V-shape at each edge of the center, as shown in **Figure C**. Hold the bow tightly at the center and twist the individual loops so that each one is right side out.

3. Place the bow against the front of the wreath at the point where the other ribbon ends are tied together. Tie them around the bow at the V-shaped clips, and make a square knot to secure. Clip a V-shape at each end of the bow ribbon.

4. Glue the bird's nest to the wreath at the bottom (opposite the bow), and fill it with nesting material. Glue the bird into the nest.

5. If you wish to add more decorations to the wreath, we suggest that you try out the arrangement before glueing anything in place permanently.

Making a Vine Wreath

1. If you are making a vine wreath you'll first need to find a cylindrical object (like a small trash basket), about 10 inches in diameter, around which to form the wreath. In addition, you'll need some thin nylon cord or string.

2. To make the wreath, wrap one vine around the cylindrical object as many times as the length will allow (**Figure D**). Weave the ends over and under the vine to secure temporarily. Weave a second vine over and under the first one, and continue adding vines until the wreath is as full as you desire.

3. Remove the wreath from the form and wrap it with cord (**Figure E**), to secure while the vines dry. It may take two or three days to dry completely. When the wreath is dry you can remove the cord or not, whichever you prefer.

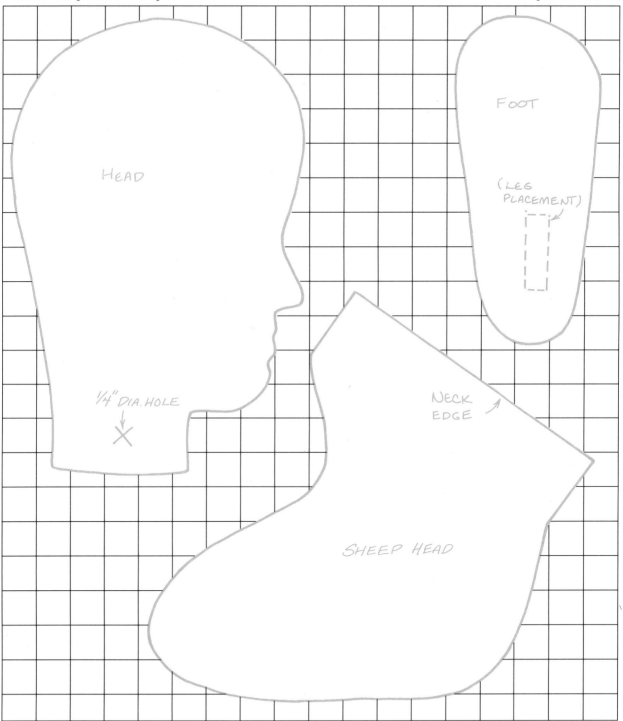

HEAD

FOOT

(LEG PLACEMENT)

¼" DIA. HOLE

NECK EDGE

SHEEP HEAD

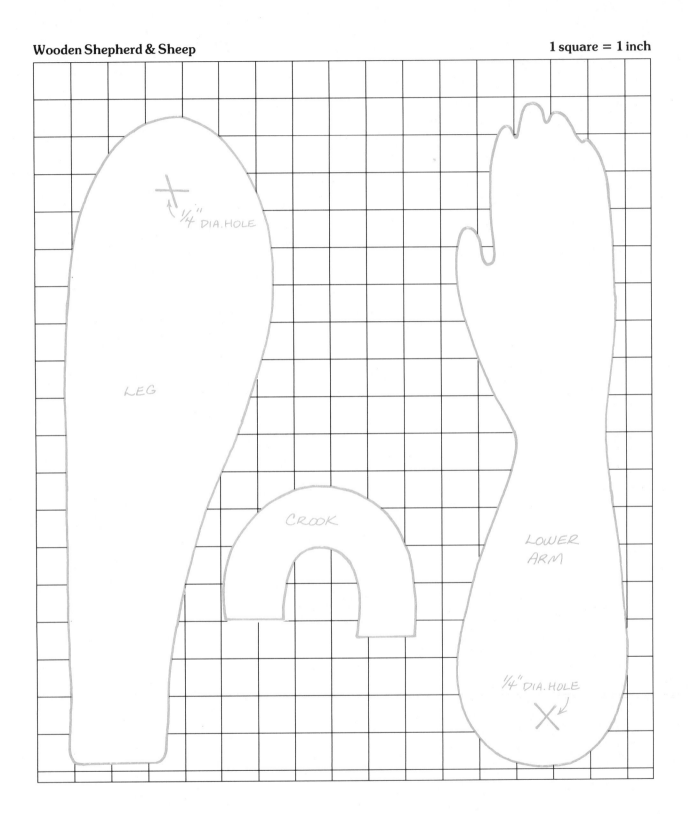

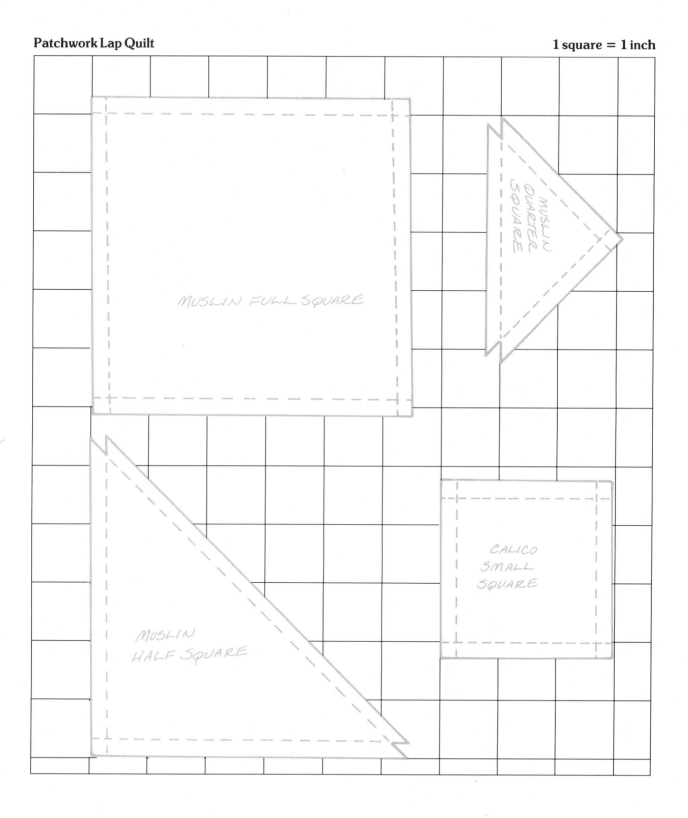

WESTFIELD MEMORIAL LIBRARY,
WESTFIELD, NEW JERSEY

863764

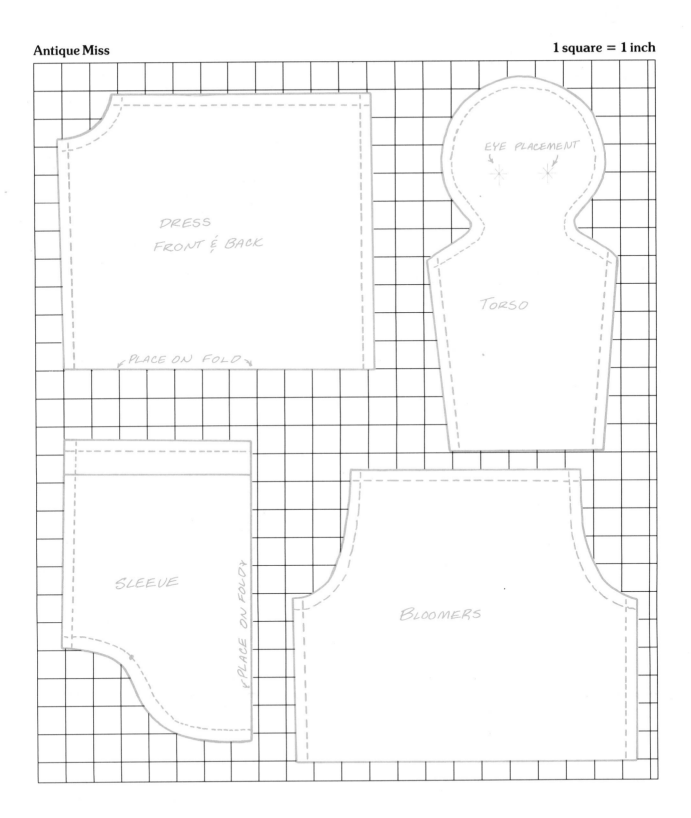

DRESS
FRONT & BACK

←PLACE ON FOLD→

EYE PLACEMENT

TORSO

SLEEVE

←PLACE ON FOLD→

BLOOMERS

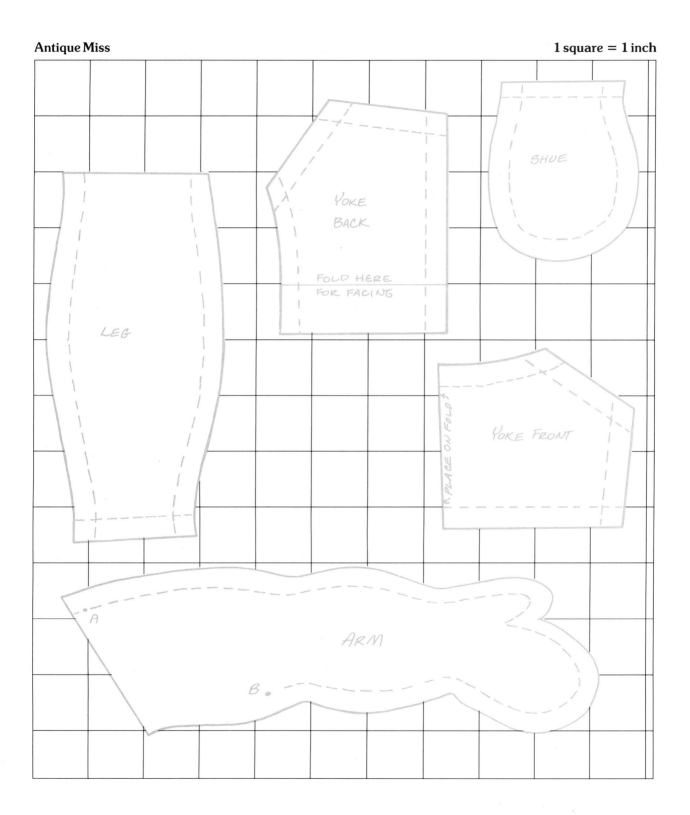

A Victorian Christmas

T he modern concept of the Victorian era is of a people and time that were stuffy, pompous, and way-too-formal. But compared to the earlier iron-fisted Puritans, the Victorians were really a rather fun-loving group. Christmas, as it turned out, had everything a good Victorian could desire.

The British Victorians polished Christmas until it glowed with a new warmth – thanks in part to Queen Victoria's husband, Prince Albert, who reignited the Christmas flame in merrie olde England. The Victorians brought to the holidays a revival of the feasting, fellowship, and fun that the Middle Ages had enjoyed.

In keeping with the Victorian Christmas spirit, in this section we have combined frills and lace with modern-day fun and a festive atmosphere. The crocheted ornaments and angel will trim your tree in a most Victorian manner. The quilted Jessica bear, Antique Miss doll, and wooden drumbox and flute are great presents for any little girl or boy, and the Victorian Christmas stocking is simple to create and beautiful to display.

Victorian Christmas

Victorian Stocking

Christmas Carolers

Drumbox

Crocheted Angel & Snowflakes

Jessica Bear

CELEBRATIONS OF CHRISTMAS

Menus and Melodies

A Victorian Menu

The Victorian Christmas dinner was a very special affair. The table was set with the family's best china, silverware, and linens, and throughout the house were evergreen boughs, holly, bright ribbons and decorations. A cluster of mistletoe was hung from the chandelier, and as a special touch (if the cost was not prohibitive), were freshly cut flowers.

Following an early morning breakfast, the children opened their presents, and then went to church. When they returned they were greeted by savory smells drifting through the house, all in preparation of the holiday dinner that would soon be ready.

Christmas dinner was served in the early afternoon, and it was a grand feast. A beautifully browned turkey, stuffed hams, and on occasion, a roast were the central stars of the dining table. To accompany the turkey, there was a dressing of oysters, chestnuts, or corn-meal mixture. Side dishes of two or three different styles of potatoes, vegetables, gravies, pickled mangoes, peaches, relishes, and platters of oysters complimented the main courses.

Dinner might take a couple of hours to finish, and second, third, and (occasionally) fourth helpings were not uncommon. When the main courses were consumed, the traditional plum pudding with its halo of blue flame was presented. Other pies and puddings and sweets were also served, and everyone ate their fill. Coffee, wines, and brandies were served to the men, and since this was pre-women's lib, the women and children would leave the men to their cigars, liquors, and conversation.

A typical menu for the Victorian dinner might be:
Roast Turkey with Oyster Dressing
Stuffed Ham
Stewed Oysters
Vegetables: Mashed Potatoes, Beets, Braised Celery, Candied Sweet Potatoes
Cranberry and Apple Pie
Pumpkin Pie
Plum Pudding
Fruits, Candies, and Nuts

Braised Celery

2 large onions	4 cups celery,
1 Tbsp. cornstarch	cut into pieces
2 cups bouillon	4 Tbsp. butter,
2 cups water	melted

Place sliced onions in baking dish. Brown celery in melted butter. Blend cornstarch with a little water, add remaining water and bouillon. Combine with browned celery and cook for 5 minutes. Pour over onions and bake at 325° for about 1 hour. Serves 6 to 8.

Cranberry and Apple Pie

1½ cups cranberries	1½ cups diced
½ cup water	cooking apples
Pastry dough	1 cup sugar

Cook cranberries and apples in water until tender. Add sugar and cool slightly. Line 9-inch pie pan with pastry and pour in filling. Cover with ½-inch strips of pastry dough in lattice design. Bake at 450° for 10 minutes; reduce heat to 350° and bake 30 to 40 minutes longer, or until pastry is brown.

For the Victorian Christmas, home-canned preserves, jams, jellies, and candies were given as gifts as well as gracing the dining table. Modern favorites such as peanut brittle and fudge were as popular then as now, and in many ways (with the exception of microwave cooking), the preparation was also the same.

Chocolate Fudge

2 cups sugar	Corn syrup (2 Tbsp.
⅔ cup milk,	to ⅓ cup,
cream or water	to taste)
3 Tbsp. cocoa (or 2	⅛ tsp. salt
squares chipped	1 tsp. vanilla
chocolate)	2 or 3 Tbsp. butter

Combine all ingredients except butter and vanilla in sauce pan. Cook over low heat, stirring constantly, until sugar dissolves and mixture begins to boil. Cook without stirring until candy reaches soft-ball stage. Add butter, and let candy cool. Add vanilla. Beat until the gloss is gone and it begins to feel grainy. Turn into buttered square pan and mark into squares.

Twelfth Night parties, celebrating the end of the Christmas season, were very popular. A special cake was baked for this occasion. The Epiphany cake contained small surprises placed in the batter before the cake was baked. The surprise could be as simple as a bean, which designated the man who found it as king for the duration of the party; or a pea, which designated the woman who found it as queen of the party.

In some instances, various items were wrapped in foil or paper and represented certain qualities of the finder. A button or a ring represented faithfulness, and wealth was symbolized by a dime or a coin. A small heart denoted devotion, and a thimble indicated that the finder possessed great patience. Woe to the person who bit into a clove, for it was the symbol of the fool.

Epiphany Cake
(A yellow cake, rich in sour cream.)

2 eggs	1 cup sugar
1 tsp. vanilla	1 cup sour cream
1½ cups	½ tsp. baking soda
sifted flour	½ tsp. salt
1 tsp. baking powder	

Beat the eggs and sugar. Sift the dry ingredients. Add the vanilla to the sour cream. Combine with the egg mixture and the dry ingredients. Add surprises. Bake in a square pan at 350° for 35 to 45 minutes.

Music to Enjoy

During the Victorian revival of the Christmas celebration, many new carols were composed and old ones rediscovered. Carol singing once again became popular. In fact, the majority of today's most popular carols originated, or were adapted, in the late 19th century. The following recorded albums contain beautiful Christmas music reminiscent of the Victorian era.

A Christmas Carol
Ralph Richardson and Paul Scoffield
Caedmon Records #1135
This record offers a dramatization of Dickens' greatest Christmas work.

Christmas With Marilyn Horne and the Mormon Tabernacle Choir
Columbia Records, #IM-37836.
Presenting such Victorian favorites as "Hark, the Herald Angels" and "Silent Night."

The Joy of Christmas
Leonard Bernstein with the New York Philharmonic Orchestra and Mormon Tabernacle Choir
Columbia Records #MS-6499
This record includes such traditional children's favorites as "Patapan," "The Animal Carol," and "Once in Royal David's City."

The following lyrics were sung on Twelfth Night celebrations, during the selection of the king and queen:

"Was-haile!
Your places, lads and lasses, take
To find your fortune in the cake.
Was-haile!
Jock gets the bean,
and chooses Kate for queen,
Drink-haile!
Now foot it in the reel,
Each frolic heel;
Ye maskers, that a-mumming go,
Stay yet, and point the toe;
"Bounce, buckram, velvets dear,
For Christmas comes but once a year!
Was-haile! Drink-haile! Noel!
Goodnight! Sleep well!
God keep us all, Immanuel!"

Quilted Jessica Bear

Just picture the glowing smiles and happy faces when your little ones find this adorable girl-bear under the tree on Christmas morning. Jessica is as simple to make as she is to love. While some wear their hearts on their sleeves, Jessica wears one on her tummy and one on her muzzle.

Materials

1 yard of pre-quilted unbleached muslin for the body
¼ yard of unbleached muslin for the front of the ears and the back of the muzzle
¼ yard of solid-color cotton fabric for the hearts (We used scarlet.)
Small amount of fusible interfacing material
½ yard of ½-inch-wide ivory-colored lace trim
2 yards of 1½-inch-wide ivory-colored lace trim
1 yard of ¾-inch-wide satin ribbon (We used fuschia.)
Two ¾-inch-diameter black domed shank buttons for the eyes

Small amount of pink felt for the tongue
One-half bag of polyester fiberfill
4-ply wicking thread or ivory embroidery floss
Regular sewing thread in ivory and white
Chenille needle, size 20
Hot-melt glue and a glue gun (or white glue)
Embroidery hoop (optional)

Cutting the Pieces

1. Scale drawings are provided on pages 78-81 for the Arm, Leg, Muzzle, Tongue, Big Heart, Small Heart, Head, Body, and Ear. Enlarge the drawings to make full-size paper patterns. (Refer to the Tips & Techniques section on enlarging scale drawings.)

2. Cut the pieces as listed in this step from the specified fabrics. Fold the fabric into a double thickness, so you can cut two of each piece at a time, and the resulting pieces will be matching pairs. Pay attention to the "place on fold" notations on the scale drawings. Transfer any placement markings or instructions to the fabric pieces.

Pre-quilted muslin: Head - cut two
Muzzle Front - cut one
Ear Back - cut two
Arm/Leg - cut eight
Body - cut two

Plain muslin: Ear Front - cut two
Muzzle Back - cut one

Pink felt: Tongue - cut one

Cotton fabric: Big Heart - cut one
Small Heart - cut one

Fusible interfacing: Small Heart - cut one

Making the Body

1. Place the Big Heart piece right side up on a flat surface. Pin the ½-inch-wide lace trim to it, aligning the straight edge of the lace with the outer edge of the Heart (**Figure A**). Stitch ¼ inch from the edge of the Heart. Clip the corner and curves, and carefully press the lace to the outside.

2. Place one of the Body pieces right side up on a flat surface. Pin the lace-trimmed heart to the center of the Body piece, and blind stitch the heart in place. This will be the Body Front.

3. Work a combination of large and small French

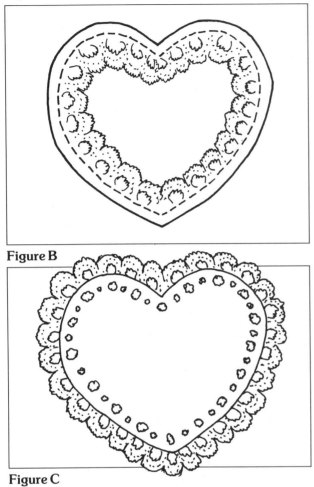

Figure C

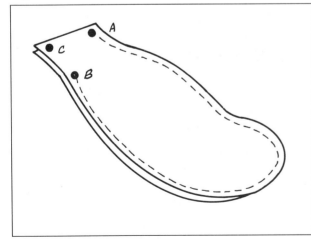

knots around the perimeter of the heart, about ¼ inch from the edge (**Figure B**). Make sure the knots are as evenly spaced as possible. (Refer to the Tips & Techniques section on French knots if necessary.)

4. You will be making the arms and legs next; note the lettered start and stop points as you follow the instructions in this step. Place two Arm/Leg pieces right sides together and stitch the seam along the long contoured edge, beginning at point A and continuing around to point B. Leave the seam open between points B and C, and leave the straight shoulder edge open (**Figure C**). Clip the curves and turn the arm right side out. Press the seam allowances to the inside between points B and C.

5. Realign the layers of the arm at the shoulder edge, matching the seams (**Figure D**). Baste across the shoulder end, about ½ inch from the edges.

6. Repeat the procedures in steps 4 and 5 to create three more arm/leg assemblies, using the remaining Arm/Leg pieces.

7. Place the Body Front piece right side up on a flat surface. Pin two of the arm/leg assemblies on top, aligning the straight basted edge of each arm with the edge of the Body Front piece (**Figure E**). Note that the front of the arm (the toes) should curve toward the Body piece. The upper edge of each arm should lie about 2 inches from the neck opening. Baste the arms to the Body piece over the existing basting lines.

8. Pin the two legs to the Body Front piece in the same manner (toes curving toward the Body piece), placing them toward the lower portion of the Body about 5½ inches apart. Baste the legs to the Body.

9. Place the Body Back piece on top of this assembly, right side down, sandwiching the arms and legs between the Body pieces. Pin the Body pieces together around the entire outer edge and stitch the seam, leaving a neck opening between the arms.

10. Clip the curves and turn the body right side out. Press the seam allowances to the inside along the opening in the neck.

11. Stuff the arms and legs with fiberfill through the short openings in the seams, leaving about 1 inch unstuffed at the top of each limb. Whipstitch the opening edges of each limb. Stuff the body through the neck opening. Do not stitch the neck opening.

Making the Head

1. Begin by making the ears. Place one Ear Back

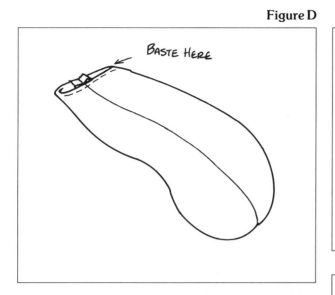

BASTE HERE

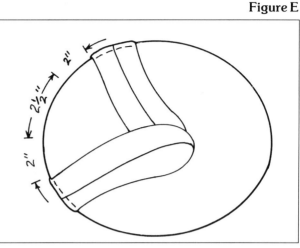

2"
2½"
2"
2"

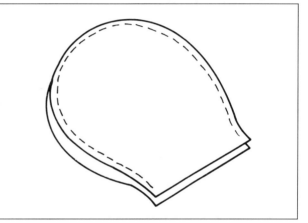

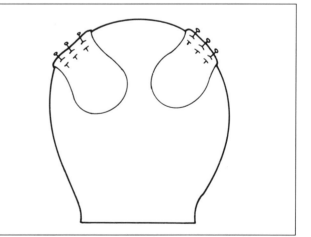

piece and one Ear Front piece right sides together. Stitch the seam along the long curved edge, leaving the straight edge open (**Figure F**). Clip the curve and turn the ear right side out. Baste the layers together across the straight edge. Do not stuff the ear.

2. Make a second ear in the same manner, using the remaining Ear Front and Ear Back pieces.

3. Place one Head piece right side up on a flat surface and pin the ears along the placement marks, plain muslin side down (**Figure G**). Baste the ears in place over the existing basting lines, and remove the pins.

4. Pin the remaining Head piece right side down on top of this assembly, sandwiching the ears between the Head pieces. Stitch the seam along the long curved edge, leaving the short straight neck edge open. Clip the curves and turn the head right side out.

5. Stuff the head firmly with fiberfill, leaving about 1 inch unstuffed at the neck opening. Baste across the neck opening, about 1 inch from the edges, to secure the stuffing.

6. Place the Muzzle Front piece right side up on a flat surface. Place the Small Heart cut from fusible interfacing on top, in the center of the muzzle. Place the Small Heart cut from the pre-quilted muslin on top of that. Fuse the Heart to the Muzzle Front, following the manufacturer's instructions.

7. Work evenly spaced French knots along the outer edge of the heart, as closely as possible to the edge. (The Muzzle piece is too small to fit in an embroidery

Figure H

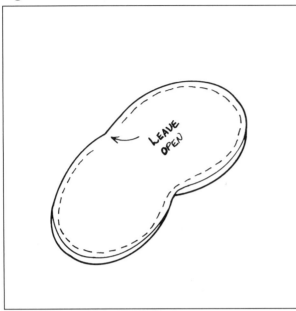

Figure I

Figure J

hoop, so you'll have to take extra care in working the French knots.

8. Place the two Muzzle pieces right sides together and stitch the seam (**Figure H**), leaving a short opening for turning. Clip the curves and the corner, turn the muzzle right side out, and stuff. Press the seam allowances to the inside along the opening edges, and whipstitch them together.

9. Place the muzzle against the front of the head (the plain muslin sides of the ears face front) along the placement lines. The "scalloped" edge of the muzzle should be at the bottom. Pinch the sides of the muzzle toward each other so the center of the muzzle humps upward, to create a more dimensional effect (**Figure I**). Whipstitch the muzzle to the head around the curved upper portion only, leaving the scalloped edge unstitched, as shown.

10. Figure J shows the finished face. Stitch the buttons to the face, just above the upper edge of the muzzle. Glue the straight edge of the Tongue underneath the muzzle, so that the rounded edge extends about ½ inch below the lower edge of the muzzle.

11. To attach the head to the body, insert the neck into the neck opening on the body. Be sure the face is toward the front of the body. Begin at the center back, and whipstitch around the neck several times.

Finishing

1. Run a line of basting stitches along the long straight edge of the 1½-inch-wide lace. Pull the thread to gather the lace, and place it around Jessica's neck, hiding the whipstitches. Tack together the ends of the lace, to secure it to the neck.

2. Tie a knot at each end of the colored ribbon. Wrap the ribbon around Jessica's neck, covering the gathered edge of the lace, and tie it in a bow at the front.

Victorian Stocking

Ribbons and lace, buttons and bows evoke the soft, feminine charm of Victorian ladies in the parlor at their handiwork. You can give this simple project special meaning by using trims from your treasure-trove of Grandmother's heirlooms.

Materials

Note: We used the taffeta and wool fabrics listed here because they were taken from Grandmother's wedding dress. If you have some heirloom fabric of the proper weight, by all means substitute.

20 x 22-inch piece of cream-colored heavy-weight taffeta for the stocking front and cuff
14 x 20-inch piece of cream-colored lightweight wool fabric for the stocking back
1½-yard length of cream-colored corded piping

Trims:

Here is where you can work in heirloom items of your choice. We have listed all of the trims we used – some old and some new – but feel free to substitute.

5½-inch-diameter cream-colored lace medallion
A lace-trimmed handkerchief, white or cream-colored
5 x 20-inch piece of cream-colored eyelet fabric
22-inch length of 2-inch cream-colored eyelet trim
22-inch length of ⅝-inch-wide cream-colored ribbon lace trim
22-inch length of 1¼-inch-wide cream-colored lace trim (We used gathered lace trim.)
22-inch length of ⅜-inch-wide blue satin ribbon
1-yard length of ⅜-inch-wide lilac-colored satin ribbon with decorative edging
1-yard length of very narrow blue satin ribbon
1-yard length of ³⁄₁₆-inch-wide blue velvet ribbon
An antique pearl-drop hat pin
Handful of buttons in various sizes and colors

Cutting the Pieces

1. A scale drawing of the Stocking pattern is provided on page 82. Enlarge the drawing to make a full-size pattern (see Tips & Techniques).

2. Cut from taffeta one Stocking Front, using the full-size pattern, and one Cuff, 7½ x 20 inches.

3. Cut from wool fabric one Stocking Back, using the full-size pattern.

4. We used about one quarter of the handkerchief as part of the stocking decoration. Measure from a corner of the handkerchief 6 inches along each adjacent edge, and mark these two points. Cut out the 6-inch-square corner section.

Assembly

1. Place the Stocking Front right side up on a flat surface. Place the handkerchief square right side up on top of the heel portion (**Figure A**), and trim the hankie to match the contoured heel edge, as shown. Baste the hankie in place ½ inch from the heel edge, and tack down the free corner.

2. Pin and then baste the piping to the Stocking Front, as shown in **Figure A**. Note that the raw edges of the piping are aligned ¼ inch from the edge of the Stocking, and the corded edge extends in toward the center. Cut off and save the excess piping.

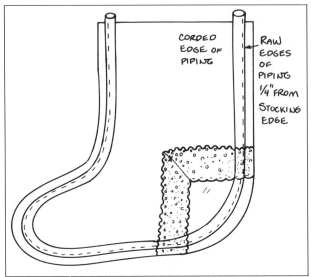

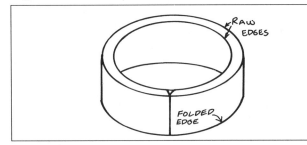

Figure C

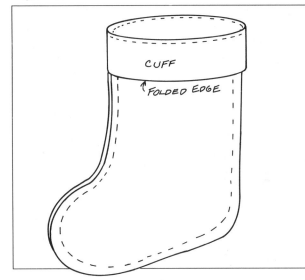

3. Place the Stocking Back right side down on top of the Stocking Front; the piping and hankie trim will be sandwiched between the fabric layers. Pin or baste the layers together along the long contoured edge, leaving the straight top edge open. Use a zipper foot on your machine, and stitch the seam along the contoured edge, as close as possible to the cord inside the piping. Clip the curves, press the seam, and leave the stocking turned wrong side out.

4. Measure around the open top of the stocking and compare this measurement to the length of the taffeta Cuff piece. If necessary, trim the length of the Cuff so that it is exactly 1 inch longer than the stocking-top measurement. Fold the Cuff in half widthwise, placing right sides together, and stitch a ½-inch-wide seam along the short edge only. Press the seam open.

5. The Cuff piece is now a cylinder. Fold the Cuff down over itself lengthwise, all the way around, placing wrong sides together (**Figure B**). Adjust it evenly so that the ends of the existing seam match, as shown. Baste the raw edges together around the cuff.

6. The stocking should still be turned wrong side out. Slip the cuff down over the top of the stocking (**Figure C**), aligning the basted raw edges of the cuff with the raw top edge of the stocking. Stitch a ½-inch seam all the way around the top. Press the seam allowances toward the stocking.

7. Turn the stocking right side out and turn the cuff to the right side of the stocking. Adjust the cuff so that it is not folded along the cuff-to-stocking seam, but about 1 inch above, as shown in **Figure D**. Press the fold line.

Trimming the Stocking

1. Turn the stocking wrong side out, extending the cuff outward (**Figure E**). Wrap the 2-inch-wide eyelet trim around the cuff as shown, placing the lower edge about ⅛ inch below the pressed fold line of the cuff. Fold under the ends of the eyelet (they should overlap at one of the stocking side seams), and baste in place.

2. Wrap the 1¼-inch gathered lace trim around the top of the cuff (**Figure F**), placing the gathered edge just below the folded cuff edge. The lace should extend up beyond the cuff, as shown. Turn under the ends of the lace at a stocking side seam, and baste in place.

3. Weave the 22-inch length of ⅜-inch blue satin ribbon through the 22-inch length of ⅝-inch ribbon lace.

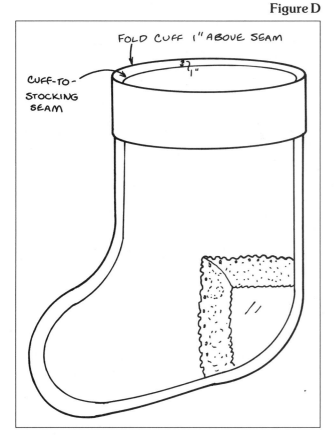

FOLD CUFF 1" ABOVE SEAM

CUFF-TO-STOCKING SEAM

1"

PRESSED FOLD LINE

EDGE OF EYELET 1/8" BELOW FOLD LINE

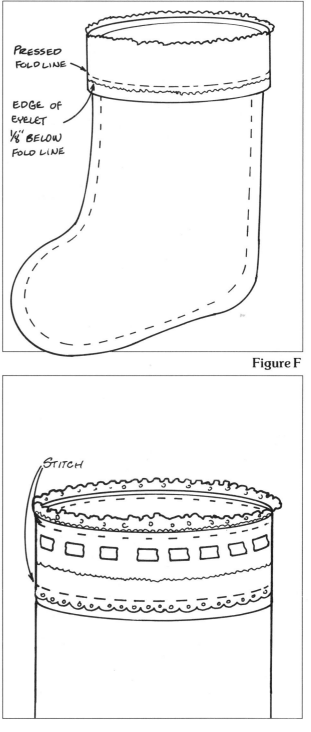

STITCH

Place the ribbon lace around the top of the cuff (**Figure F**), aligning the top edge of the lace just below the folded cuff edge. (Note that the 1¼-inch lace extends out beyond the ribbon lace.) Turn under and overlap the ends at the stocking side seam, and pin or baste the lace in place.

4. It will be easier to machine stitch the trim in place if you will first turn the stocking right side out, with the cuff extending outward. Machine stitch around the cuff through all layers of trim and fabric, close to the folded top edge and about ¼ inch above the lower edge of the 2-inch eyelet, as shown in **Figure F**. (Note that in **Figure F** the stocking is shown wrong side out.)

5. Fold the cuff to the right side of the stocking along the pressed fold line. Remove all of the basting stitches that show.

6. The 5 x 20-inch piece of eyelet fabric is gathered to form a fan shape. To finish one long edge of the eyelet, we worked a scalloped line of closely spaced

Figure G

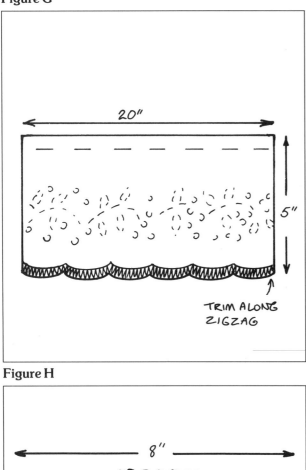

20"

5"

TRIM ALONG
ZIGZAG

Figure H

8"

Figure I

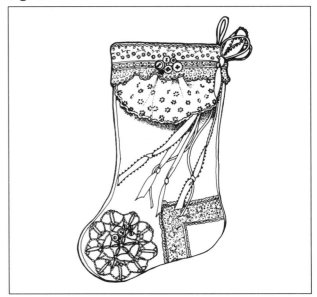

7. Place the fan-gathered eyelet against the front of the stocking, inserting the gathered top edge just underneath the cuff (**Figure I**). Hand stitch the eyelet to the underside of the cuff. Stitch five or six buttons to the front of the cuff on top of the ribbon lace, as shown.

8. Tack the lace medallion to the toe area of the stocking front (**Figure I**), and stitch five or six buttons on top.

9. The three 1-yard lengths of ribbon are attached as shown in **Figure I**. Cut both ends of each ribbon at an angle, and tie a half knot about 3 inches from each end. Align all three ribbons, fold them in half, and tie them together in a half knot about 3 inches from the folded center point. Place this knot against the stocking cuff, near the edge that includes the heel, and secure using the pearl-drop hat pin as shown. Fan out the lower ends of the ribbons and tack each one to the stocking front (tack at the knot near the lower end of the ribbon). Be sure that the ribbons are not stretched tightly between the upper and lower knots.

10. We used the leftover length of corded piping to make a hanger loop. Fold it in half and insert the aligned raw ends inside the stocking cuff at the heel-edge side seam, allowing the folded loop end to extend up beyond the top of the cuff. (It should be hidden behind the top loops of ribbon.) Tack the hanger loop to the cuff close to the top edge.

machine zigzag stitches and then trimmed the fabric along the stitches, as shown in **Figure G**. Run a line of basting stitches about ½ inch from the opposite long raw edge, and pull up the stitches to gather the edge tightly. This should pull the fabric into a fan shape, as shown in **Figure H**

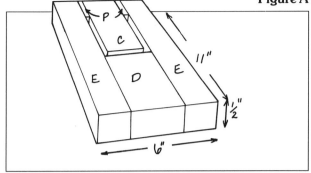

Figure A

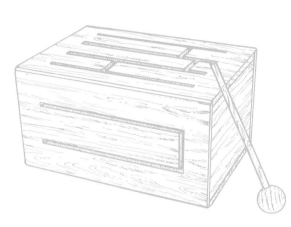

Wooden Drum Box

Although musical instruments have evolved over the centuries, ancient drum styles remain great favorites of both children and performing musicians. This drum box produces eight clear tones.

Materials

5-foot length of ½-inch-thick hardwood lumber, at least 7 inches wide

15-inch length of ¼-inch-diameter wooden dowel rod for the mallets

Two spherical wooden drawer pulls, 1 inch in diameter (These will serve as the mallet heads, and will produce clear, sharp tones. For a softer sound, substitute hard rubber balls.)

Four small rubber bumper pads

Carpenter's wood glue; sandpaper; clear wood sealer; and wood stain or vegetable oil

Cutting the Parts

The drum box consists of a solid floor and end walls, and a slotted lid and side walls. The slots produce the different tones. We made each slotted wall from several rectangular pieces and small spacers. Cut from ½-inch hardwood the parts listed in this section, and label each one with its code letter for reference during assembly.

Code	Dimensions	Quantity
End Walls:		
A	5 x 7 inches	2
Floor:		
B	7 x 11 inches	1
Side Walls:		
C	2 x 5⅜ inches	1
D	2½ x 5⅜ inches	1
E	1¾ x 11 inches	2
F	1⅜ x 2 inches	1
G	2 x 9⅜ inches	1
H	1¾ x 11 inches	2
Lid:		
I	1½ x 2⅜ inches	1
J	1½ x 3⅜ inches	1
K	1½ x 4⅜ inches	1
L	1½ x 6⅜ inches	1
M	1½ x 7⅜ inches	1
N	1½ x 8⅜ inches	1
O	¾ x 11 inches	2
Spacers:		
P	¼ x 1⅜ inches	14

Assembly

1. One side wall consists of the C, D, and E parts and two P spacers. Glue them together along the edges as shown in **Figure A**, and clamp the assembly while it

Figure B

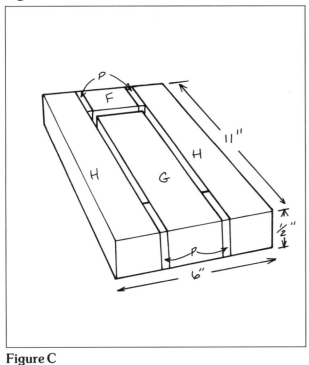

Figure C

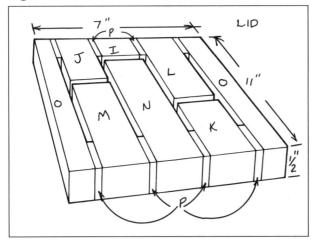

dries. There should be a ¼-inch space between the C piece and the surrounding D and E pieces, except where the two P Spacers go.

2. To assemble the second side wall (**Figure B**), glue together the F, G, and H parts with four P spacers, as shown. Clamp the assembly while the glue dries.

Figure D

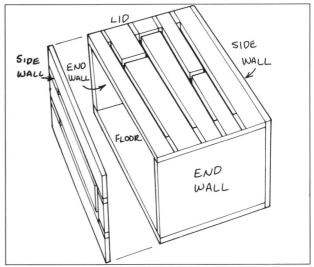

3. To assemble the lid (**Figure C**), glue together and clamp the I through O parts with eight P spacers.

4. Use clear wood sealer to coat one surface of each assembled side wall and the lid, for a sharper, clearer tone. (The coated surface will go on the inside when you assemble the walls to form the box.) Coat one side of each A end wall and the B floor, as well.

5. The box is assembled as shown in **Figure D**. Make sure that you turn each part with the sealed surface facing center. Glue and nail the two A end walls to the top of the B floor, flush at the ends, as shown. Attach the lid over the end walls. Add the side walls over the open sides of the box. Recess the nails and fill the holes with wood filler.

6. Use a wood rasp followed by sandpaper to round off the corners and long edges of the assembled drum box. Sand all remaining edges and surfaces. Glue a rubber bumper to each corner of the floor. Finish with wood stain or vegetable oil. The drum box should be oiled regularly, to keep the wood from drying out.

7. To create the mallets, cut the ¼-inch dowel rod into two equal lengths. Drill a ¼-inch-diameter socket, ½ inch deep, into each wooden drawer pull or rubber ball. (If you are using rubber balls it will be easier to cut out the sockets using a sharp pocket knife, rather than trying to drill them.) Glue a rod into the socket. Sand and finish the mallets as you did the box. When playing the drum box, you will get the best tones by striking the slotted walls and lid at the closed ends of the slots.

Crocheted Angel & Snowflakes

Trim your tree in Victorian splendor with these crocheted ornaments.

Materials

One large ball of bedspread crochet cotton in white
Size 1 steel crochet hook
Four or five cotton balls
Starch; waxed paper; and stainless steel pins

CHRISTMAS ANGEL

Head

Note: Use two strands of thread throughout.

Ch 5, join with sl st to form ring.

Rnd 1: Ch 1, 12 sc in ring, join with sl st in 1st sc.

Rnd 2: Ch 1, * 1 sc in 1st st, 2 sc in 2nd st, repeat from * around, join (18 sc).

Rnd 3: Ch 1, * 1 sc in each of next 2 sts, 2 sc in next st, repeat from * around, join (24 sc).

Rnd 4: Ch 1, * 1 sc in each of next 3 sts, 2 sc in next st, repeat from * around, join (30 sc).

Rnd 5: Ch 1, Work 1 sc in each st around, join.

Rnd 6: Ch 1, repeat Rnd 5.

Rnd 7: Ch 1, * sc in each of next 3 sts, dec over next 2 sts, repeat from * around, join (24 sc).

Rnd 8: Ch 1, * sc in next 2 sts, dec over next 2 sts, repeat from * around, join (18 sc).

Rnd 9: Ch 1, * sc in next st, dec over next 2 sts, repeat from * around, join (12 sc).

Rnd 10: Ch 1, repeat Rnd 9 (8 sc). Stuff head with cotton balls, not firmly, just enough to hold the shape.

Rnd 11: Ch 1, work 1 sc in each st, join to form neck.

Rnd 12: Ch 1, * sc in 1st st, 2 sc in next st, repeat from * around, join (12 sc). From here on, beginning ch 3 counts as 1st dc.

Rnd 13: Ch 3, * dc in 1st st, 2 dc in next st, repeat from * around, join (18 dc).

Shape Sleeves and Bodice

Rnd 14: Ch 3, dc in next st, 2 dc in next st, * (ch 1, dc in next st), repeat from * 7 times, 2 dc in next st, dc in next st, * (ch 1, dc in next st), repeat from * 7 times, join (20 dc).

Rnd 15: Ch 3, dc in next dc, * 2 dc in each of next 2 dc, dc in next dc, (ch 1, dc in sp, ch 1, dc in dc) 7 times. Repeat from * ending last repeat in brackets 6 times. Ch 1, dc in sp, ch 1, join to beg ch 3 (38 dc).

Rnd 16: Ch 3, dc in next 5 sts, ch 1, (dc in next dc, ch 1) 13 times, dc in next 6 sts, ch 1, repeat directions in brackets 13 times, join.

Rnd 17: Ch 3, dc in next 5 sts, ch 3, skip next 13 dc, dc in next 6 dc, ch 3, skip next 13 dc, join to beg ch 3. This form the waist.

Rnd 18: Ch 3, dc in next 5 sts, dc in each ch st, dc in next 6 sts, dc in each ch st, join (18 dc).

Rnd 19: Ch 3, * dc in next st, 2 dc in next st, repeat from * around, join (27 dc).

Rnd 20: Ch 4, dc in joining. * Skip next dc, dc in next dc, ch 1, dc in same dc (V st made) repeat from * around, join (13 V sts).

Rnd 21: Sl st to sp of 1st V st, ch 4, dc in same sp, * ch 1, V st in sp of next V st. Repeat from * around, ch 1, join.

Rnd 22: Sl st to 1st sp, ch 3, dc in same sp, ch 1, 2 dc in same sp, * 2 dc, ch 1, 2 dc in next sp (shell made) repeat from * around, join.

Rnd 23: Sl st to 1st sp, ch 3, dc in same sp, ch 1, 2 dc in same sp, * ch 1, shell in sp of next shell, repeat from * around, ch 1, join.

Rnd 24: Sl st to 1st sp, ch 3, in same sp make dc, ch 2, 2 dc, * ch 1, in next sp make shell of 2 dc, ch 2, 2 dc. Repeat from * around, ch 1, join.

Rnd 25: Sl st to 1st sp, ch 3, in same sp make dc, ch 2, 2 dc, * ch 2, in next sp, make shell of 2 dc, ch 2, 2 dc, repeat from * around, ch 2, join.

Rnd 26: Sl st to 1st sp, ch 3, in same sp make 2 dc, ch 2, 3dc, * ch 1, in next sp make shell of 3 dc, ch 2, 3 dc, repeat from * around, ch 1, join.

Rnd 27: Sl st to 1st sp, ch 3, in same sp make 2 dc, ch 2, 3 dc, * ch 2, in next sp make shell of 3 dc, ch 2, 3 dc, repeat from * around, ch 2, join.

Rnd 28: Sl st in next sp, ch 3, in same sp make 2 dc, ch 2, 3 dc, * ch 2, sc in sp between shells, ch 2, in next sp make shell of 3 dc, ch 2, 3 dc, repeat from * around, ch 2, sc (in sp between shells), ch 2, join.

Rnd 29: Sl st to 1st sp, ch 3, in same sp make 2 dc, ch 2, 3 dc, * ch 3, sc in sc, ch 3. In next sp make shell of 3 dc, ch 2, 3 dc, repeat from * around. Ch 3, sc in sc, ch 3, join. End off.

Sleeve Ruffle

With the side of the angel facing you, attach thread at the right side of the waist through the remaining loop of the original ch 3 that formed the waist. Ch 2, sl st to underarm, work dc in each of 2 remaining waistline loops, sl st at underarm on opposite side. Continue along sleeve, * ch 2, in next dc work shell (2 dc, ch 1, 2 dc), ch 2, sc in next dc, repeat from * around (7 shells). End off at underarm.

Repeat these directions for the other sleeve and side of waist.

Wings

Find the center of the back bodice. Attach thread on the outermost bodice dc in second row from neck. Wings are worked vertically along posts of this dc and the one below it.

Row 1: Ch 3, work 2 dc along post of 1st dc, work 3 dc along post of 2nd dc, ch 4, turn (6 dc).

Row 2: * Work dc in 1st dc, ch 1, repeat from * across, ch 4, turn (7 dc).

Row 3: Dc in 1st dc, * in next dc; dc, ch 1, dc (V st made), repeat from * across ending with V st in last dc, ch 1, dc in same place, ch 4, turn.

Row 4: V st in space of next 5 V sts, ch 1, sl st in sp of next V st, ch 1, work V st in sp of next 2 V sts, ch 1, dc in same sp, ch 1, turn.

Row 5: Sk 1st sp, (in next sp work shell of 2 dc, ch 1, 2 dc) twice, ch 1, sl st in sl st of previous row, ch 1. Repeat directions in brackets four more times. Ch 1, sl st in last sp, ch 1, turn.

Row 6: (In next sp, make shell of 3 dc, ch 1, 3 dc) four times. Ch 1, sc in sl st, ch 1. Repeat directions in brackets two times. Ch 1, sl st in beg ch 1 of previous row. End off.

Repeat directions above for the second wing along the opposite side of the bodice.

Finishing

With a needle and thread, make a large loop at the top of the angel's head so she can hang to dry.

Starch the angel and the wings, using either a heavy cooked starch (about 1 tablespoon powdered starch to 2 cups water) or a starch of white glue mixed half and half with water. The starch method gives more stiffening but greater flexibility.

Wring out the angel without crushing the head. Crumple pieces of paper and stuff the bodice and the sleeves, shaping the crochet as you go. Stuff a small ball of waxed paper inside the angel to shape the waist. Use a large ball of waxed paper to fill out the skirt.

DO NOT USE WAXED PAPER WITH WHITE GLUE. The paper will stick and be glued in place. With glue, constantly check while drying to reshape.

The angel may be air-dried or hung from a hook or bent paper clip in a warm oven with the pilot light on.

When stiff and nearly dry, remove the waxed paper and complete the drying. If the wings tend to "flop," whipstitch them in place with a couple of tiny stitches, using a matching thread color.

Halo

Bend a small piece of thin wire into a circle approximately the size of a quarter. Join the ends of the wire by twisting them around each other.

With metallic gold thread, join to wire and work sc over the wire until the circle is completely covered. Attach the completed halo to the back of the angel's head, using a matching thread color.

SNOWFLAKE ORNAMENTS

Materials

One standard ball of size 10 white cotton crochet thread (will make about twenty-five snowflakes)
One size 8 steel crochet hook
One large box of rust-proof straight pins
A roll of paper towels
A piece of corrugated cardboard, 14 x 18 inches

One can of spray starch
A roll of wax paper
One 8-oz. bottle of white school glue
A small sponge brush, approximately 1½ inches wide
One spool of 8-pound transparent fishing line

Snowflake #1

Ch 7, join with sl st to form ring.

Rnd 1: Ch 3, 2 dc in ring * ch 3, 3 dc in ring * 4 more times, ch 3, sl st in top of beg ch 3.

Rnd 2: Sl st in next 2 dc & in next ch 3 sp, ch 3, 2 dc, ch 3, 3 dc all in same ch 3 sp, ch 1 * 3 dc, ch 3, 3 dc, all in next ch 3 sp * 4 more times, sl st in top of beg ch 3.

Rnd 3: Turn work over & sl st in ch 1 sp just made, turn work back over to right side * ch 2, 3 dc in next ch 3 sp; ch 3, 3 dc in same ch 3 sp, ch 2, sl st in next ch 1 sp * 5 more times.

Rnd 4: Sl st in next 3 chs & in next dc, ch 1 * sc in same sp, sc in next dc (make sc in each of next 2 dc next 5 times), 2 sc in next ch 3 sp, ch 4, tr in 4th ch from hook, ch 4, sl st in same sp as tr, ch 5, tr in 4th ch from hook, ch 4, sl st in same sp as tr, sl st in next ch, ch 4, tr in 4th ch from hook, ch 4, sl st in same sp as tr, sl st in base of 1st cluster, 2 sc in same ch 3 sp, sc in each of next 2 dc, ch 6, sl st in 3rd ch from hook, ch 3 * 5 more times, end with sl st in beg sc.

Snowflake #2

Ch 7, join with sl st to form ring.

Rnd 1: Ch 3, 2 dc in ring * ch 3, 3 dc in ring * 4 more times, ch 3, sl st in top of beg ch 3.

Rnd 2: Sl st in next 2 dc & in next ch 3 sp, ch 3, 2 dc, ch 3, 3 dc, all in same ch 3 sp, ch 1 * 3 dc, ch 3, 3 dc all in next ch 3 sp, ch 1 * 4 more times, sl st in top of beg ch 3.

Rnd 3: Turn work over & sl st in ch 1 sp just made, turn work back over to right side, ch 1 * sc in same ch 1 sp (next 5 times, sc in next ch 1 sp), sc in each of next 3 dc, work as follows in next ch 3 sp: sc, ch 6, tr in 4th ch from hook, ch 4, sl st in same sp as tr, 2 dc, ch 3, dc in 3rd ch from hook, ch 3, sl st in same sp as dc, ch 4, tr in 4th ch from hook, ch 4, sl st in same sp as tr, ch 3, dc in 3rd ch from hook, ch 3, sl st in same sp as dc, sl st in base of 1st dc of this cluster, 2 dc, ch 4, tr in 4th ch from hook, ch 4, sl st in same sp as tr, ch 2, sc; sc in each of next 3 dc * 5 more times, end with sl st in beg sc.

Snowflake #3

Ch 7, join with sl st to form ring.

Rnd 1: Ch 3, 2 dc in ring * ch 3, 3 dc in ring * 4 more times, ch 3, sl st in top of beg ch 3.

Rnd 2: Sl st in next 2 dc & in next ch 3 sp, ch 3, 2 dc, ch 3, 3 dc all in same ch 3 sp, ch 1 * 3 dc, ch 3, 3 dc all in next ch 3 sp, ch 1 * 4 more times, sl st in top of beg ch 3.

Rnd 3: Turn work over & sl st in ch 1 sp just made, turn work back over to right side * ch 2, 3 dc in next ch 3 sp, ch 6, sl st in 6th ch from hook, twirl work & work into 6-ch ring just made from right-hand side to left: sc (ch 3, tr, ch 3, sc) total of 5 times; 3 dc in same ch 3 sp, ch 2, sl st in next ch 1 sp * 5 more times, end with sl st in beg ch 1 sp.

Blocking Instructions

1. Place paper towels on the corrugated cardboard. Place the snowflakes on top of the paper towels, leaving plenty of space around each one.

2. Begin in the center of the snowflake, and secure with a pin at the tip of each major and minor point. Very gently stretch the snowflake as you insert the pins. Spray with starch until all snowflakes are saturated. Let them dry completely before removing the pins.

3. Assemble a sheet of wax paper large enough to block at least four snowflakes, a sponge brush, and white school glue. Place each dry starched snowflake on a piece of wax paper, and use a sponge brush to press white school glue into each one. Remove each snowflake, and wipe off the excess glue from the reverse side. Place each snowflake on another piece of wax paper, making sure each lies flat, and allow them to dry completely.

4. Once the snowflakes have dried thoroughly, repeat the glueing process on the reverse side. Again, allow them to dry completely.

5. To make hangers for the snowflakes, cut a 12-inch length of 8-pound transparent fishing line for each. Insert one length of fishing line through one of the six major points of a finished snowflake, and thread it through the snowflake until you have formed an even double strand. Tie a knot in the strand approximately 1 or 2 inches from the end. Follow the same procedure to make hangers for the remaining snowflakes.

Christmas Carolers

Your family, neighbors, and holiday visitors are sure to be enchanted by this nearly life-size group of Victorian carolers – they're so lifelike, you'll swear you hear the strains of "Good King Wenceslas" wafting out from somewhere in time. A bit of fabric and stuffing, some easy-to-make wooden stands, and clothing purchased at a thrift shop will fill the bil!.

Materials

Note: Amounts listed are for the group of four carolers: two adults and two children.

4 yards of medium-weight double-knit flesh-tone fabric, at least 45 inches wide, for the bodies

1¼ yards of medium-weight shiny black fabric, at least 44 inches wide, for the boots

Two pairs of regular-weave flesh-tone pantyhose

Three skeins of rug yarn for the hair (You can use all the same color, or two or three different colors.)

Ten large bags of polyester fiberfill

Heavy-duty flesh-tone thread; and thread to match the yarn colors

Cosmetic cheek blusher; and powdered eye shadow in light brown and gray

4-foot length of 2 x 12 pine lumber for the stands

Eight 3-foot lengths of ¾-inch wooden dowel rod

14-foot length of "12-2" copper electrical cable (This is fairly stiff, but flexible, plastic-sheathed flat cable, which we inserted into the carolers' clothing to hold the arms in position.)

Clothing

We shopped the local resale stores and found a wealth of Victorian-style clothing. Size is not critical, as even the adult carolers are no larger than a child of about twelve. The smaller carolers are about the size of a six-year-old. You can pin and tuck larger clothing to make it fit, and add holiday accents of lace trim, holly sprigs, fur-fabric cuffs and collars, and the like. The clothing we purchased is described in the following paragraphs – if you want to be ultra-authentic, visit the library to find pictures of Victorian period clothing.

For the adult female we purchased a pale-pink nylon satin outfit consisting of a gathered skirt and quilted overblouse, a short black fur-fabric cape, a gray-and-red striped neck scarf, cranberry-colored knit mittens, a gray hood (cut from a coat), and a red plaid belt. We cut strips from the cape to make matching cuffs.

For the adult male we purchased gray wool trousers, a gray overcoat with fur collar and cuffs, a red-and-white striped neck scarf, black knit gloves, and a very funky old gray top hat.

For the female child we purchased a quilted cranberry-colored dress, a white furry coat collar with pom-pom ties, and a white furry muff.

For the male child we purchased green wool trousers, a gray tweed jacket, cranberry-colored knit mittens, a black knit stocking cap, a gray-and-red plaid neck muffler, and a pair of wire-rim eyeglasses.

Cutting the Pieces

1. A scale drawing of the Adult Boot pattern is pro-

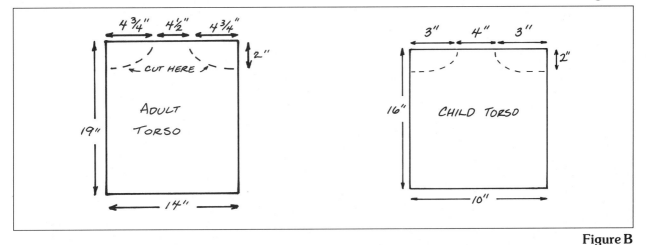

vided on page 83. Enlarge the drawing to make a full-size pattern (see Tips & Techniques). To make a pattern for the Child Boot, trace a slightly smaller version of the Adult Boot pattern, making the straight top edge 7 inches across (this measurement includes a ½-inch seam allowance at each side).

2. Cut from the specified fabrics the body pieces listed in this step, and label each one. The quantities listed are for two adults and two children.

Description	Dimensions	Quantity
Flesh-tone fabric:		
Adult Torso	14 x 19 inches	4
Adult Leg	16 x 21 inches	4
Adult Arm	13 x 24 inches	4
Child Torso	10 x 16 inches	4
Child Leg	13 x 17 inches	4
Child Arm	9 x 17 inches	4
Black fabric:		
Adult Boot	use pattern	8
Child Boot	use pattern	8

3. To create a shoulder-and-neck shape, modify each Adult and Child Torso as shown in **Figure A**.

Making the Bodies

Note: All seams are ½ inch wide.

1. To assemble an adult caroler's body you will need the following adult-size fabric pieces: two Torsos, two Legs, two Arms, and four Boots. Fold one Arm piece in half lengthwise, placing right sides together. Stitch the seam along one end, curve the stitching line around

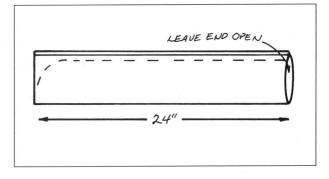

the corner, and continue to stitch the seam along the long edge (**Figure B**). Leave the opposite end open, as shown. Trim the seam allowances to ½ inch along the curve, and clip the curves and corners.

2. Turn the arm right side out and press the seam allowance to the inside around the open end. Stuff the arm with fiberfill right up to the open end, but not too tightly. It is not necessary to manipulate the stuffing to create a realistic-looking arm, as it will be covered completely by clothing.

3. Make another arm in the same manner, using the second Adult Arm piece.

4. Fold one Leg piece in half lengthwise, placing right sides together, and stitch the seam along the long edge only. Turn the leg tube right side out; it will be finished after the boot has been partially assembled.

5. Pin two Boot pieces right sides together. Stitch the seam along the front, bottom, and back edges, leaving a 3-inch opening at the bottom, directly below the top

Figure C

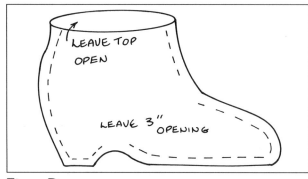

Figure D

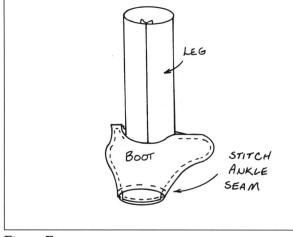

Figure E

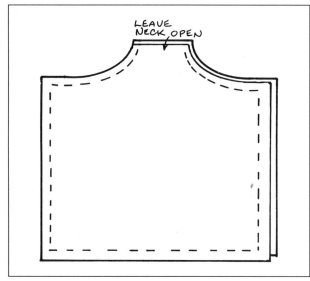

edge (**Figure C**). Leave the straight top edge open, as well. Clip the curves and corners, and leave the boot turned wrong side out. Press the seam allowances to the wrong side of the fabric along each side of the 3-inch opening at the bottom.

6. Slip one end of the leg tube into the opening at the bottom of the boot, as shown in **Figure D**. Note that the boot is wrong side out and the leg is right side out, so the fabrics are right sides together. Align the ankle edge of the boot with the lower open end of the leg tube, making sure that the leg seam is placed as shown. Stitch the ankle seam all the way around the aligned leg and boot edges, as shown. Press the seam and turn the boot downward, so it is right side out.

7. Whipstitch together the opening edges along the bottom of the boot, and press the seam allowance to the inside around the top of the leg. Tightly stuff the boot and leg all the way to the top.

8. Repeat the procedures described in steps 4 through 7 to create another leg-and-boot assembly.

9. Pin the two Torso pieces right sides together. Stitch a continuous seam all the way around (**Figure E**), leaving the neck edge open. Clip the curves and corners, and turn the torso right side out. Press a 1-inch allowance to the inside around the neck opening. Stuff the torso firmly with fiberfill up to about an inch of the pressed neck edge.

10. Whipstitch the arms and legs to the torso, stitching around each one several times for extra strength. Be sure that the toes face the same direction.

11. Follow the same procedures to assemble the second adult and the two child carolers, using the appropriate size body pieces.

Making the Heads

1. To make the female adult's head, cut one leg from a pair of pantyhose. Tie a knot at the top of the leg and cut across the hose about 12 inches below the knot. Turn the hose inside out, so the knot is on the inside.

2. Stuff the hose with fiberfill to form a head, approximately 17 inches around and 8 inches in diameter lengthwise. (See Tips & Techniques for specific instructions on forming a stuffed-pantyhose head.) Tie the hose in a knot below the stuffing and cut off the excess about an inch below the neck knot.

3. To soft-sculpt the facial features, thread a long sharp needle with a generous length of heavy-duty flesh-tone thread, and follow the entry and exit points illustrated in **Figure F**.

a. Enter at 1, where the hose is knotted at the neck, push the needle through the center of the head, and exit at 2. (Points 2 and 3 are about 4 inches below the knot at the top of the head, and there is about 2 inches of space between them.)

b. To form the bridge of the nose, pinch up a ridge between 2 and 3. Reenter at 2, push under the ridge, and exit at 3. Use the needle to push stuffing up into the nose ridge, and pull the thread to define it. Reenter at 3 and exit at point 2.

c. Extend the nose ridge downward between 4 and 5. Pull the thread across the surface and enter at 4. Push the needle underneath the ridge, exiting at 5.

d. Pull the thread across the surface, enter at 3 and exit at 2. Pull the thread to define the nose and lock the stitch at 2.

e. To shape the end of the nose, reenter at 2 and exit at 5. Make a short curved line of tiny running stitches between points 5 and 7 (indicated by dotted lines in **Figure F**). Reenter at 7 and exit at 6. Pull the thread across the surface, enter at 7 and exit at 4. Pull gently to gather the hose between 5 and 7, and lock the stitch at 4.

f. Renter at 4, make tiny running stitches between points 4 and 6, reenter at 6 and exit at 5. Pull to gather, and lock at 5.

g. To form the nostrils, reenter at 5 and exit at 6. Pull the thread across the surface and enter about ¼ inch directly above 6 on the end of the nose. Push the needle through the nose and exit at 3. Pull the thread to form the nostril.

h. Reenter at 3 and exit at 2. Reenter at 2 and exit at 7. Pull the thread across the surface and enter about ¼ inch directly above 7 on the end of the nose. Push the needle through the nose and exit at 2. Pull to form the second nostril and lock the stitch at 2. Do not cut the thread.

4. Continue working with the same thread to form the eye lines and mouth, following the entry and exit points illustrated in **Figure F**.

a. Pull the thread across the surface and enter at 8. (Point 8 is about 1¼ inches to the left of point 2, and slightly above.) Push the needle through the head and exit at point 3. Pull to form the left eye line.

b. Pull the thread across the surface, enter at 9 and exit at 2. Pull to form the right eye line and lock at 2.

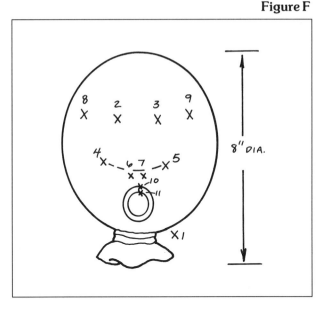

c. The mouth in indicated by the double circle in **Figure F**. It is open, as if singing. Reenter at 2, push the needle through the head, and exit at 10. (Point 10 is about 1 inch directly below the nose.) Pinch up a tiny ridge between points 10 and 11, reenter at 10 and exit at 11.

d. Work with a small section at a time, pinching up a tiny ridge in a circular shape, as shown, and stitching back and forth underneath it as you did between points 10 and 11. The finished mouth circle should be about 1¼ inches in diameter.

e. When you have completed the mouth, lock the stitch at the final exit point. Reenter there, push the needle through the head, and exit at point 1. Lock the stitch and cut the thread.

5. Final facial details will be added later. For now, put aside the adult female's head and proceed with the three other heads. They are very similar to the first one, with the following exceptions:

a. The adult male's head is made in the same manner and is about the same size. When sculpting the features, make the nose a bit longer and wider at the bottom. Allow a little extra room between the nose and mouth.

b. Both child-size heads should be slightly smaller. Make their noses very short and round, allowing only about ½ inch of vertical space between points 2-3 and 4-5 (see **Figure F**).

Figure G

Final Assembly

1. To complete the adult female, insert the neck knot at the bottom of the head into the open neck edge of the torso. Make sure that the face points in the same direction as the toes. It may be necessary to stuff a little more fiberfill into the torso, so the head is firmly supported. Start at the center back and whipstitch around the neck several times to secure it to the body. Attach the remaining heads to their respective bodies in the same manner.

2. To form the adult female's hair, unfold one skein of yarn and place it across the top of the head, as shown in **Figure G**. Spread the yarn forward and backward, as shown – it need not go all the way down to the normal hairline at the back if she will be wearing a head covering. Thread a needle with a matching thread color and backstitch along the center part line to attach the yarn to the head. On each side of the center part, arrange the yarn to cover the head evenly, forming a slight curve along the forehead and eye line, and spot glue to hold it in place. Gather the yarn together at what would be the bottom of the ear, and tie in a large knot, as shown for one side in **Figure G**. Finish both sides in this manner.

3. Cut a 4-foot length of electrical cable and bend it into a slight curve. Dress the caroler in her finery, inserting the cable across the back of her neck and shoulders, and down into the sleeves of her coat or dress. You can bend the cable to arrange the arms as you like – we made them curve forward so she could hold a large piece of sheet music. It's a good idea to stitch the cable to the body, if possible, so it won't slip out of position.

4. To create her hands, stuff each mitten or glove with fiberfill up to the base of the thumb. Insert the ends of the arms into the mittens, making sure that the thumbs point in the right direction, and whipstitch in place. Pull down the sleeves or add a fur cuff to cover the arm-to-mitten stitches.

5. Brush brown eye shadow on the eyelid area above each sculpted eye line. Make more distinct lines of brown shadow to define the eyebrows and exaggerated lower lashes. Brush the inside of the mouth circle with brown shadow, as well. Brush cheek blusher across each cheek and along the mouth ridge.

6. To form the adult male's hair, cut about eighty 16-inch lengths of yarn. Place them evenly across the top of his head and backstitch along the center part to attach. Spot glue along the sides of the head, from the center part to what would be the tops of his ears. Allow the hair to fall freely below the ears.

7. To form his beard, loop a continuous length of yarn and backstitched it to the face along the beard line, as shown in **Figure H**. Allow the tops of the loops to fall down over the backstitching. For the mustache, cut about thirty 8-inch lengths of yarn and tie them together at the center. Tack the mustache to his face, just underneath the nose.

8. Dress the adult male in his clothing, using another 4-foot length of cable to shape the arms. Form his hands by stuffing the gloves and stitching them to the arms, as you did for the adult female.

9. To define his facial features, brush gray eye shadow on the eyelid areas and directly on top of each eye line. Brush in rather thick brown eyebrows and mouth circle. Use blusher across each cheek, along the ridge of the nose, and along the mouth.

10. The female child's hair is very much like her mother's, except that she has bangs. Use only half or three-quarters of a yarn skein for her hair. Cut off a 4-yard length for the bangs, and attach the remainder to her head as you did the mother's, knotting the yarn at each side (*see* **Figure G**). To form the bangs, wrap the 4-yard length into a continuous loop about 8 inches across, and tie it off at the center. Stitch it to her head just in front of the center part.

11. Dress the female child in her caroling duds, using a 3-foot length of cable for shape. Stuff the mittens and stitch them to the arms.

12. Use brown eye shadow to define the eyelids, eyebrows, and lower lashes. Use blusher across the cheeks and along the mouth circle.

13. For the male child's hair, cut the remaining yarn into 12-inch lengths. Spread them across the top of his head and backstitch along the center part. Arrange the yarn around his head and forehead, trimming the front strands to form the bangs. Spot glue where necessary.

14. Dress the young lad, using a 3-foot length of cable for shape. Stuff and attach the mittens to form the hands. Define the facial features as for the other carolers — we added a few freckles across his cheeks. Glue or tack his eyeglasses in place.

Making the Stands

1. To make a stand for one adult, cut a 13-inch length of pine 2 x 12. Drill into one side of the wood two ¾-inch-diameter sockets, about 1 inch deep, spacing them as shown in **Figure I**. Glue a 3-foot length of ¾-inch dowel rod into each socket. Paint the stand or seal it with a few coats of clear wood sealer and allow to dry.

2. Place the adult female caroler on top of the stand, inserting the dowel rods up under her clothing so that the tops rest just under her arms. You may wish to stitch the dowels to the body underneath the clothing.

3. Make a second stand for the adult male. Insert the dowels up through his trouser legs.

4. Each child-size stand is made in the same manner, but slightly smaller. For the base, cut a 10-inch length of pine 2 x 12 and drill the sockets where indicated in **Figure J**. Cut two 29-inch lengths of ¾-inch dowel and glue them into the sockets. Seal the stands and install the child-size carolers as you did the adults.

5. Arrange the carolers on your porch, in your yard, or in your home. We purchased some sheet music to glue into their hands. A nice touch for an outdoor setting is to broadcast Christmas carols — at a reasonable volume, so your carolers aren't arrested for disturbing the peace of the season!

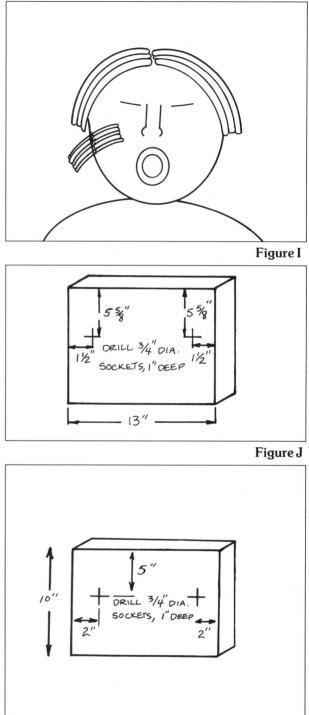

Figure I

Figure J

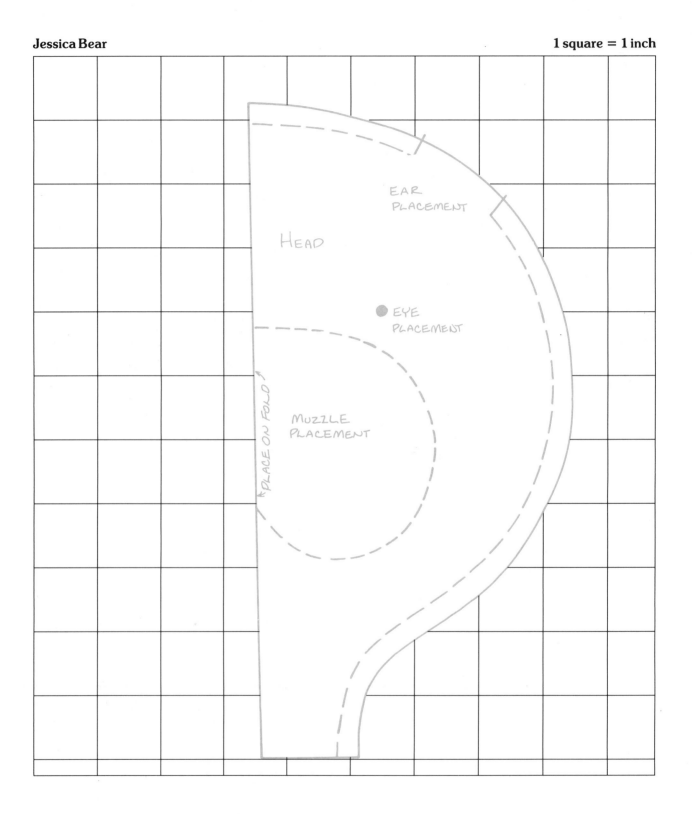

HEAD

EAR
PLACEMENT

● EYE
PLACEMENT

← PLACE ON FOLD →

MUZZLE
PLACEMENT

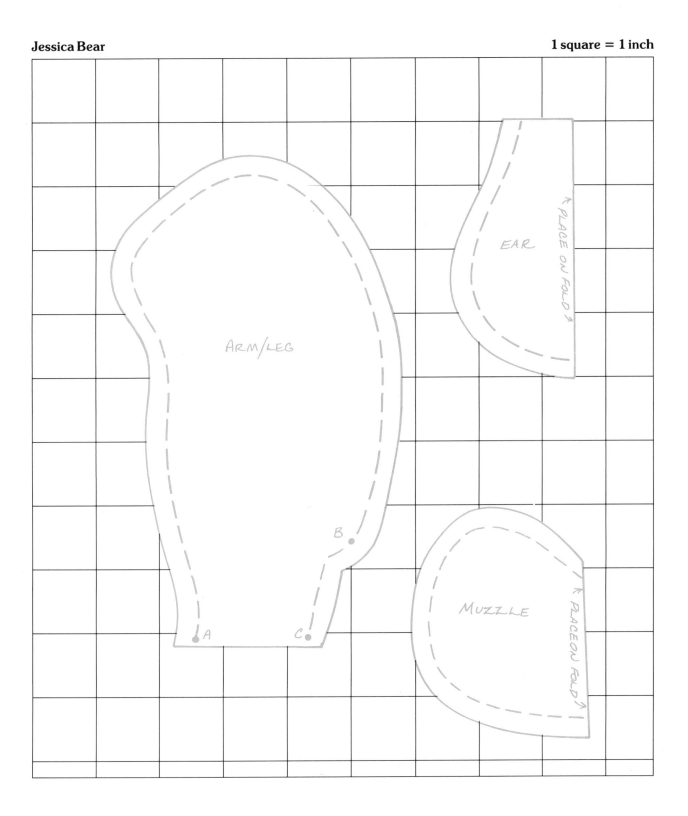

ARM/LEG

EAR

PLACE ON FOLD

MUZZLE

PLACE ON FOLD

A

B

C

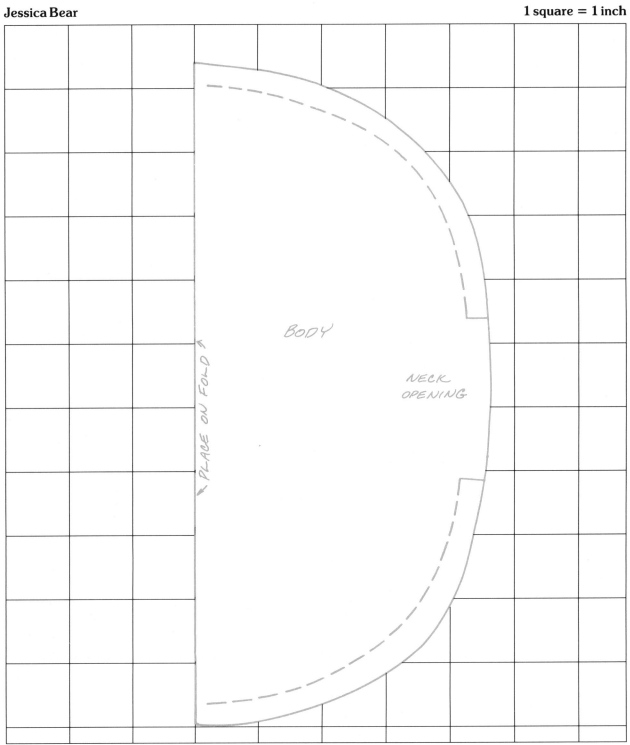

BODY

PLACE ON FOLD

NECK
OPENING

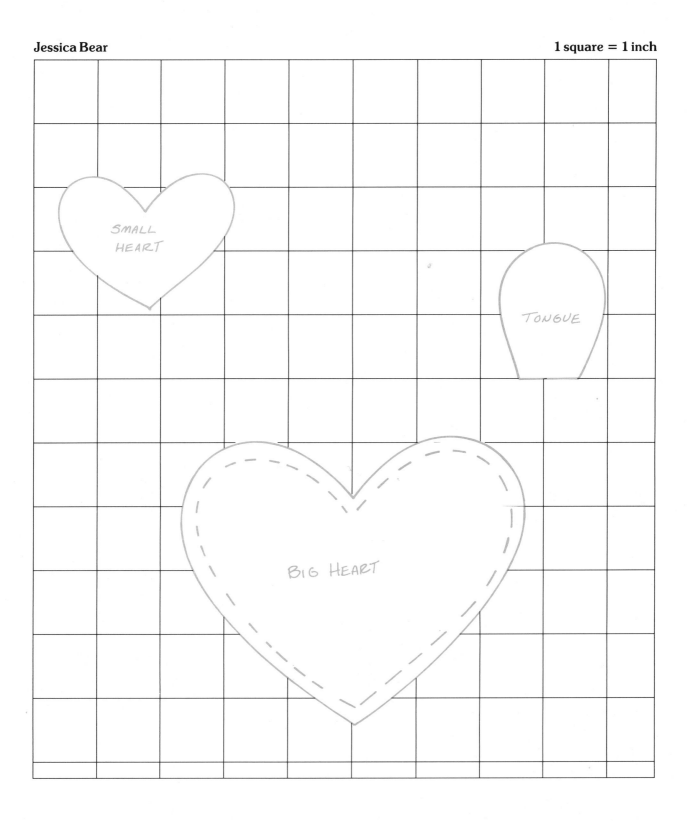

SMALL HEART

TONGUE

BIG HEART

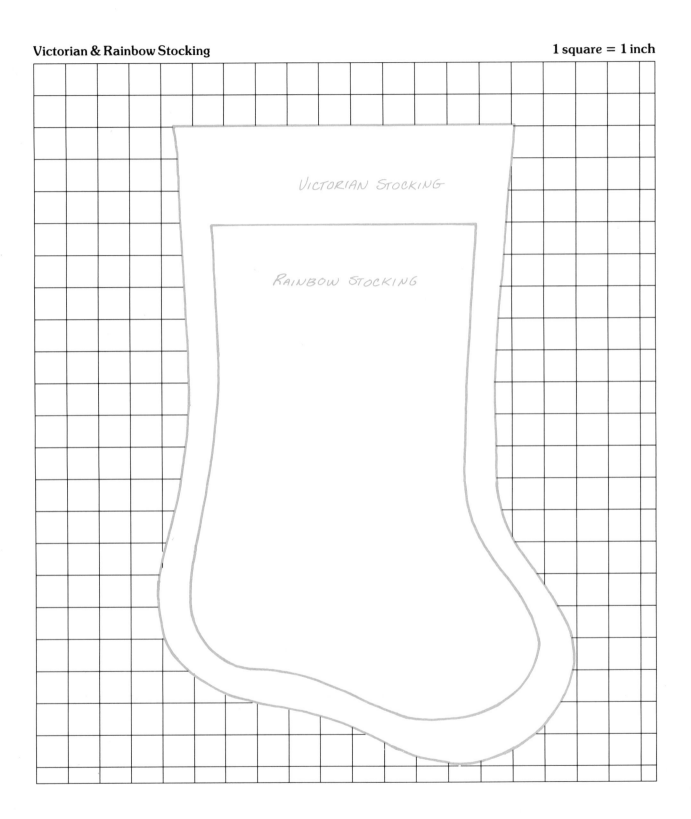

Victorian Stocking

Rainbow Stocking

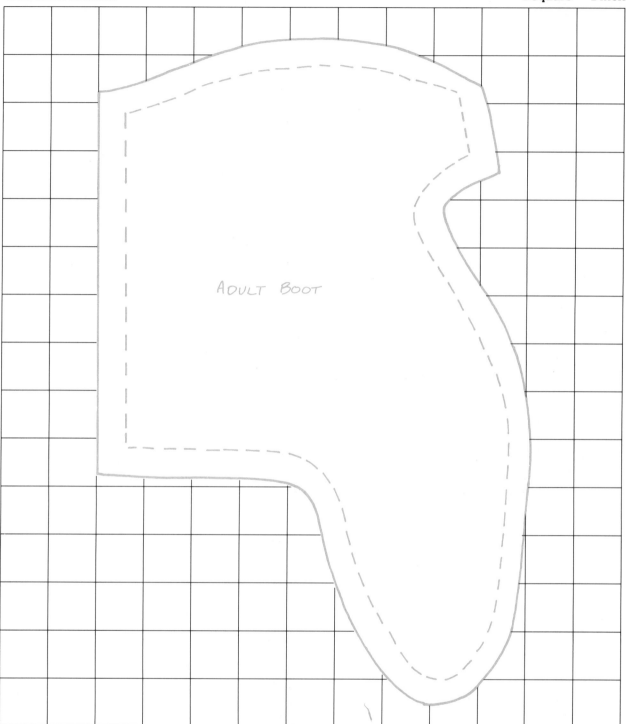

ADULT BOOT

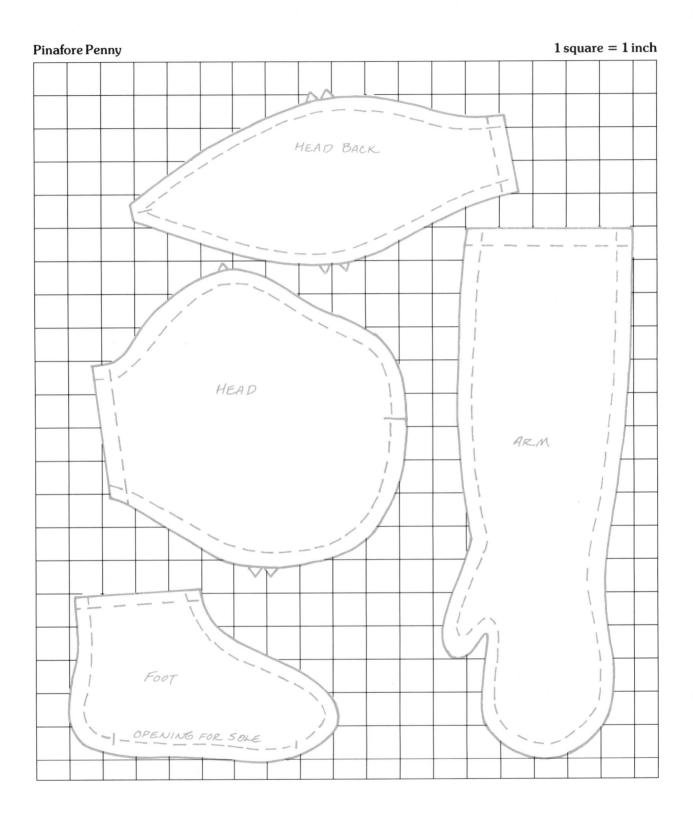

HEAD BACK

HEAD

ARM

FOOT

OPENING FOR SOLE

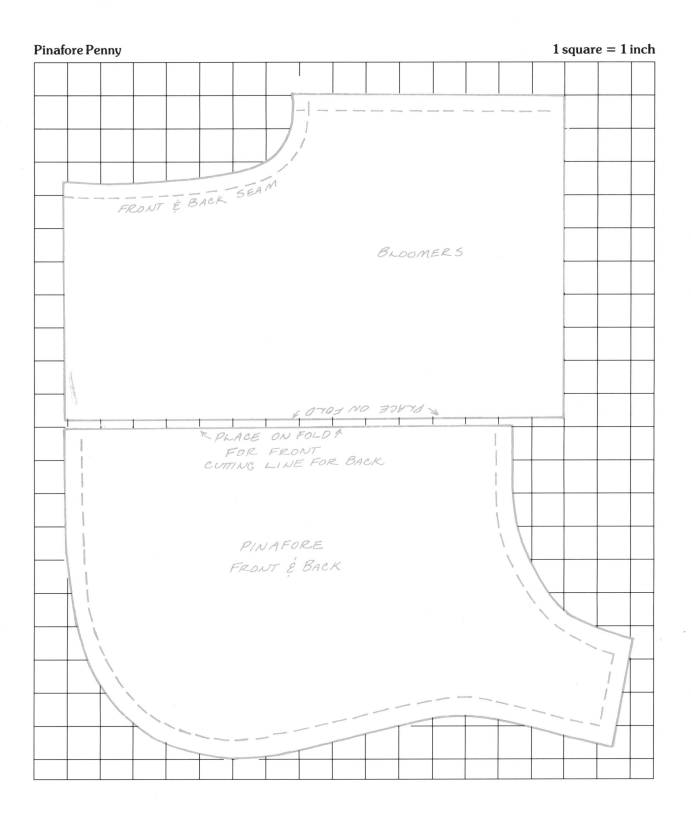

BLOOMERS

FRONT & BACK SEAM

PLACE ON FOLD

PLACE ON FOLD
FOR FRONT
CUTTING LINE FOR BACK

PINAFORE
FRONT & BACK

CENTERS

CENTERS

POCKET

FULL-SIZE PATTERNS

NOSE

EYELASH

CHEEK

EYELID

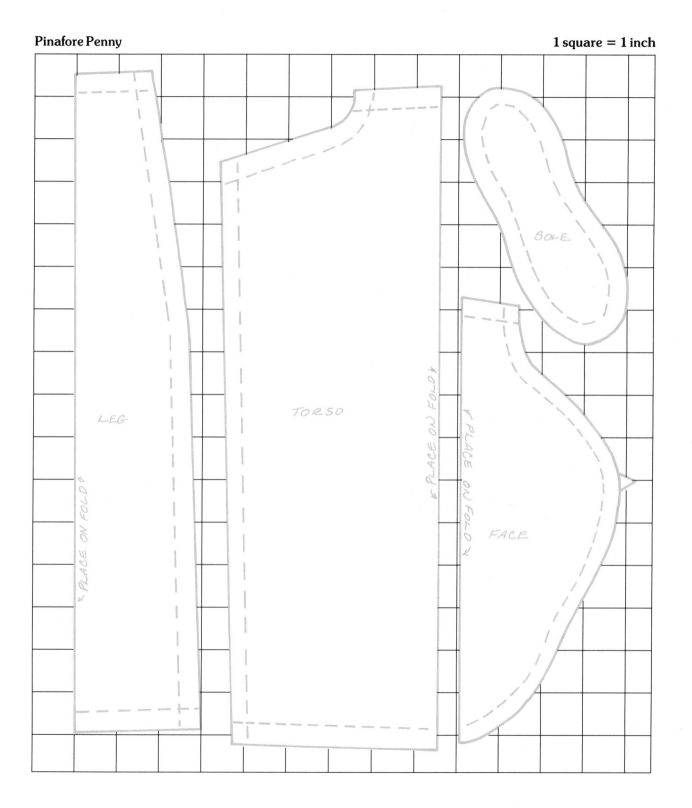

A Traditional Christmas

T radition is defined as "...the handing down of stories, beliefs, and customs from generation to generation." In light of that definition, we can see that what is considered traditional by some might be very different from what is considered traditonal by others. Modern celebrations owe many traditions to the immigrants who poured into America in the nineteenth century. Their potpourri of old-world customs were adapted to fit the new spirit of Yankee enthusiasm and the bounty of natural resources available in the new world.

The traditions of Christmas make the season special, regardless of where or how they began. Ask any child to name a Christmas tradition and the majority will say gifts or presents. Few children (or adults for that matter) will be able to tell you that the tradition began during the ancient Roman Saturnalia festivals with the practice of exchanging "good luck" gifts of fruits and pastries.

As time and generations come and go, people will add to, delete from, change, and create new customs that will in time become traditions. In this section we have featured projects that fit into the traditional concept of Christmas; a shiny red wagon and a beautiful doll for the children, a handsome furniture accessory for the adults, and (of course) Santa Claus!

Traditional Christmas

Mr. Santa

Traditional Christmas

Big Red Wagon

Afghan & Quilt Rack

Pinafore Penny

Santa & Reindeer

Mr. Santa

Menus and Melodies

Traditional Menus

With the melting-pot atmosphere in the United States, it is easy to see that foods considered traditional in one area might not be thought of as such in another area. Tastes, customs, and traditions vary from border to border and coast to coast, all of which make this nation the unique accumulation that it is.

In the fiftieth state, Hawaii, Christmas began in 1786 when Captain Portlock, a British sea captain, gave gifts and trinkets to the island children in Waimea Bay on Christmas Eve. The next day his men feasted on roast pig and coconut punch in celebration of the birth of Christ. This mixture of European and Hawaiian customs set the stage for future Christmas celebrations. To many Hawaiians, Christmas dinner takes the form of the luau, and might feature roast pig (kailua), sweet potato pudding (koele paloa), and Portugese sweet bread (pao doce).

Christmas in New England is epitomized by the images derived from Currier and Ives prints; snow covered villages, a church steeple towering above the rooftops, and laughing children sledding or ice skating on a frozen pond.

To give you an idea of the variety (and similarity) of the holiday dinners served across the United States, here are two menus: New England and Deep South.

A New England Menu
Oysters Rockefeller
Standing Rib Roast with Stuffed Mushroom Crowns
Potatoes au Gratin
Creamed Onions
Cranberry Salad Ring
Coffee Nut Muffins
Pumpkin Nut Pie
Boston Cream Pie
Beverage

Pumpkin Nut Pie
(Pumpkin pie might very well be one dish that is considered traditional in all parts of the country.)

1½ cups mashed cooked pumpkin	1⅔ cups milk
1 tsp. cinnamon	2 eggs, lightly beaten
½ tsp. ginger	¼ tsp. nutmeg
9-inch pastry pie shell, uncooked	⅔ cup sugar
	⅛ tsp. salt
	⅓ cup chopped nuts

Sift dry ingredients together and stir into eggs. Add milk and pumpkin. Add nuts. Line pan with pastry and pour in filling. Bake at 450° for 10 minutes; reduce temperature to 325° and bake 35 minutes longer, or until knife inserted in center comes out clean. Cool. Top with whipped cream before serving, if desired.

Cranberry Salad Ring

2 cups cranberries
1 cup sugar
½ cup chopped nuts
¾ cup diced celery
Mayonnaise

1½ cups cold water
1 Tbsp. unflavored
   gelatin
Lettuce

Wash cranberries, add 1 cup cold water. Cook until tender. Add sugar and cook 5 minutes. Soften gelatin in ½ cup cold water, dissolve in hot cranberries. Chill until mixture begins to thicken. Add nuts and celery. Mix thoroughly. Pour into oiled ring mold. Chill until firm. Place lettuce leaves on salad plate and unmold ring in center. Place mayonnaise in center of ring (or serve separately), and garnish with sprig of parsley, pineapple ring, nut meats, chopped celery, etc.

Coffee Nut Muffins

3 cups cake flour,
   sifted
1 cup of nut
   meats, chopped
2 Tbsp. shortening,
   melted

4 tsp. baking powder
¾ cup brown sugar
1 egg
1¼ cups strong,
   cold coffee
½ tsp. salt

Sift dry ingredients together and add nut meats. Beat egg, add coffee and shortening, and add to dry ingredients. Mix only enough to dampen all the flour. Bake in greased muffin pans in 400° oven, 20 to 25 minutes. Makes 16 large or 30 small muffins.

A Southern Menu

Roast Turkey with Cornbread Dressing
Mashed Potatoes and Giblet Gravy
Seasoned Rice
Scalloped Oysters
Asparagus au Gratin
Pecandied Yams
Ambrosia
Pumpkin Pie
Pecan Pie
Beverage

Pecandied Yams

(Perhaps nothing is as southern as pecans.)

⅓ cup brown sugar
¼ tsp. salt

4 tsp. cornstarch
¾ cup orange juice

¾ cup orange
   marmalade
⅓ cup pecan halves

2 Tbsp. butter
   or margarine
2½ pounds yams

Cook the yams, peel, and cut into thick slices. Combine brown sugar, cornstarch, and salt in a sauce pan. Stir in orange juice and marmalade. Cook until thickened and bubbly, stirring to prevent sticking and burning. Remove from heat. Stir in butter. Arrange yams in 12-inch skillet. Pour orange sauce over yams. Sprinkle with pecans. Cover and simmer till yams are glazed and heated through, basting often. Makes 12 servings.

Ambrosia

(This recipe is very simple, and simply delicious. It can be made in as large a quantity as needed. Make it the day before, cover, and let sit in refrigerator for the flavors to blend.)

6 navel oranges
Sugar

One package flaked
   coconut

Peel the oranges. Cut the pulp from the membrane, one section at a time. Cut the sections into smaller pieces. Layer the oranges, coconut, and sugar into a serving bowl. Build as many layers as needed to fill the bowl. Reserve some of the coconut for the next day. To serve, stir the layers to coat all pieces, and then sprinkle the reserved coconut over the top.

Music to Enjoy

The recorded albums listed here include selections of favorite traditional holiday songs.

The Meaning of Christmas
Fred Waring and the Pennsylvanians
Capitol Records #SM-1610
Here are many early favorites such as "Carol of the Bells," "Kentucky Wassail Song," and Clement Moore's poem "'Twas the Night Before Christmas."

Lanza Sings Christmas Carols
Mario Lanza
RCA Victor #LSC-2333
This record features the popular tenor singing carols written by American composers. Included are such favorites as "Away in a Manger," "We Three Kinds of Orient Are," "It Came Upon a Midnight Clear," and "O Little Town of Bethlehem."

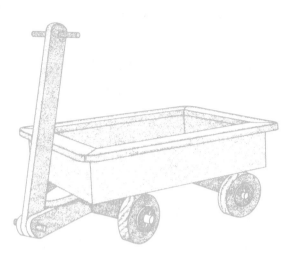

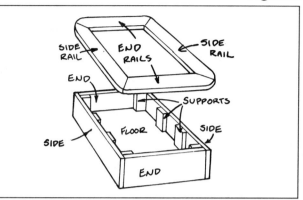

Big Red Wagon

Luckily, this is a very easy project to build. We say "luckily" because you're probably going to end up making several: one for the kids, one for the family gardener, one for hauling the trash and the firewood. This is our only prototype that hasn't been kid-tested—the kids haven't had a chance to get near it yet. (It's MINE!) Overall size is 13 x 21 x 29 inches.

Materials

26 x 38-inch piece of ¾-inch exterior-grade plywood or waferwood

1-foot square of ¼-inch plywood or waferwood

3 linear feet of pine 2 x 4

3 linear feet of pine 2 x 8

15 linear feet of pine 1 x 3 (If your dealer doesn't stock this size, purchase a 1 x 4 instead.)

4-foot length of 1-inch-diameter wooden dowel rod

1-foot length of ¾-inch-diameter wooden dowel rod

10-inch length of ¼-inch-diameter wooden dowel rod

(**Note:** All hardware should be galvanized, or made of brass, bronze, or stainless steel.)

One ⅝ x 2½-inch round-head stove bolt, with a hex nut and three flat washers

Nine flathead wood screws, ¾-inch long

A handful each of 2d, 3d, and 4d finishing nails

Six 4d and four 8d common nails

Carpenter's wood glue; beeswax or hard soap for lubricant; and exterior paint in your choice of colors

Cutting the Parts

1. Cut the parts listed here from ¾-inch plywood. Label each part as it is cut to avoid confusion during the assembly process.

Description	Dimensions	Quantity
Floor	16 x 24 inches	1
Side Wall	5 x 25½ inches	2
End Wall	5 x 16 inches	2

2. Drill a ¾-inch-diameter hole through the Floor, 3 inches from one end. Center the hole between the long edges of the floor.

3. Scale drawings are provided on page 121 for the Hinge Support, Washer, and Wheel. Enlarge the scale drawings to make full-size paper patterns. (See the Tips & Techniques section on enlarging scale drawings.)

4. Cut one Hinge Support from ¾-inch plywood.

5. Cut eight circular Washers from ¼-inch plywood. Drill a 1-inch-diameter hole through the center of each Washer. Enlarge each hole slightly so that a 1-inch-diameter dowel rod will turn easily when inserted through the Washer.

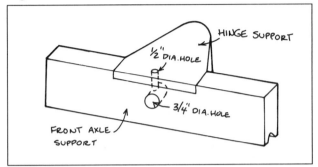

Figure C

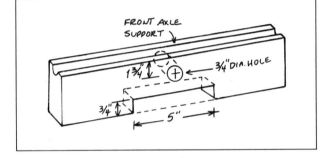

6. Cut four circular Wheels from 2 x 8. Drill a 1-inch-diameter hole through the center of each Wheel, enlarging the hole slightly as you did for the Washers.

7. Cut the parts listed here from 1 x 3.

Description	Dimensions	Quantity
Support	2½ x 4¼ inches	8
Side Rail	2½ x 27½ inches	2
End Rail	2½ x 19½ inches	2
Handle	2½ x 24 inches	1
Hinge	2½ x 10 inches	2

8. Flat miter both ends of each Rail at a 45-degree angle, so that they will form a frame when assembled, as shown in **Figure A** . In addition, round off the outer corners of each Rail as shown.

9. Round off both ends of the Handle and one end of each Hinge. In addition, drill a ¾-inch-diameter hole through the Handle, 1¼ inches from each end. Drill the same size hole 1¼ inches from the rounded end of each Hinge.

10. Cut two Axles, each 20 inches long, from 1-inch-diameter wooden dowel rod. Drill a ¼-inch-diameter hole ¾ inch from each end of both Axles.

11. Cut one Hinge Pin, 5 inches long, and one Han-

dlebar, 7 inches long, from ¾-inch-diameter wooden dowel rod.

12. Cut four Axle Pins, each 2½ inches long, from the ¼-inch-diameter wooden dowel rod.

13. Cut two Axle Supports, each 14 inches long, from 2 x 4. Each Axle Support must be grooved to accommodate an Axle. Cut a 1-inch-wide V-shaped groove along one long edge of each Axle Support, as shown in **Figure B**. You can do this in one pass with a router, or two angled cuts with a circular saw.

14. On the front Axle Support only, cut a rectangular slot 5 inches long and ¾ inch deep into the center of the ungrooved edge, as shown in **Figure C**. Drill a ¾-inch-diameter hole through the same Axle Support, 1¾ inches from the grooved edge, being careful to avoid the slot and axle groove.

Assembly

Once the sawdust has settled, the assembly of the wagon is as easy as 1, 2, 3 (literally).

One – The Wagon Box and Axle Supports

1. Use glue and 4d finishing nails to attach the Side and End Walls to the Floor, butting the edges, as shown in **Figure A**. The edges of the Floor are covered by the Walls, as shown.

2. Secure the Supports to the wagon box assembly using 3d finishing nails. Position one Support in each corner and two equally spaced along each side, as shown in **Figure A**.

3. Assemble the Rail pieces over the wagon box and attach by driving 3d finishing nails through the Rails and into the Supports (**Figure A**).

Two – The Steering Assembly

1. Fit the Hinge Support into the rectangular slot in the front Axle Support, attaching it with glue and 4d nails, as shown in **Figure D**. Drill a ½-inch-diameter hole through the Hinge Support, and continue drilling into the Axle Support until the drill bit emerges into the ¾-inch hole.

2. Position the front Axle Support on the underside of the wagon box, aligning the holes (**Figure E**). Insert the stove bolt through the hole in the Floor as shown, placing one metal washer under the bolt head, one between the Floor and the Axle Support, and one washer and the nut at the end of the bolt. Tighten the nut so that it will hold the assembly together, but allow it to swivel freely.

3. Glue the two Hinges to the Hinge Support, leaving a 1-inch space between them (**Figure F**). Secure with 4d nails driven through the Hinge Support, and 8d nails through the Axle Support.

4. To install the Handle, insert one end between the Hinges, aligning all three holes, as shown in **Figure F**. Insert the Hinge Pin through the holes, leaving equal extensions on each side. Do not use glue, for if you do, the handle action will be permanently frozen. Do use glue, however, to secure the Handlebar in the hole at the other end of the Handle.

Three – Axles and Wheels

1. Position the rear Axle Support on the underside of the Floor, about 3 inches from the rear edge, centered between the sides. Attach it to the floor using glue and screws.

2. Glue the Axles to the Axle Supports, leaving equal extensions on each end. Insert screws through each Axle into the Axle Support (**Figure G**).

3. The wheel assembly is shown in **Figure G**. To install one Wheel, slip a Washer over the end of the Axle, pushing it all the way up to the Axle Support. Lubricate the end of the Axle and slip on the Wheel, followed by another Washer. Secure the assembly by inserting an Axle Pin into the hole near the end of the Axle. Glue the Axle Pin in place. Repeat this procedure to install the remaining Wheels.

4. Paint your wagon using exterior paints. You can personalize the wagon with the owner's name or initials by using a contrasting color paint and the alphabet provided on pages 120-121. Enlarge the letters to the size you prefer.

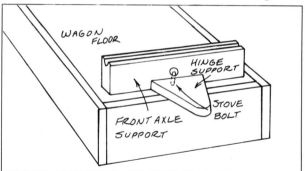

Figure E

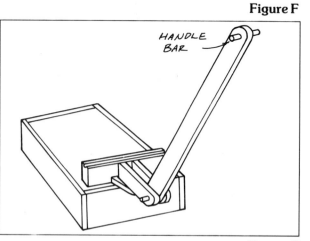

Figure F

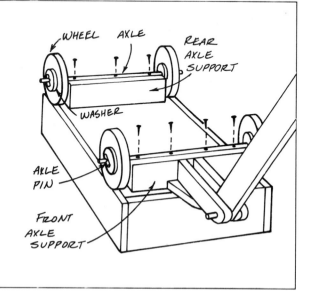

Figure G

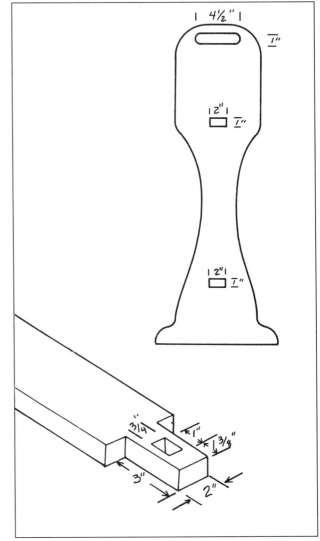

Afghan & Quilt Rack

The afghan and quilt rack are easy projects to construct. The afghan will help you use up those odds and ends of yarn, and you'll only need two crochet stitches: chain and half double (hdc). The finished afghan will measure approximately 48 by 72 inches. The rack stands 34 inches tall and 38 inches long, and can be disassembled for easy portability.

Materials

For the quilt rack:

13 square feet of ¾-inch oak (Dimensions of all parts are listed in "Cutting the Parts, step 1." For any part that is wider than the stock you purchased, simply join two narrower boards using a blind spline, and then cut the part.)
1-foot length of ¼-inch-diameter wooden dowel rod
Four flathead Phillips wood screws
Carpenter's wood glue
Medium and fine sandpaper

For the afghan:

15 skeins (or an equivalent amount) of crochet yarn (This is a good project to use up those odds and ends of yarn. Varying the weights and colors will result in a unique, attractive design.)
Size 1 crochet hook (We have not specified a stitch gauge, so use a smaller hook if you want a more solid look, or a larger hook if you want a lighter, more open look. Adjust the number of chain stitches to the length you prefer.)

THE QUILT RACK

The quilt rack consists of two contoured uprights connected by two horizontal supports and the rack assembly. The lower end of each upright is sandwiched between two feet, and the horizontal supports are joined to the uprights with pegged mortise and tenon joints. Triangular glue blocks attached to the uprights support the rack assembly. You can disassemble the mortise and tenon joints if you do not use glue.

Cutting the Parts

1. Scale drawings are provided on page 123 for the Upright, Peg, Glue Block, and Foot. Enlarge the drawings to make full-size paper patterns. (Refer to the Tips & Techniques section on enlarging scale drawings.) Cut the parts listed here from the ¾-inch oak.

Description	Dimensions	Quantity
Upright	use pattern	2
Foot	use pattern	4
Glue Block	use pattern	4
Peg	use pattern	4
Horizontal Support	4 x 42¼	2
Upper Rack	3¾ x 36¼	1
Lower Rack	3 x 36¼	1

2. Refer to **Figure A** for the additional cutting instructions in this step. Cut one 1 x 4½-inch handhold and two 1 x 2-inch mortises in each Upright. Cut a 2 x 3-inch tenon at each end of each Horizontal Support. To accommodate the Pegs, cut a ¾ x 1-inch slot in each tenon, 1⅜ inches from the end, as shown.

Assembly

1. The lower end of each Upright is sandwiched between two Feet to provide a more solid base. Glue the Feet in place (**Figure B**).

2. Align and glue two Glue Blocks together to form an identical piece twice as thick as the originals. Do the same with the other two Glue Blocks.

3. Center one of these assembled glue blocks against one side of one Upright, 2¾ inches below the handhold (**Figure C**). Attach with temporary holding nails only (no glue or screws yet), because you'll probably have to adjust the blocks later. This will be the inside of the Upright. Attach the remaining block to the other Upright in the same manner.

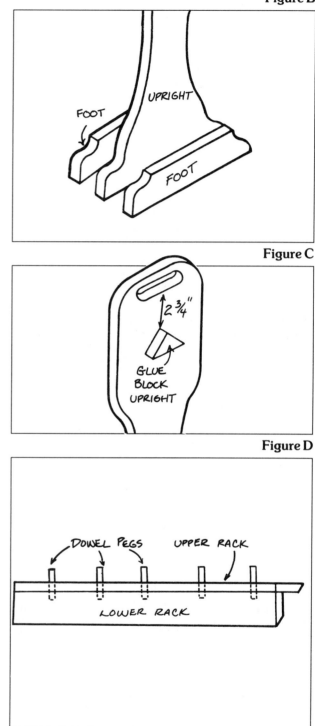

Figure B

Figure C

Figure D

Figure E

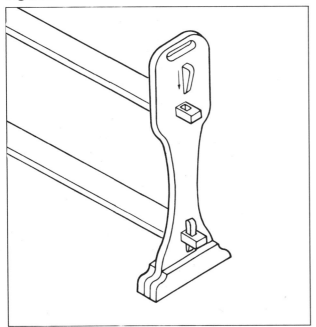

Figure F

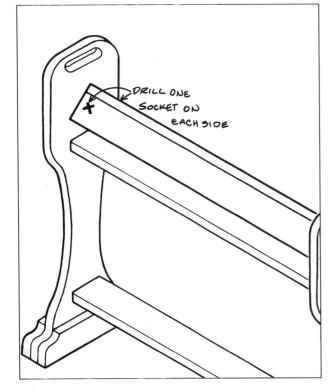

DRILL ONE SOCKET ON EACH SIDE

4. The rack is formed by joining the Upper and Lower Racks in an inverted V-shape. Glue the wider Upper Rack over one long edge of the Lower Rack, and secure the joint with five dowel pegs (**Figure D**) spaced evenly along the joint. We cut the dowel pegs 1¼ inches long.

5. Assemble the Uprights and Horizontal Supports (**Figure E**), and insert the Pegs through the slots in the tenons. Insert the assembled rack between the uprights and lower it down onto the glue blocks. This is the moment of truth, in which you'll be able to tell immediately if you've (or we've) erred somewhere along the way. It may be necessary to perform one or more of the following corrective measures. If the rack doesn't want to sit straight, adjust one or both glue blocks to get a proper alignment. If the rack is too long or short, trim either the rack or the supports to achieve a good fit. When everything is aligned, fitted, and ready to live happily ever after, permanently attach the glue blocks to the uprights, using screws and glue.

6. The rack is held in place by two wooden pins inserted into sockets drilled through each end of the rack into the glue blocks (**Figure F**). Each pin consists of a 1¼-inch-long shank cut from dowel rod and a ½-inch-diameter cap cut from oak. We cut each cap about ⅜ inch thick, and beveled the upper edge.

7. Sand the wood, and then finish the surface in whatever manner you prefer. We used a walnut Danish oil, but you might prefer a lighter or darker stain, or no stain at all.

Making the Afghan

You'll use only two different stitches for the afghan; a chain stitch and a half double crochet (hdc) worked in lengthwise rows. (See the Tips & Techniques section on crochet if you are unsure about either of these crochet stitches.)

1. Start by chaining on. Make a chain as long as you want the finished afghan to be.

2. Work the second (and all subsequent rows) in half double crochet.

3. Change yarn colors as often as you wish. However, since different weights of yarn will produce different stitch sizes, we don't suggest that you change yarn weights except at the beginning of a row.

4. Continue working rows of hdc until the afghan is as wide as you want it to be.

5. Use a steam iron and gently press the afghan, or have it blocked by a dry cleaning establishment.

CELEBRATIONS OF CHRISTMAS

Mr. & Mrs. Santa

If good things come in small packages, then this life-size Santa and wife must be super-good! Don't let the size intimidate you, they're really quite easy to put together...just stock up on lots of fiberfill.

Materials

For Santa:

Two pairs of flesh-tone queen-size support pantyhose

One leg cut from a pair of regular flesh-tone pantyhose

5 yards of 36-inch-wide (or 3 yards of 60-inch-wide) red fabric for Santa's suit (We used polyester double-knit. The fabric need not be stretchy, but it will make your job a little easier.)

1¾ yards of 36-inch-wide white fake fur fabric

10 pounds of polyester fiberfill (For the hair and beard, purchase an extra bag of fiberfill or use a medium-length white wig.)

One pair of men's average-size black galoshes or boots

One black leather belt (You can make one from a strip of black felt 2 inches wide by 3 yards long, and a very large buckle.)

One pair of men's black mittens (To make the mittens, you'll need four rectangles of black felt, each 7 x 10 inches, or a heavy-weight black plastic bag.)

Long sharp needle; heavy-duty beige thread; and red sewing thread

Acrylic paints in white, black, red, and light blue; and a fine- tipped artist's brush

Cosmetic cheek blusher; and a brown eyebrow pencil

Hot-melt glue and a glue gun (or white glue)

23-inch length of 1-inch-diameter wooden dowel rod

One medium-size unopened bag of potting soil (We used this to give Santa a little extra weight in the posterior. This provides stability when he's sitting. You can use just about anything that's reasonably heavy for this purpose – it won't show.)

Cutting the Pieces

1. Scale drawings are provided on page 122 for the Coat, Pants, Hat, and Mitten. Enlarge the drawings to make full-size paper patterns. (Refer to the Tips & Techniques section on enlarging scale drawings.)

2. Cut the pieces as listed in this step from the specified fabrics. Fold the fabric into a double thickness, so you can cut two of each piece at a time, and the resulting pieces will be matching pairs. Pay attention to the "place on fold" notations on the scale drawings and patterns. Transfer any placement markings or instructions to the fabric pieces.

Red fabric: Coat - cut two
     Pants - cut two
     Hat - cut one

Black felt or plastic: Mittens - cut four (If you did not purchase mittens)

Fake fur: Pant Cuff - cut two, 8 x 20 inches
    Sleeve Cuff - cut two, 8 x 15 inches
    Hat Band - cut one, 8 x 30 inches
    Hat Pompom - cut one, 8-inch-diameter circle
    Coat Front - cut one, 8 x 28 inches
    Waist Trim - cut three, 8 x 36 inches

Making the Body

1. Use one pair of support pantyhose for the legs and torso. Stuff each leg with fiberfill, working from the toe upward. To keep the legs equal in size, work with one handful of fiberfill at a time, and distribute it as evenly

Figure A

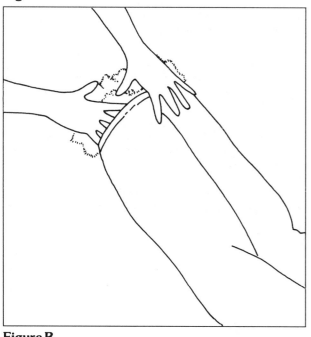

Figure B

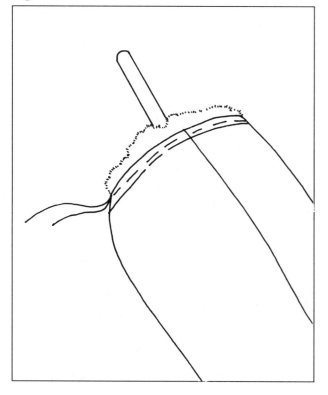

Figure C

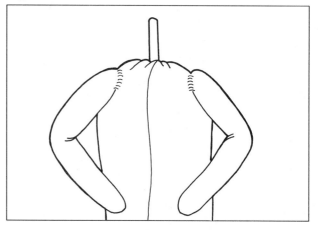

as possible. You can manipulate the shape of the legs when they are sufficiently stuffed, but don't worry about trying to make them perfect – Santa's legs will be covered by trousers.

2. Continue stuffing the panty portion of the hose to form the torso (**Figure A**), pulling the hose upward as you work. (This will be the entire torso – the waistband of the hose will be the neck.) As you begin stuffing the torso above the legs, place it on a chair to make sure that the figure will bend at the top of the legs and sit properly when finished.

3. After you have stuffed the hips, insert the wooden dowel rod in the center of the torso. The rod will provide internal support for the finished figure, and help to hold the head in place. Continue to stuff the torso, working around the center dowel rod and stretching the pantyhose as you work.

4. When you have stuffed the torso, the dowel rod should project about 6 inches above the torso in the center of the neck opening (**Figure B**). Baste around the neck opening ¼ inch from the edge, using heavy-duty thread. Pull the thread to gather the neck opening around the dowel rod.

5. Cut the legs from the second pair of support pantyhose, and stuff each one to form an arm. Keep the arms as equal in size as possible. (Later, if you find that the arms are not quite full enough, you can add stuffing between his arms and the sleeves of his suit.) Tie a knot in the hose at the top of each stuffed arm.

6. Use heavy-duty thread to whipstitch an arm to each side of the body (**Figure C**), placing the arms at a slight angle to the shoulders.

Making the Head

1. The head is made from the single leg of regular-weave pantyhose. Tie a knot in the hose at the panty line, and cut off any excess hose about 1 inch above the knot. Cut off the hose 14 inches below the knot. Turn the hose so the knot is on the inside.

2. Stuff generous amount of fiberfill inside the hose, manipulating the shape until a head is formed (**Figure D**). (See the Tips & Techniques section on working with pantyhose.) The completed head should be approximately the same size as your own. Tie the hose loosely at the neck, as shown, using thread or string. The string will later be untied to insert the dowel rod.

Santa's Facial Features

1. To soft-sculpt Santa's facial features, use a long sharp needle and heavy-duty flesh-tone thread. Follow the entry and exit points illustrated in **Figure E**.

   a. Enter at point 1 where the hose is tied at the neck, push the needle straight through the center, and exit at point 2 on the front.
   b. To form the nose, pinch up a vertical ridge, and stitch back and forth underneath the ridge between points 2, 7, 3, and 5. Make your final exit at 3.
   c. Use the tip of the needle to carefully lift fiberfill up into the ridge. Pull the thread and lock the stitch at 3.
   d. To form the nostrils, reenter at 3, and exit at 4. Enter just above 4 and exit at 3.
   e. Reenter at 3 and exit at 5.
   f. Reenter at 5 and exit at 6. Enter just above 6 and exit at 7. Pull the thread gently to form the nostrils, and lock the stitch at point 7. Do not cut the thread.

2. To form Santa's mouth, continue working with the same thread, and follow the entry and exit points illustrated in **Figure E**.

   a. Reenter at 7 and exit at 8.
   b. Pull the thread across the surface, enter at 9, and exit at 2.
   c. Pull the thread until a smile appears. Lock the stitch, but do not cut the thread.

3. To form the eyes and eyelids, follow the entry and exit points illustrated in **Figure E**.

   a. Pull the thread across the surface, enter at 10, and exit at 2. Pull the thread gently to form an

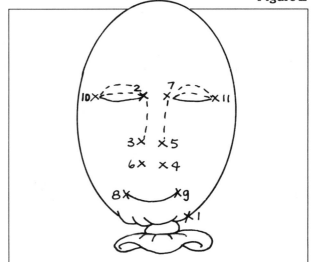

eye line, and lock the stitch.
   b. Pinch up a narrow curved ridge over the eye line. Reenter at 2, stitch back and forth underneath the ridge, and exit at 10.
   c. Reenter at 10, exit at 2, pull the thread, and lock the stitch.
   d. Reenter at 2, and exit at 7.
   e. Repeat steps a through d to form the second eye line and eyelid on the opposite side of the face, between points 7 and 11. When you have completed the steps, lock the stitch at 11, and cut the thread.

Figure F

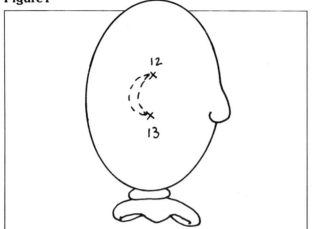

Figure G

Figure H

4. To form the ears, follow the entry and exit points illustrated in **Figure F**.

　　a. Enter at 1, where the hose is tied at the neck, push the needle through the center of the head, and exit at 12. Pinch up a small ridge at an angle on one side of the head, just below the eye line.

　　b. Stitch back and forth underneath the ridge between points 12 and 13. Exit at 13 and lock the stitch. Do not cut the thread.

　　c. Push the needle through the head, exit at point 1, lock the stitch, and cut the thread.

　　d. Repeat steps a through c on the other side of the head to form the second ear.

5. Santa's eyebrows are tufts of white fiberfill (or small sections of the wig) that are glued to his face above the eyes. Glue the fiberfill or wig in place, and then trim the eyebrows.

6. Paint Santa's eyes using acrylic paint and a fine-tipped brush (**Figure G**). Paint each eye background solidly with white paint. Allow the paint to dry. Use blue paint to fill in the iris of each eye, and allow it to dry before adding a small black pupil in the center. The remainder of Santa's features will be added later.

Attaching the Head

1. Untie the string around the neck, and center the head over the dowel rod that extends above the neck opening. Force the rod into the cavity in the center of the head (**Figure H**).

2. Begin at the back, and carefully whipstitch around the neck several times to secure the head to the body.

Making Santa's Suit

We used a very simplified construction for Santa's coat. It does not provide a tailored fit, to be sure, but it's very simple to make. Besides, Santa's ample form doesn't take very kindly to the tailored look. The width of the seams is not crucial; a ½-inch seam will do.

1. To make the coat, first pin the Coat pieces right sides together. Stitch the shoulder and upper arm seam on each side, as shown in **Figure I**, leaving a 12-inch neck opening at the center.

2. Stitch the underarm and side seam on each side, as shown. Clip the corners, and press the seams open. Press the seam allowances to the wrong side of the fabric along the center neck opening.

3. Turn the coat right side out. Choose one side as

104　　　　　　　　　　　　　　CELEBRATIONS OF CHRISTMAS

Figure I

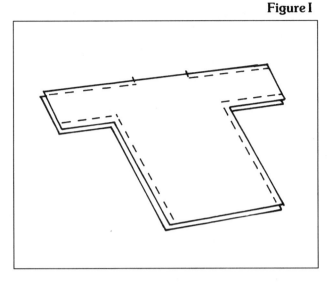

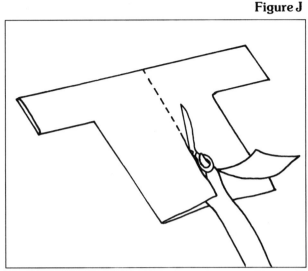

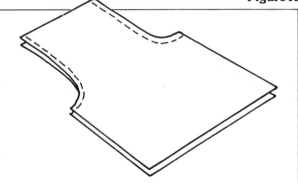

Figure L

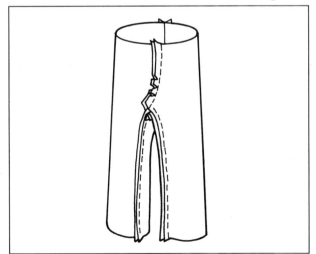

the front, and cut it open along the center line, from the lower edge all the way to the neck opening (**Figure J**). Put the coat aside for the moment.

4. To make the pants, place the two Pant pieces right sides together, and stitch the center front and back seams (**Figure K**). Clip the curves, and press the seams open. Do not turn the pants right side out.

5. Refold the pants, aligning the center front and back seams, and stitch the continuous inner leg seam, as shown in **Figure L**. Clip the curves, press the seams, and turn the pants right side out.

6. To make Santa's hat (**Figure M**), fold the Hat piece along the "place on fold" line, with right sides together. Stitch the seam along the long straight edge, leaving the lower edge open and unstitched. Press the seam, and turn the hat right side out.

7. To make the pompom, run a line of basting stitches near the circular edge of the Pompom piece. Pull the thread to gather the edge slightly, so the wrong side of the fur fabric is on the inside. Stuff a handful of fiberfill inside the pompom, and pull the thread to gather the fabric tightly around the fiberfill. Tie off the thread, and take a few stitches to secure the assembly. Stitch the pompom to the tip of the hat.

8. (If you purchased mittens, skip this step and continue with step 9.) To make the mittens, place two Mitten pieces together and stitch the seam around the long contoured edge, leaving the straight wrist edge open and unstitched. (If you are working with plastic, follow the same procedures, but use glue instead of thread.)

Figure M

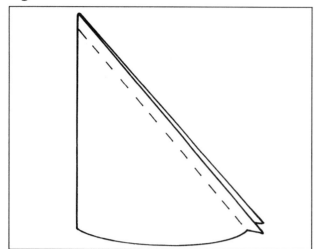

Figure N

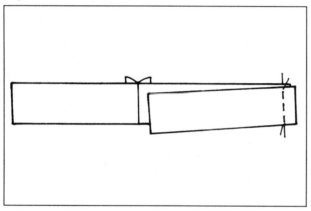

Clip the curves, and turn the mitten right side out. Stuff it with fiberfill up to about ½ inch of the open edge. Make a second mitten in the same manner, using the two remaining Mitten pieces.

9. We made fur trim pieces for the pant cuffs, the sleeve cuffs, the waist, the coat front, and the hat band. Each trim piece is made in the same manner, and finished when the suit is assembled. Fold one Pant Cuff piece in half lengthwise, placing right (furry) sides together. Stitch a ½-inch-wide seam along the long edge only. Turn the tube right side out, and stuff it lightly with fiberfill, leaving about 1 inch unstuffed at each open end. Make a second cuff in the same manner, using the remaining Pant Cuff piece.

10. To make the sleeve cuffs, fold, stitch, and stuff

each of the Sleeve Cuff pieces in the same manner as you did the pant cuffs.

11. To make the waist trim (**Figure N**), first place two of the Waist Trim pieces right sides together, and stitch a ½-inch seam along one short edge. Press the seam open, and stitch the remaining Waist Trim piece to one end of this assembly in the same manner. You should now have one long strip that measures 8 x 106 inches. Fold the strip in half lengthwise, stitch, and stuff this strip in the same manner as you did the cuffs.

12. Fold, stitch, and stuff the Center Front trim piece in the same manner as you did the others.

13. Fold, stitch, and stuff the Hat Band trim piece in the same manner as you did the others.

Finishing Santa

1. Begin by wrangling Santa into his pants. They will be somewhat short for him, but his boots and pant cuffs will cover the lower edge of the pants. Pin the waist edge of the pants to the body in a few places so they won't fall down as you're working on the feet.

2. To finish the feet, bend one foot into an L-shape at the ankle (**Figure O**). Whipstitch the top of the foot to the front of the leg, as shown. Pull the thread tightly, lock the stitch, and cut the thread. Repeat the procedures for the other foot. When both feet have been sewn, put Santa's boots on his feet.

3. Work from the open ends of the pant legs as you stuff extra fiberfill between the pants and legs, up to about knee level. Tuck the ends of the pant legs into the tops of the boots.

4. On one leg, wrap a stuffed-fur cuff around the pant so that it covers the top of the boot (**Figure P**). Overlap the ends of the cuff at the back, inserting one end into the other until the cuff forms a fairly tight band around the leg and boot, as shown. Glue or stitch the cuff in place. Finish the remaining leg in the same manner.

5. Work from the waist edge as you stuff extra fiberfill into the top of the pants, down to the knees. Don't add extra stuffing to the posterior — use the bag of potting soil, with a little stuffing around it for a smooth line. This will make Santa fairly heavy, and will keep him sitting in an upright position, so place Santa in a chair that's convenient to your work. When you're satisfied with the stuffing job, whipstitch the waist edge of the pants to the body.

6. Slip Santa into his coat, and push up the sleeves. Insert the end of one arm into the open wrist edge of one stuffed mitten. Whipstitch around the wrist to secure the mitten in place. Attach the remaining mitten to the end of the other arm.

7. Work from the open end of one sleeve as you stuff a little extra fiberfill between the arm and sleeve, up to the elbow. Adjust the sleeve so the open end falls at the wrist stitching. Wrap one of the stuffed-fur sleeve cuffs around the wrist seam so that it covers the end of the sleeve and part of the mitten. It need not be as tight as the pant cuffs. Secure it as you did the pant cuffs. Finish the end of the other arm in the same manner.

8. Work from the open front of the coat as you stuff a little extra fiberfill into each sleeve, from the elbow up to the shoulder. You can add additional padding to Santa's chest, shoulders, sides, and back by glueing fiberfill to his body. Don't be afraid to use lots of fiberfill – he's well-known as a late-night snacker.

9. When you're satisfied with the stuffing, overlap the front opening edges of the coat and pin them together. Whipstitch the neck edge of the coat to Santa's neck, and whipstitch the front opening edges together.

10. The lower edge of the coat should overhang the waist edge of the pants just slightly. If it overlaps by quite a bit, fold a hem to the wrong side of the coat and stitch or glue it in place. Wrap the fur waist trim around the lower edge of the coat, overlapping the ends at the center front. Glue or whipstitch the trim in place. You may wish to tack the lower edge of the coat to the pants in a few places, to help support the extra stuffing.

11. Glue or whipstitch the coat front trim along the center front of the coat.

12. Because Santa's waist is so big around, we used the black belt as a front decoration only. Cut the belt in half at the center back, and buckle the two pieces together. Glue the belt to Santa's waist, with the buckle in the front. If you prefer a whole belt, cut several 2-inch-wide strips of black felt and glue them around his waist, then glue a buckle to the center front.

13. To finish Santa's face, paint his lips using very light red acrylic paint. Use the eyebrow pencil to outline his eyes.

14. To make Santa's hair and beard, use either a wig or fiberfill. Cut pieces from the wig or use tufts of fiberfill for the hair. Glue them to his head around the sides, where the edge of the hat will be. There's no need to glue hair to the top of his head, as it won't show. Form a large, billowy piece of fiberfill or use the remaining portion of the wig as Santa's beard. Glue it to his chin and cheeks, and over his mouth as a mustache.

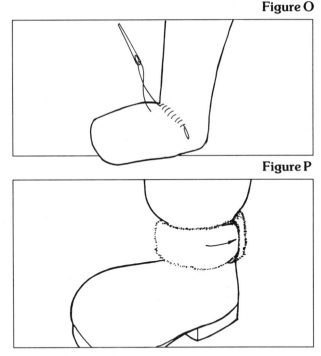

Figure O

Figure P

15. Stuff Santa's hat with fiberfill and glue it to his head. Wrap the hat band trim around the edge of the hat, overlapping the ends at the back, and glue or whipstitch it in place. Fold the point of the hat to one side, and glue or tack it to the hat near the hat band.

Mrs. Santa

Although Mr. and Mrs. Santa have different characteristics, their bodies are made in the same manner. Mrs. Santa has a (slightly) slimmer body than her husband and, of course, more feminine features. We purchased her size 10 clothing at a thrift shop: long red skirt, fancy white blouse, pair of black boots, red vest, and apron. You can add extra decoration to her clothing using various trims.

If you wish to construct Mrs. Santa, follow the same procedures for the body as you did for Mr. Santa, adding the appropriate feminine features where necessary. You can use white gloves for her hands. Or if you prefer, you can form them from stuffed pantyhose and soft-sculpt fingers on each hand. Soft-sculpt the facial features in the same manner as Santa's, making her features softer and more feminine. Add a longer white wig (or fiberfill), and a pair of wire-rim glasses.

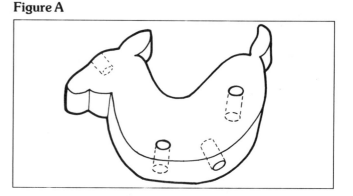

20 red chenille stems and one white chenille stem, each 12 inches long

5-foot length of ¼-inch wooden dowel rod

2 yards of ¼-inch red velvet cord

Acrylic paints in red, white, and black; artist's fine-tipped paint brush; carpenter's wood glue; and wood stain or paint

Small wooden ball, approximately ½ inch in diameter, to use for Rudolph's nose

Black sewing thread

Six wire brads, ½ inch long

Santa & Reindeer

"On Dasher, on Dancer..." so goes Santa's famous call. You can now have your own wooden replica of Santa and five of his reindeer to add to the holiday decorations in your home. Rudolph leads his high-stepping fellow reindeer as they tow Santa and his sleigh across the Christmas Eve sky. Santa's black velvet toy bag can hold Christmas cards, candy, or small gifts.

Materials

5½-foot length of standard 1 x 10 white pine

1½ x 3-foot piece of ¼-inch interior-grade plywood, smoothed on both sides

3 x 13-inch piece of ⅜-inch interior-grade plywood, smoothed on both sides

5 x 6-inch piece of black satin fabric; a short length of plaid corded piping; and a sprig of holly (for Santa's toy bag)

Making the Reindeer

1. Full-size patterns for Santa's Body, Arm, and Leg are provided on page 238. Trace the patterns onto tracing paper. Scale drawings are provided on pages 236-237 for the Reindeer Body, Foreleg, Hind Leg, Toy Bag, and Sleigh Side. Enlarge the drawings to make full-size paper patterns. (Refer to the Tips & Techniques section on enlarging scale drawings.) Transfer any placement markings or instructions to the patterns.

2. Cut five Reindeer Bodies from 1 x 10 pine. Drill two ¼-inch-diameter holes through each Reindeer Body where indicated on the pattern.

3. Cut ten Forelegs and ten Hind Legs from the ¼-inch plywood. Drill a ¼-inch hole through each Leg where indicated on the pattern.

4. To accommodate the dowel supports (which will be added later) drill a ¼-inch-diameter socket approximately ½ inch deep into the lower edge of each Reindeer Body, as shown in **Figure A**. Drill one reindeer at a slight angle, so the head will tilt up when it is installed on a vertical support rod.

5. To accommodate the antlers (which will also be

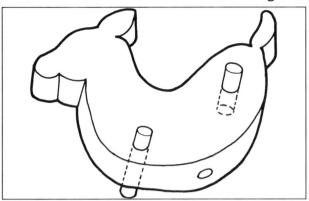

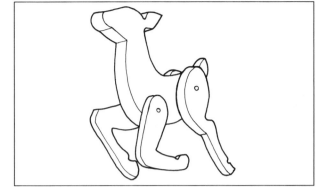

Figure D

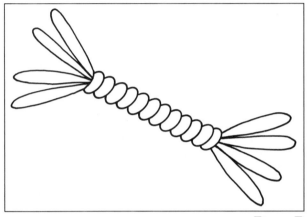

Figure E

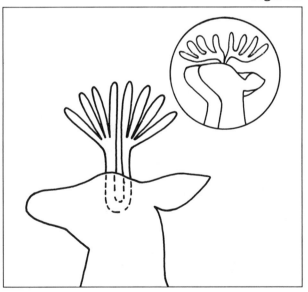

added later) drill a ¼-inch-diameter socket approximately ½ inch deep into the top of each reindeer's head (**Figure A**).

6. Cut twenty lengths of ¼-inch-diameter wooden dowel rod, each 1¼ inches long. Glue one length into each hole in one Reindeer Body (**Figure B**), leaving equal extensions on each side.

7. Slip two Forelegs onto the front dowel rod, one leg on either side of the body, as shown in **Figure C**. Install the Hind Legs in the same manner. Don't glue them in place, so you can position them later.

8. Install Legs on the remaining Reindeer Bodies in the same manner.

Making the Antlers

1. To make one set of antlers, cut two 12-inch red chenille stems in half. Place the four halves side by side, and twist them together tightly from the mid-point to within 2 inches of the ends (**Figure D**).

2. Bend the antler assembly in half, and insert the twisted end into the socket in the head of one reindeer, as shown in **Figure E**. Bend the ends into the shape of antlers, as shown in the inset.

3. Repeat all the steps in this section to make and install antlers on the remaining reindeer.

Making the Sleigh

1. Cut two Sleigh Sides from ¼-inch plywood.

2. Cut the following sleigh pieces from ⅜-inch plywood: one Floor, 3 x 6¼ inches; one Seat Back, 3 x 3½ inches; and one Fender, 1½ x 3 inches. Bevel one 3-inch edge of the Floor and Fender at a 15-degree angle. Bevel one 3-inch edge of the Seat Back at a 25-

Figure F

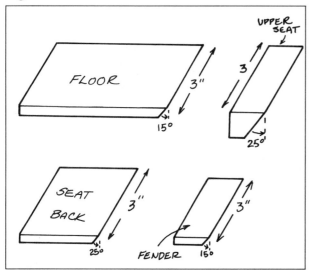

Figure G

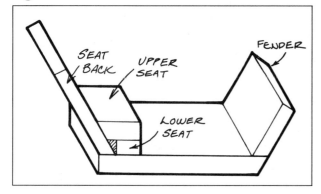

degree angle (**Figure F**).

3. Cut the following sleigh seat pieces from 1 x 10 pine: one Upper Seat, 1¾ x 3 inches; and one Lower Seat, 1 x 3 inches. Bevel one 3-inch edge of the Upper Seat at a 25-degree angle (**Figure F**).

4. The interior parts of the sleigh are assembled first, and the sides are added last. To assemble the interior parts, refer to **Figure G**. First, glue the beveled edge of the Seat Back to the Floor, flush at one end, as shown. Glue the Upper and Lower Seat pieces in place, aligning the front edges. Nail the Seat Back to the Upper Seat, and nail the Floor to the Lower Seat. Finally, glue the beveled edge of the Fender to the Floor, flush with the front end, and secure the joint with brads.

5. Glue one Sleigh Side piece to the interior assem-

bly, as shown in **Figure H**. Glue the remaining Side, checking to be sure it is level by temporarily placing the sleigh upright on its runners. Allow the glue to dry thoroughly before drilling the socket.

6. Drill a ¼-inch-diameter socket, ¼ inch deep, into the underside of the sleigh Floor, centered 1¼ inches from the front edge. Drill an identical socket ½ inch from the back edge.

Making Santa

1. Cut one Santa Body from 1 x 10 pine.

2. Drill two ¼-inch-diameter holes through the Body at the points indicated on the pattern.

3. Cut two Arms and two Legs from the ¼-inch-thick plywood.

4. Drill a ¼-inch-diameter hole through each Arm and each Leg where indicated on the patterns.

5. Cut two 1¾-yard lengths of ¼-inch-diameter wooden dowel rod. Glue them into the holes in Santa's body, leaving equal extensions on each side. Install the Arms and Legs in the same manner as you did for the reindeer's arms and legs.

6. Paint Santa in his traditional red suit, trimmed with white fur. We gave him black boots and belt, a white beard and hair, and a cheery pink face. In case you're unsure of your artistic abilities, we've provided a few guide lines on the scale drawing.

Making Santa's Toy Bag

1. Cut two Bag pieces from black satin fabric.

2. Place the Bag pieces right sides together and stitch the seam along the long, curved edge, using black thread. Leave the straight top edge open and unstitched. Clip the curve, and turn the bag right side out. Press gently.

3. Fold a ½-inch seam allowance to the wrong side around the top of the bag and stitch close to the edge, leaving a short opening between the beginning and end of the stitching line. Insert the white chenille stem through the casing, as shown in **Figure I**.

4. Gather the top of the bag along the chenille stem by gently pulling the bag closed. Secure the closed bag by twisting the ends of the chenille stem together.

Final Assembly

1. Cut two Base pieces, each 4 x 20 inches, from pine. These pieces are drilled to accommodate the dowels that support the figures (**Figure J**). Drill a ¼-inch-diameter socket, ½ inch deep, about 2 inches from the front end of one Base, and centered between the sides. Drill a second socket of the same size approximately 7½ inches behind the first one. Drill a third socket 7½ inches from the second one.

2. In the remaining Base, drill the first socket ¾ inch from the front end. Drill a second socket 8¼ inches from the first one. Drill a third socket 5½ inches from the second one, and a fourth socket 4½ inches behind the third socket.

3. Cut the following lengths of dowel rod: 10¼, 7½, 6½, 4½ (cut two), 3½, and 2½ inches.

4. Glue the lengths of dowel rod into the sockets in the Base pieces: In the Base piece with three sockets, glue the 10¼-inch rod in the front end socket, the 6½-inch rod in the center socket, and a 4½-inch rod in the back socket. In the remaining Base piece, glue the 7½-inch rod in the front socket, the remaining 4½-inch rod in the next socket behind, then the 2½-inch rod followed by the 3½-inch rod.

5. Glue the reindeer onto the upper ends of the dowels, as shown in **Figure J**. It doesn't matter which reindeer goes on which rod, except that the one with the angled socket should be the last one on the three-rod Base. The two shortest rods are for Santa's sleigh; install it in the same manner as the reindeer (**Figure J**). Position the reindeer legs in different galloping, prancing, and dancing poses. The legs don't have to be glued; changing their positions from time to time may keep your family wondering if reindeer really can fly!

6. Stain or paint the reindeer, sleigh, dowel rods, and base, and allow to dry thoroughly.

7. Glue the small wooden ball to the tip of Rudolph's nose. (If you're not sure which reindeer is Rudolph, just ask anyone under the age of five, or refer to **Figure J**.) Paint the nose bright red.

8. Tie one end of the red velvet cord around Rudolph's neck. Tie a loop 8 or 9 inches down the line, and hang it over the second reindeer's neck. Continue in this manner until you have hitched up the entire team. Place Santa in the sleigh, tie a loop at the free end of the cord, and hang it on Santa's hand, as shown in **Figure J**.

9. Form a hook at the free end of the white chenille stem on Santa's bag. Hang the hook over Santa's hand, and the toy bag over the back of the sleigh.

10. Sprinkle a little spray-on snow over the whole thing, if you like.

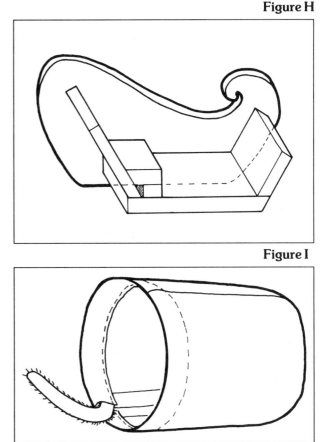

Figure I

Figure J

Pinafore Penny

What little girl wouldn't be delighted to find this lovable 3-foot-tall stuffed-fabric doll under her Christmas tree? Penny's yarn hair and felt facial features are easy to create. Her frilly embroidered eyelet pinafore is pretty enough for a real child to wear. Penny wears size 4 clothing.

Materials

1½ yards of flesh-tone stretchy knit fabric for the body
¾ yard of 36-inch white eyelet fabric for the pinafore
¾ yard of 36-inch white cotton fabric for the bloomers and the pocket
3½ x 4½-inch piece of fusible lining fabric
Small amount of felt in black and pink
3 yards of 1¾-inch-wide white eyelet trim
¾ yard of 2½-inch-wide white eyelet trim
4 yards of 1-inch-wide white satin ribbon
1 yard of white bias binding tape
1½ yard of ¼-inch-wide elastic

Three skeins of rug yarn for the hair (We used brown.)
Embroidery floss in red, pink, pale green, and yellow
Long sharp needle; heavy-duty thread in flesh-tone and a color that matches the rug yarn; and regular sewing thread to match the fabrics
Cosmetic cheek blusher
Hot-melt glue and a glue gun (or white glue)
A small embroidery hoop (optional)
Water-soluble fabric marking pen

Cutting the Pieces

1. Full-size patterns are provided on page 86 for the Eyelash, Eyelid, Nose, and Cheek. Trace the patterns onto tracing paper. Scale drawings are provided on pages 84-87 for the Head, Foot, Arm, Face, Leg, Torso, Sole, Bloomers, Pinafore, Head Back, and Pocket. Enlarge the drawings to make full-size paper patterns. (Refer to the Tips & Techniques section on enlarging scale drawings.)

2. Cut the pieces as listed in this step from the specified fabrics. Fold the fabric into a double thickness, so you can cut two of each piece at a time, and the resulting pieces will be matching pairs. Pay attention to the "place on fold" notations on the scale drawings. Transfer any placement markings or instructions to the fabric pieces.

Stretchy knit: Head - cut two
Arm - cut four
Head Back - cut one
Leg - cut four
Face - cut one
Foot - cut four
Nose - cut one
Sole - cut two
Torso - cut two
Eyelid - cut two

White cotton: Bloomer - cut two
Pocket - cut one

Eyelet fabric: Pinafore Back - cut two
Pinafore Front - cut one

Black felt: Eyelash - cut two

Pink felt: Cheek - cut two

3. To make the bias-cut Neck Binding piece, cut a

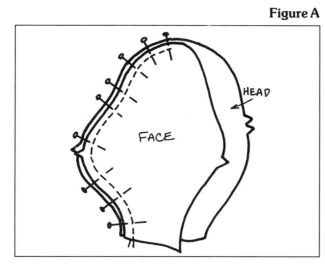

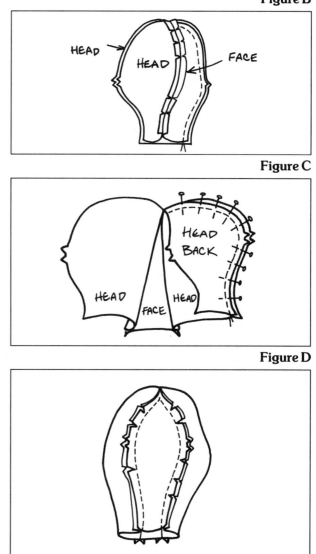

12-inch square from the remaining gingham, using the selvage as one edge so that you have a perfectly square piece of fabric. Fold the square in half along the diagonal and cut through both layers of fabric, 1⅛ inches from the fold. You will not need the triangular portions that have been cut away. The unfolded center portion will serve as the Neck Binding piece.

Making the Head

1. Place one Head piece right side up on a flat surface. Pin the Face piece right side down on top, matching the notches, as shown in **Figure A**. Stitch the seam as shown, easing the curve. Clip the curves, and press the seam open.

2. Place the second Head piece right side up on a flat surface. Place the head-and-face assembly on top, right side down. Align the free long edge of the Face piece with one long edge of the unattached Head piece, matching notches, as shown in **Figure B**. Stitch the seam, as shown, easing the curve. Clip the curves, and press the seam open.

3. Pin the Head Back piece to the head-and-face assembly, placing right sides together and matching notches along one edge, as shown in **Figure C**. Stitch the seam, easing the curve. Clip the curve, and press the seam open.

4. Pin the remaining free edge of the Head Back to the remaining free edge of the head assembly, placing right sides together (**Figure D**). Stitch the seam, as shown, leaving the neck edge open. Clip the curves,

and press the seam open. Turn the head right side out, and stuff firmly with fiberfill.

5. Penny's facial features are shown in **Figure E**. To create her little round nose, first run a line of basting stitches all the way around the Nose piece, about ⅜ inch from the edge. Do not cut off the tails of thread. Place a small wad of fiberfill in the center of the Nose piece, on the wrong side of the fabric, and pull up the basting threads to gather the fabric around the fiberfill. Tie off the gathering threads securely.

Figure E

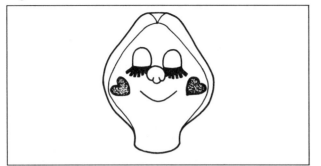

Figure F

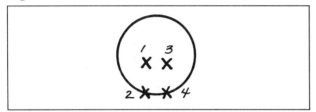

Figure G

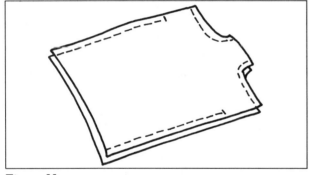

Figure H

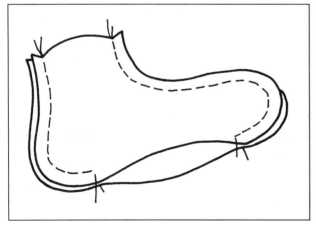

6. To sculpt two small nostril lines on the nose, thread a long sharp needle with heavy-duty flesh-tone thread. Follow the entry and exit points illustrated in **Figure F**.

    a. Insert the needle in the back of the nose (where it is gathered), and exit on the front at point 1 (just below the center).

    b. Pull the thread across the surface, down toward the bottom of the nose, and enter at point 2.

    c. Push the needle through the inside of the nose, and exit at point 3.

    d. Pull the thread across the surface, down toward the bottom of the nose, and enter at point 4.

    e. Push the needle through the nose to the back, and exit at the gathers. Pull the thread to form the nostril indentations, and lock the stitch at the back of the nose. Cut the thread.

7. Glue and blind stitch the nose to the face, placing the gathered side against the face (**Figure E**).

8. To create the closed eyes, turn under and press a very narrow hem along each edge of both Eyelid pieces. Glue the hemmed Eyelids to the face, as shown, and blind stitch in place. Cut several slits into each felt Eyelash piece to separate the lashes. Glue an Eyelash to each attached Eyelid, along the straight lower edge.

9. To create the mouth line, thread an embroidery needle with red floss and work a lightly curved line of split stitches, back stitches, or chain stitches where indicated in **Figure E**.

10. Glue a heart-shaped Cheek Spot to each of Penny's cheeks, where indicated in **Figure E**. Use cosmetic cheek blusher to add a little soft color to the cheeks and nose. Use the blusher sparingly; you can always add more, but if you apply too much, it's difficult to remove. Her hair will be added later.

Making the Torso, Arms, and Legs

1. Pin the two Torso pieces right sides together, and stitch the shoulder and side seams, as shown in **Figure G**. Be sure to leave neck and arm openings where indicated, and leave the lower edges open, as shown. Clip the curves, and leave the torso turned wrong side out.

2. Place two Arm pieces right sides together, and stitch a continuous seam all the way around, leaving only the short straight edge open. Clip the curves and the inside corner at the thumb. Turn the arm right side out. Repeat these procedures to assemble a second arm, using the two remaining Arm pieces.

3. To make one leg, place two Leg pieces right sides

together and stitch the two side seams, leaving both ends open. Press the seams open, and turn the leg tube right side out.

4. Pin two Foot pieces right sides together. Stitch the seams, as shown in **Figure H**, leaving an opening at the bottom for the Sole, and leaving the ankle edge open. Clip the curves, and press the seams open. Leave the foot turned wrong side out.

5. Slip the partially assembled foot over the lower end of the leg tube, as shown in **Figure I**. The fabrics should be right sides together, and the lower raw edge of the leg should be aligned with the raw ankle edge of the foot, as shown. Stitch the ankle seam, clip the curves, and turn the foot downward so that it is right side out.

6. Turn the entire leg-and-foot assembly wrong side out. Pin or baste a Sole piece into the opening at the bottom of the foot, as shown in **Figure J**, placing right sides together. Stitch the seam all the way around the Sole. Clip the curves, and press the seams. Turn the assembly right side out, and stuff the leg and foot. Manipulate the stuffing so that the leg is nice and round. Baste across the open upper end of the leg to hold the stuffing in place.

7. Repeat the procedures described in steps 3 through 6 to assemble and stuff a second identical leg-and-foot assembly, using the remaining Leg, Foot, and Sole pieces.

Body Assembly

1. The torso should still be wrong side out, and the arms should be right side out. Slip the arms inside the torso, as shown in **Figure K**, making sure that each thumb points upward. Pin the open shoulder end of one arm to the arm opening at one edge of the torso, as shown. Pin the other arm in place in the same manner, and stitch around each arm by hand or machine.

2. Turn the torso-and-arm assembly right side out. Place the two legs on top of the torso, with the toes pointing toward the body (**Figure L**). Stitch across the top of each leg to attach it to the front layer of the torso only. Turn the legs downward, and press the seam allowance to the inside of the torso around the lower edge. Whipstitch the pressed front and back lower edges of the torso together, securing the back of the legs with the whipstitches.

3. Turn and press the seam allowance to the inside

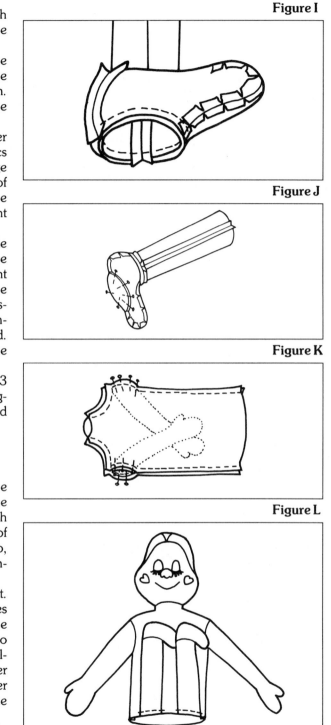

Figure I

Figure J

Figure K

Figure L

Figure M

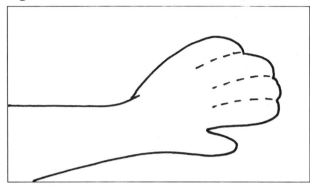

Figure N

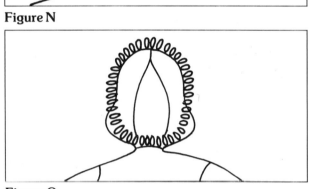

Figure O

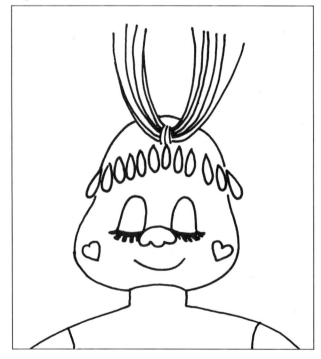

around the open neck edge of the torso. Work through the torso to stuff the arms and hands, using a long thin object to be sure the thumbs and hands are stuffed. Stuff the torso to within ½ inch of the open neck edge.

4. Insert the neck edge of Penny's head down into the neck opening of the torso, making sure that her face points in the same direction as her toes. It may be necessary to add extra stuffing at the neck, so the head won't wobble. Start at the center back, and whipstitch around the neck several times to secure the head.

5. Penny's fingers are soft-sculpted, as shown in **Figure M**. Thread a long sharp needle with heavy-duty flesh-tone thread. Start at the base of one finger line, and stitch up and down through the hand, working out to the end of the finger, as shown. At the outer end of the finger, lock the stitch, and push the needle through the inside of the hand to the base of the next finger. Sculpt three finger lines on each hand.

Adding the Hair

Penny's long yarn hair is pulled into a ponytail on the top of her head, with the rest of the hair falling straight to the shoulders. Her face is framed in short curls.

1. To make the curls, begin with a continuous length of rug yarn, a long sharp needle, and a length of heavy-duty matching thread. Tack the end of the yarn to the base of the head in the back. Form a 2-inch loop of yarn, and stitch it to the head. Continue to work around the hairline, forming closely spaced loops and stitching them in place, until you reach the starting point again (**Figure N**). Work a second row around the head, so you have a double row of closely spaced loops.

2. Cut the remaining yarn into 2½-foot lengths, and divide the strands into separate bunches, each containing eight or nine strands. Fold one bunch in half, and stitch the folded center point to Penny's head at the base of one loop, near the center front of the head, as shown in **Figure O**. Continue stitching additional bunches of yarn along the hairline, at the bases of the loops, working from the top center down to about mouth level on each side. Gather up all the yarn strands at the top center, forming a ponytail, and tie them together using a spare piece of yarn.

3. Draw a pencil line down the back center of Penny's head. Stitch bunches of yarn to the head along the line, spacing them closely together.

4. Cut all the remaining yarn strands in half, so each

is 15 inches long. Fold each bunch in half, and stitch these to Penny's head just above the hairline, beginning at mouth level, and working around the back of the head.

5. Allow the yarn that you attached in step 4 to hang downward. Spread out the yarn that is stitched along the "center part," arranging it evenly across the head on each side. Secure the hair by glueing or stitching it in place in a few spots. Allow the ponytail to fall backward over the top of the head.

6. Cut a 15-inch length of white satin ribbon, and wrap it around the ponytail over the yarn tie. Tie the ribbon in a big bow at the top. You can add a flower or second ribbon to the ponytail.

Making the Bloomers

1. Pin two Bloomer pieces right sides together, and stitch the center front and back seams (**Figure P**). Clip the curves, and press the seams open.

2. Measure around Penny's leg, about 4 inches below the top. Cut two pieces of elastic, each about 1 inch shorter than this measurement. Place one length of elastic across one of the bloomer legs, on the wrong side of the fabric, and about 2½ inches from the lower edge. Hold both ends of the elastic and stretch it as you stitch it in place, using a zigzag stitch setting on your machine (**Figure Q**). Don't let your sewing machine needle take any of the stress, or it might break. Stitch the remaining length of elastic to the remaining bloomer leg in the same manner.

3. Refold the bloomers, still with right sides together, matching the center front and back seams. Stitch the inner leg seam, as shown in **Figure R**. Turn and stitch a narrow hem to the wrong side of the fabric around the lower edge of each leg.

4. Press a ¼-inch allowance to the wrong side of the fabric around the waist edge. Fold the same edge over again, about ½ inch, to form a casing for elastic. Stitch close to the pressed edge, leaving a short opening. Cut a length of elastic 1 inch shorter than Penny's waist measurement, and thread it through the casing. Stitch the ends of the elastic together, and then tuck them inside the casing.

Making the Pinafore

1. Place the Pinafore Front piece right side up on a flat surface. Place the two Pinafore Back pieces right sides down on top, and stitch the shoulder seam on

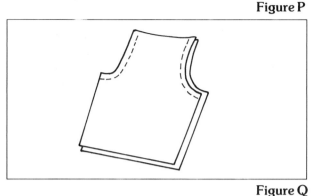

Figure P

Figure Q

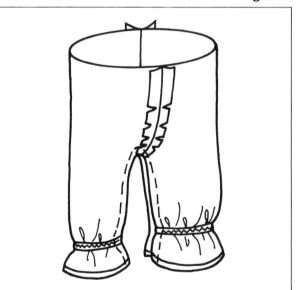

Figure R

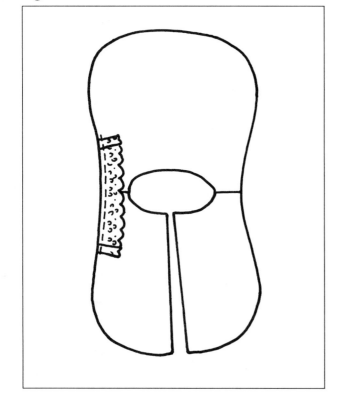

each side (**Figure S**). Zigzag stitch the edges of the seam allowances to keep them from raveling, and press the seam allowances toward the back of the pinafore on each side.

2. Press a ⅜-inch-wide facing to the wrong side of the fabric along the straight center opening edge of each Pinafore Back piece. Turn each of these edges under again, to form a double-turned facing. Topstitch each facing in place.

3. Cut two 11-inch lengths of 2½-inch-wide eyelet trim. Press the cut ends of each trim piece to the wrong side, forming ½-inch-wide hems.

4. Baste one of the trim pieces to the pinafore, placing right sides together, as shown in **Figure T**. The bound edge of the trim should be just inside the raw edge of the pinafore, and the scalloped edge should extend in toward the neck opening. The eyelet trim should extend equally beyond each side of the pinafore shoulder seam.

5. Baste the second eyelet trim piece to the opposite side of the pinafore in the same manner.

6. Cut a 40-inch length of the narrower eyelet trim and press the cut ends to the wrong side as you did for the wider trim pieces. Follow the same placement techniques to baste the narrow trim piece along the outer edge of the front pinafore between the wider trim pieces, lapping the ends over the front ends of the wider trim pieces.

7. Cut a 20-inch length of the narrower eyelet trim, and press the ends to the wrong side. Baste this trim piece along the outer edge of one back pinafore piece in the same manner as you did the others, lapping one end over the back end of the wider trim piece on that side. This trim piece should extend along the outer edge, down to the corner of the center back opening.

8. Repeat the procedures in step 7 to cut and baste a length of narrow eyelet trim to the edge of the opposite back pinafore piece.

9. Stitch the trim pieces to the pinafore in one continuous seam, about ½ inch from the pinafore edge. Turn the eyelet trim pieces outward, and press all seam allowances toward the pinafore. Topstitch about ¼ inch from the turned pinafore edge (**Figure U**). The topstitching should pass through the pinafore fabric and all seam allowances underneath.

10. Use the white bias binding tape to form a casing and finish the raw neck edge of the pinafore. Topstitch the binding in place, close to the edge. Turn the ends of the tape to the inside, but do not stitch the ends of the tape.

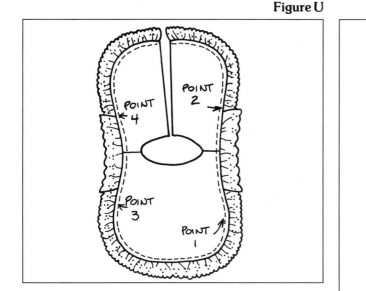

11. The neck edge will be gathered to fit, using a satin ribbon tie. Cut a 40-inch length of white satin ribbon. Attach a safety pin to one end, and then thread the ribbon through the neck casing that was formed by the bias binding tape.

12. The pinafore is secured under Penny's arms by two ribbon ties on each side. Cut four 15-inch lengths of satin ribbon. Fold under one end of one ribbon, and tack the folded end to the wrong side of the pinafore, about 1 inch below the front end of the wider eyelet trim (**Figure U**, point 1). Fold and tack a second ribbon to the wrong side of the pinafore, 1 inch below the back end of the same wide eyelet trim piece (point 2). Fold and tack the remaining two ribbon ties to the opposite side of the pinafore in the same manner at point 3 and at point 4.

Finishing

1. Dress Penny in her pinafore, placing the open edges at the back. Gather the neck edge by pulling both ends of the ribbon as you push the fabric around toward the center front. Tie the neck ribbon in a bow at the back. Tie the ribbons under her arm on each side.

2. Tie the remaining length of satin ribbon in a bow, and tack it to the center front neck edge of the pinafore.

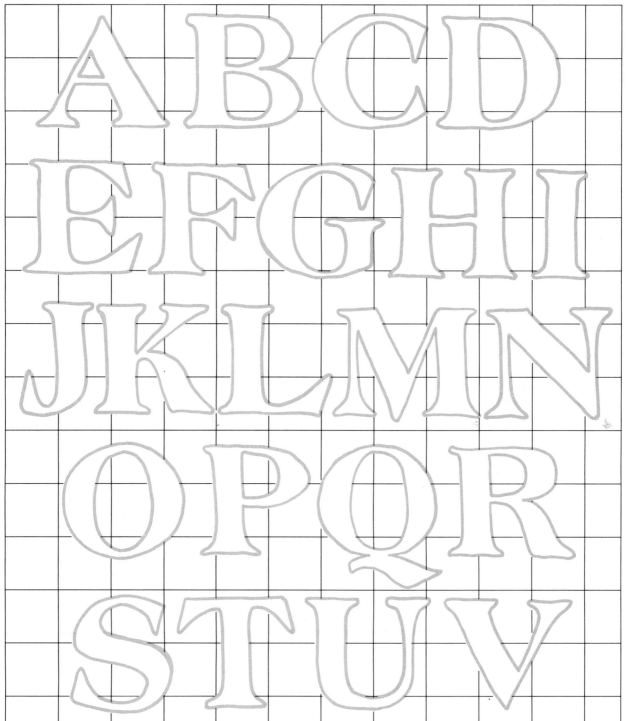

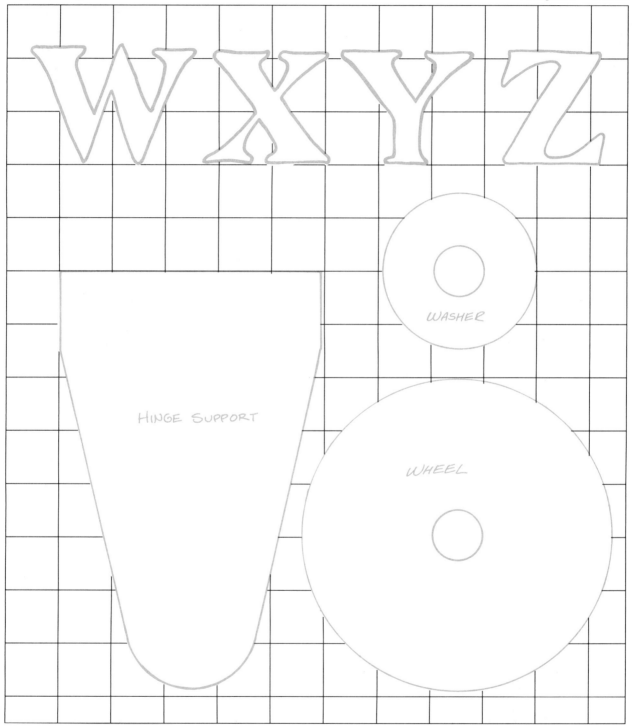

WASHER

HINGE SUPPORT

WHEEL

Mr. Santa

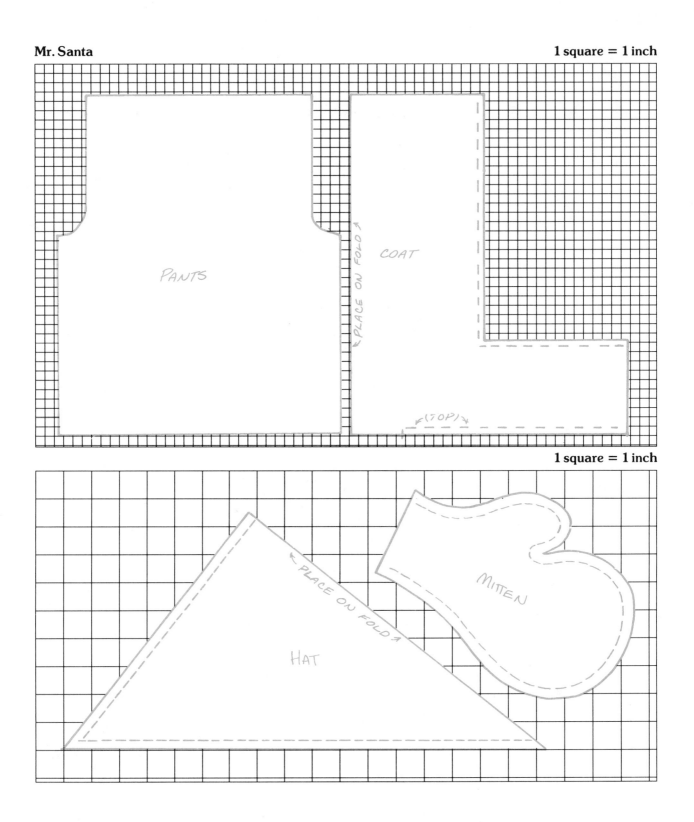

PANTS

COAT

← PLACE ON FOLD →

←(TOP)→

← PLACE ON FOLD →

HAT

MITTEN

CELEBRATIONS OF CHRISTMAS

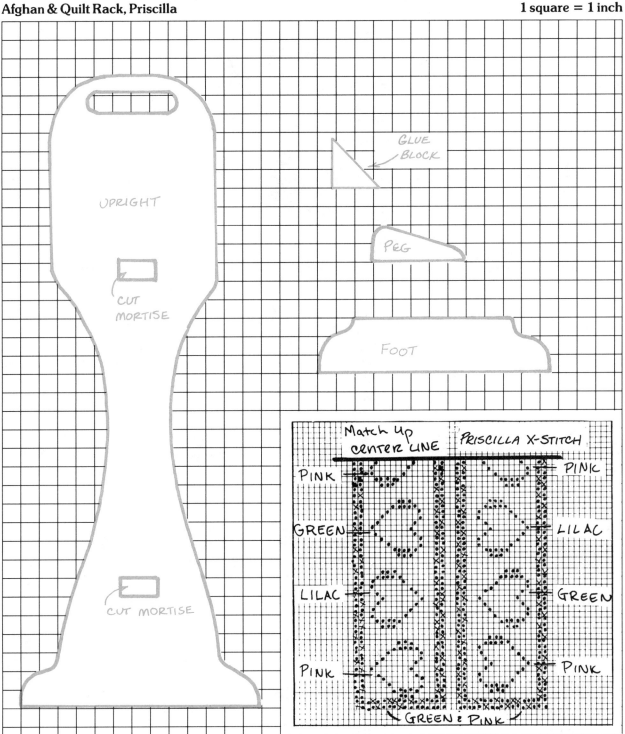

A Country Christmas

The idea of the "perfect" Christmas most often crystalizes into mental images surrounding activities in the country; horse-drawn sleigh rides through snowy fields, going into the woods to chop down your own Christmas tree, neighbors and friends gathered around the piano singing carols and sipping hot cider. In fact, Christmas celebrations since the time of the Reformation owe a huge debt to the traditions that were kept alive in the country.

Even children who grew up in the city fondly remember Christmas spent at Grandma and Grandpa's farm. It's quite possible that there are no whiter Christmases than those remembered from childhood, when the snowdrifts were higher than your head, and the crisp winter air made your cheeks tingle and turned your nose a bright red...just like Rudolph's.

As adults we know that our childhood snows were not whiter, the trees were not taller, and the days before Christmas were not at least five hours too long; but they certainly seemed that way. It's almost as if the spirit of Christmas were most alive in the sweet memories of the child who grew up in the country.

In this section we have tried to revive that country spirit, through the calicos, ruffles, ducks and geese, and the ambiance of pastoral beauty. We have updated the traditional reds and greens into modern hues of burgundy and the deep shades of the forest. Toss in freshly popped corn and cranberries to be strung for the tree, the aroma of baked cinnamon goodies drifting through the house, the hushed whispers of family members hiding handmade presents, and the enchantment of Christmas in the country will come to life.

Country Christmas

Christmas Wreath Quilt

Joy Pillows

Elf Christmas Card Holder

Stuffed Duck Wreath

Christmas Goose

Menus and Melodies

A Country Menu

If there is a typical country Christmas it surely entails decorating the family Christmas tree with new, old, handmade, and commercial ornaments; children eagerly awaiting Santa's mysterious visit and the gifts he will bring; a quiet moment of prayer either in church or at home; and a gathering of family and friends around a dinner table laden with homemade delicacies.

To many people, the terms "homemade" and "country cooking" mean the same thing. Images of mason jars full of colorful home-canned contents lined up on pantry shelves, baskets of fresh vegetables waiting to be preserved, and a cookie jar brimming with home-baked goodies immediately come to mind.

Traditions surrounding Christmas foods include recipes handed down from generation to generation, and quite often no one remembers where, when, or from whom the recipes originated. Sometimes the recipes are modernized (a "pinch" is replaced by "⅛ tsp."), and sometimes they are not. Whatever the customs and traditions, it is universal that the holidays be as pleasant and full of good things to eat as possible; standards that are deliciously blended in country cooking.

A Country Menu

Roast Turkey and Dressing
Mashed Potatoes and Giblet Gravy
Mallowed Sweet Potatoes
Buttered Green Beans
Brandied Peaches
Four-Bean Salad
Relish Tray
Yeast Rolls and Butter
Deep-Dish Apple Pie
Pumpkin Pie with Whipped Cream
Cranberry Sauce
Coffee

Deep-Dish Apple Pie

(For delicious pie crusts, one old saying goes; "Handle the pastry as a delicate rose, and light and flaky your pastry goes.")

5 cooking apples	1 cup sugar
2 Tbsp. butter	¼ tsp. nutmeg
1 Tbsp. flour	Plain pastry pie crust

Line a deep dish with pastry. Sprinkle flour and ¼ cup sugar on the bottom crust. Pare the apples, quarter, and place cut side down. Cover with remaining sugar, dot with butter and sprinkle with nutmeg. Bake in 350° oven about 35 minutes, or until apples are baked and rich syrup has formed.

Basic Cranberry Sauce

Combine 1½ cups sugar and 2 cups water in a large sauce pan. Boil 5 minutes. Add 1 pound (4 cups) whole cranberries and boil without stirring until the cranberry skins pop open; about 5 minutes. Remove from heat and cool until jelled. If you prefer a clear cranberry sauce, pour the cooked cranberries through a strainer to remove the skins.

Brandied Peaches

(These were put up during the summer when the peaches were ripe on the trees.)

Note: This is an old recipe and does not specify processing time. Check a modern canning book on hot-water bath or pressure cooker processing times.

9 pounds large clingstone peaches	9 pounds sugar
	1 quart water
2 Tbsp. whole cloves, heads removed	3 pints brandy
	2 sticks cinnamon

Peel and weigh fruit. Tie spices in a cheese-cloth bag, and boil with water and sugar. Boil until mixture is clear. Drop in peaches a few at a time, and cook until tender, but not soft. Peaches must remain whole. Repeat until all peaches have been cooked. Place fruit on platter to drain. Boil syrup until thick. Cool, add brandy and stir well. Place peaches in sterile jars and cover with syrup. Seal. Makes 4 quarts.

Yeast Rolls

1 cake yeast	½ cup lukewarm water
2 Tbsp. each shortening and sugar	½ cup scalded milk
1 egg or 2 egg yolks	3½ or 4 cups sifted flour
2 tsp. salt	

Soften yeast in lukewarm water. Add shortening, sugar and salt to milk. Cool to lukewarm and add yeast and beaten egg. Stir in flour to make a soft dough. Turn out on floured board and knead until satiny and smooth (8 to 10 minutes). Place in greased bowl, cover and let rise until doubled in bulk. Punch down. Let rest again until doubled in bulk. Punch down and let stand for 10 minutes. Shape into rolls. Let rise until doubled in bulk. Bake in 425° oven 12 to 15 minutes. Makes 24 to 36 rolls.

Mallowed Sweet Potatoes

One large can sweet potatoes	Brown sugar
Butter	One package miniature marshmallows

Empty can of sweet potatoes into large casserole dish. Sprinkle brown sugar over top. Cut butter into small pieces and sprinkle over top. Add marshmallows. Place in 350° oven for 15 minutes or until sweet potatoes are hot and marshmallows are melted. Some cooks also like to add crushed pineapple.

Four-Bean Salad

(A three-bean salad with something extra!)

Note: This recipe calls for home-canned beans; however, you can use commercially processed beans.

2 cups whole green beans	2 cups yellow wax beans
2 cups red kidney beans	2 cups garbanzos (chick peas)
1 medium green (bell) pepper	3 medium stalks celery
	2 medium onions

Dressing

1 cup vinegar	½ cup water
1 cup sugar	½ cup salad oil
1 tsp. salt	

Drain the green and yellow beans, put in pan and cover with water. Simmer 5 minutes; drain. Place kidney beans in colander and rinse well; drain. Combine vinegar, water, and sugar in pan and boil for 2-3 mintues. Remove from heat, and add cooking oil and salt. Mix well. Place green, yellow, kidney and garbanzo beans in large serving bowl. Cut into thin slices (or chop) onions, celery, and bell pepper. Place in bowl with beans. Mix well. Pour the dressing over beans. Cover bowl and refrigerate for several hours to let the flavors blend. Stir occasionally. Serves 8 to 10.

Music to Enjoy

The following recorded albums include folk, country/western, and traditional Christmas favorites.

American Folk Songs for Christmas
Folkways Records #7553
Here are twenty songs by various folk singers, from one of the most well respected record companies.

A Country Christmas
RCA Victor #AYL 1-4812
This record presents various country music artists singing Christmas favorites.

Merry Christmas
Bing Crosby
MCA Records #15024
On this record the beloved singer offers such favorites as "Jingle Bells," "White Christmas," and "I'll be Home for Christmas."

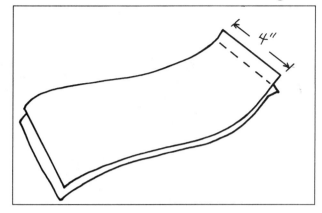

Christmas Wreath Quilt

Nine beautiful calico wreaths and Christmas trees decorate the front of this holiday quilt. It's spectacular as a wall hanging, or draped across a sofa or chair. It's easy to put together, and measures approximately 50 inches square.

Materials

¾ yard of 44-inch-wide white or off-white cotton fabric for the border pieces

3 yards of calico fabric in Christmas colors for the backing and bindings (We used green.)

Five 10½-inch-square pieces of red calico

Four 10½-inch-square pieces of cream-colored cotton fabric

½ yard of 36-inch-wide green calico for eight appliques

One 8-inch-square piece of solid-color cotton for one applique (We used grey.)

43-inch-square piece of quilt batting

Heavy-duty green thread; and regular sewing thread to match the fabrics

1 yard of ½-inch-wide red grosgrain ribbon

1½ yards of ¼-inch-wide red grosgrain ribbon

Six yards of ¼-inch-wide green grosgrain ribbon

If you wish to use the quilt as a wall hanging, you'll need the following additional materials:

4-foot length of wooden closet or curtain rod

1½ yards of 2-inch-wide grosgrain ribbon in a color that coordinates with the calicos

Cutting the Pieces

1. From the 3 yards of calico, cut one 42½-inch-square Backing piece, and two 4 x 42½-inch Side Border pieces. Cut the remaining calico into 4-inch-wide strips. Piece these strips together to form two Top/Bottom Binding pieces, each 4 x 48½ inches. To do this, place two of the strips right sides together and stitch a ½-inch-wide seam along one short edge (**Figure A**). Press the seam open. Cut the pieced strip to a total length of 48½ inches. Repeat these procedures to make a second identical strip.

2. From the remaining lengths of the pieced calico strips, cut four 4 x 4-inch Border Squares.

3. From the white or off-white fabric, you will need to cut twelve 4 x 10½-inch Border Strips, two 4½ x 35½-inch Side Borders, and two 4½ x 42½-inch Top/Bottom Border pieces.

4. Scale drawings for the Tree and Wreath appliques are provided on page 159. Enlarge them to make full-size patterns. From the green calico, cut four Tree appliques and four Wreath appliques.

5. From the solid-color cotton fabric, you will need to cut one Tree applique.

Figure B

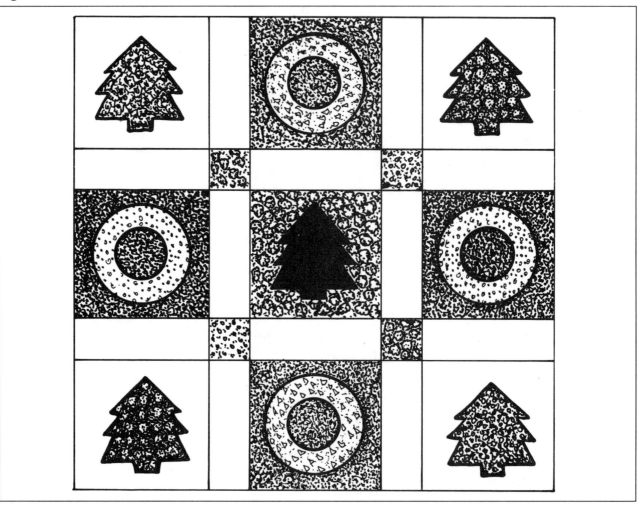

The Appliques

The first task to perform is to applique the squares. (Refer to the Tips & Techniques section on applique, if necessary.) Applique one Tree on each square of unbleached muslin. Applique one Wreath on four of the calico squares, and applique the solid-color Tree on the fifth calico square.

Making the Patchwork Quilt Top

Note: All seams allowances are ½ inch unless otherwise specified in the instructions.

1. The patchwork quilt top consists of three rows of appliqued squares plus dividing border rows. The arrangement we used is shown in **Figure B**.

2. Beginning with the top row, place one appliqued tree square right side up on a flat surface. Place one of the white Border Strips right side down on top, aligning the right-hand raw edges. Stitch the seam as shown in **Figure C**, and press the seam open.

3. Place one appliqued wreath square right side down on top of the border strip, aligning the right-hand raw edges. Stitch the seam and press it open.

4. Place another Border Strip right side down on top of the appliqued wreath square, aligning the right-hand

Figure C

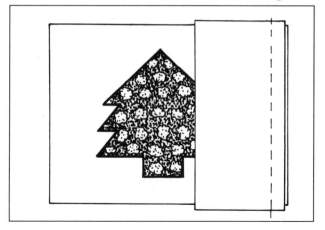

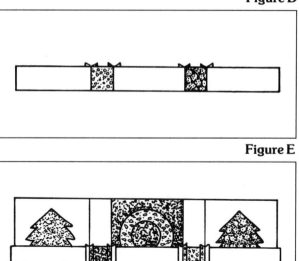

Figure F

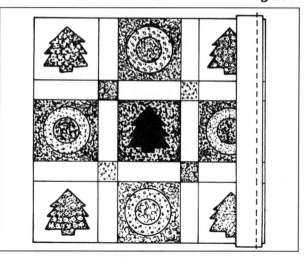

raw edges. Stitch the seam and press it open.

5. Place the second appliqued tree square right side down on top of the border strip, aligning the right-hand raw edges. Stitch the seam and press it open. This completes the first row of the patchwork quilt top.

6. Repeat steps 1 through 5 to piece the remaining two rows, following the arrangement that is illustrated in **Figure B**.

7. The appliqued rows are separated by rows of white Border Strips and calico Border Squares. To make one of these Border rows, sew together three white Border Strips and two Calico Border Squares in the same manner as you did the appliqued patchwork rows. An assembled Border row is shown in **Figure D**.

8. Repeat the procedures in step 7 to make a second row in the same manner, using the remaining Border Strips and Border Squares.

9. Place the top row of appliqued patchwork squares right side up on a flat surface. Place one border row right side down on top, aligning the lower raw edges, and stitch the seam, as shown in **Figure E**. Press the seam open.

10. Place the middle row of appliqued squares right side down on top of the border row, aligning the raw edges, and stitch the seam. Make sure the appliqued row is turned in the right direction, so when the seam is stitched and the row opened out the trees will not be upside down.

11. Stitch the remaining border and appliqued rows in the same manner.

12. All that's left to do on the patchwork top is to add

the outer white Border pieces. To begin, place the inner patchwork section that you just completed right side up on a flat surface. Press out the wrinkles. Place one Side Border piece right side down on top, aligning the right-hand edges, and stitch the seam (**Figure F**). Stitch the remaining Side Border piece to the left-hand edge of the inner patchwork section in the same manner.

13. Place one of the Top/Bottom Border pieces right side down on top of this assembly, aligning the upper

Figure G

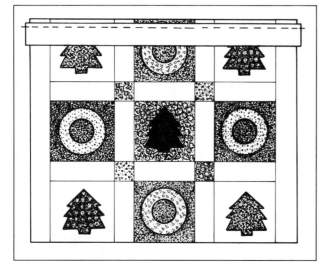

Figure H

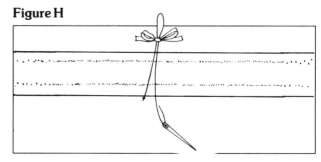

edges, and stitch the seam (**Figure G**). Press the seam open. Stitch the remaining Top/Bottom Border piece to the lower edge in the same manner.

Quilting and Finishing

1. Place the calico Backing piece wrong side up on a flat surface. Place the quilt batting over the Backing piece, and then place the assembled patchwork quilt top, right side up, over the batting. Pin all layers together. Baste from the center to each corner and then around the edges, keeping the layers smooth.

2. The layers are secured at each corner of each appliqued patch using a quick and easy method of tie-quilting (**Figure H**). Tie-quilting is usually done using yarn, but we used heavy-duty green thread, and added a decorative touch at each tie by including a small ribbon bow. Tie a 6-inch length of green ribbon in a bow. Place the bow on the quilt, and take a stitch from the back of the quilt through to the front. Catch the ribbon bow in the stitch, and then pass the needle through the quilt to the back again. Take another stitch, and then knot the stitch on the back, and cut the thread.

3. The remaining calico pieces (two Side Binding pieces and two Top/Bottom Binding pieces) are used to encase the edges of the quilt. Place the quilt right side up on a flat surface. Trim the edges around the quilt so all layers are even along each edge. Pin one of the Side Binding pieces to the front of the quilt, placing right

sides together, and align the right-hand edges. Stitch the seam through all layers. Turn the Binding piece outward over the seam allowances and press.

4. Repeat the procedures in step 3 to stitch the remaining Side Binding piece to the opposite edge of the quilt in the same manner.

5. Stitch one of the Top/Bottom Binding pieces to the upper edge of the quilt, and the remaining Binding piece to the lower edge in the same manner.

6. Press a ½-inch-wide hem to the wrong side of the fabric along each raw edge of the Binding pieces. Fold each one in half, wrong sides together, so that they encase the edges of the quilt. Tuck and fold the fabric carefully at the corners, so they present a neat appearance. Blind stitch the pressed edges of the Binding pieces to the back of the quilt.

7. If you wish to use the quilt as a wall hanging, first cut the wide green grosgrain ribbon into three equal lengths. Fold each length in half and tie the ends together in a bow, leaving a loop of ribbon large enough to insert the closet rod. Stitch the bows firmly to the quilt, placing one ribbon at each upper corner, and one in the middle of the upper edge.

8. You can paint, stain, or cover the rod with fabric. Slide the closet rod through the ribbon loops, and hang it from a wall or over a window. As a final touch, you can add a decorative finial to each end of the rod.

Finishing

1. Cut the ¼-inch-wide red grosgrain ribbon into five lengths each about 10 inches long. Tie the ribbons into small bows, leaving the ends to serve as long streamers. Tack one bow to the top of each tree.

2. Cut the ½-inch-wide red grosgrain ribbon into four lengths each about 8 inches long. Tie the ribbons into small bows, and tack one bow to the lower portion of each wreath.

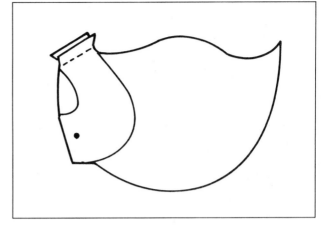

Christmas Goose

One of the traditional symbols of the holiday season is the Christmas goose. This **adorable example is amply stuffed, and wears a colorful ruffled collar and cap. Place her amid a lavish arrangement of holly and berries for an eye-catching holiday centerpiece.**

Materials

1½ yards of white cotton polyester fabric

12-inch-square piece of green calico for the bonnet

½ yard of 36-inch-wide red calico for the ruffled collar

3 x 6-inch piece of orange cotton fabric for the beak

3 yards of lace trim

Two bags of polyester fiberfill

Heavy-duty white thread; and regular sewing thread to match the fabrics

Two ¼- to ½-inch-diameter black shank-type buttons for the eyes

Long sharp needle; and regular sewing needle

Cutting the Pieces

1. Scale drawings are provided on page 158 for the Body, Head-and-Neck, Wing, Beak, and Gusset. Enlarge the drawings to make full-size paper patterns. (Refer to the Tips & Techniques section on enlarging scale drawings.)

2. Cut the pieces as listed in this step from the specified fabrics. Fold the fabric into a double thickness, so you can cut two of each piece at a time, and the resulting pieces will be matching pairs. Pay attention to the "place on fold" notations on the scale drawings and patterns. Transfer any placement markings or instructions to the fabric pieces.

    White cotton: Body - cut two
                    Head-and-Neck - cut two
                    Gusset - cut one
                    Wing - cut four

    Green calico: Bonnet - cut one

    Red calico: Collar - cut two, 6 x 35 inches

    Orange cotton: Beak - cut two

Making the Body

Note: All seam allowances are ⅜ inch unless other specified in the instructions.

1. Place one Head-and-Neck and one Body piece right sides together, and stitch the neck seam (**Figure A**). Press the seam open.

2. Repeat step 1, using the remaining Head-and-Neck and Body pieces.

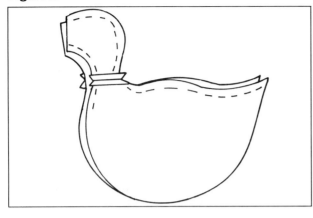

Figure C

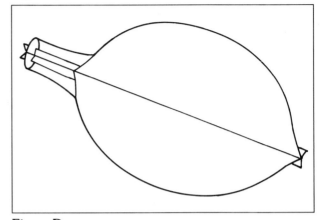

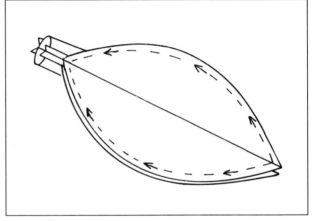

3. Place the two body assemblies right sides together, aligning the upper edges (**Figure B**). Stitch the seam along the upper edge, from the tail to the top of the head. Stitch the seam from the bottom of the head to 2 inches below the neck seam, as shown. Leave the bill opening unstitched, and leave the long lower edges of the body open and unstitched.

4. Place the partially assembled body upside down on a flat surface. Open out the lower edges of the two body sides, so the right sides of both body pieces are facing upward (**Figure C**).

5. Place the Gusset on top, right side down, aligning it with the edges of the body pieces (**Figure D**). Stitch the seam along one side from the tip of the tail to the neck (in the direction of the arrows). Stitch the seam along the remaining open side in the same direction, from the tip of the tail to the breast.

6. Clip the curves, press, and turn the goose right side out through the beak opening.

7. The beak opening is a bit small to stuff the fiberfill through, so cut a 4- or 5-inch slit down the center of the gusset on the lower side. Stuff the goose tightly with fiberfill. Take care to stuff the neck tightly through both the bill opening and the body slit. You might hum a few bars of "Christmas is Coming, the Goose is Getting Fat," then whipstitch the slit closed.

Making the Head

1. Place two Beak pieces right sides together, and stitch along the curved edge (**Figure E**), leaving the straight edge open and unstitched. Clip the curve, turn

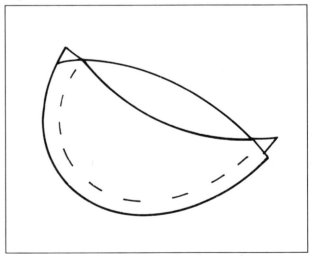

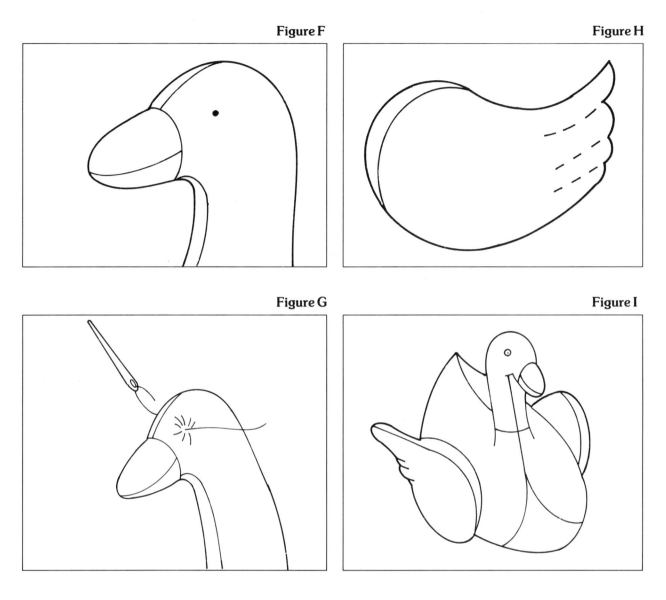

Figure F

Figure H

Figure G

Figure I

the beak right side out, and press gently. Press the seam allowances to the inside along the open edges.

2. Stuff the beak with fiberfill. Place it on the head, as shown in **Figure F**, and whipstitch it to the head.

3. To sculpt the eyes, use a long sharp needle and heavy-duty thread. Take a few stitches back and forth through the head, about 1 inch above the beak (**Figure G**). Pull the thread gently to form an eye indentation on each side, lock the stitch, and cut the thread.

4. Use black thread (if you're using black buttons),

and sew a small button over the eye indentation on each side of the head.

Making the Wings

1. To make one wing, pin two Wing pieces right sides together. Stitch the seam around the entire edge, leaving a small opening for stuffing. Clip the curves, turn the wing right side out, and press the seam allowances to the inside along the opening edges. Stuff the wing lightly with fiberfill, and then whipstitch the opening edges together.

2. To sculpt the wing, run a line of long, straight machine stitches through the wing along each of the three dotted lines, as shown in **Figure H** and on the Wing pattern.

3. Repeat steps 1 and 2 to make another wing in the same manner, using the remaining Wing pieces.

4. To attach one wing, place it alongside the goose's body, as shown in **Figure I**. Tack the wing to the body at the shoulder, using heavy-duty thread. You may stitch the wing to the body near the back edge as well, but we found it looked more natural without doing so.

Making the Bonnet

1. Press a narrow hem to the wrong side of the green calico Bonnet piece all the way around the outer edge. Stitch the hem.

2. Cut a 35-inch length of lace, and pin it to the wrong side of the hem (**Figure J**). Gather the lace slightly to fit the bonnet circumference. Stitch the lace to the bonnet.

3. Run a line of hand basting stitches around the perimeter of the bonnet, about 1 inch from the hemmed edge (**Figure K**). Place a ball of fiberfill in the center of the bonnet, and pull the basting thread to gather the bonnet around the fiberfill. Do not cut the thread.

4. Place the bonnet on the goose's head and take a few small stitches to secure the bonnet in place. Knot the stitch, and cut the thread.

5. To make the ruffled collar, place one Collar piece right side up on a flat surface, and pin one 36-inch length of lace along one long edge, with the lace toward the inside (**Figure L**). Pin the second 36-inch length of lace along the opposite long edge in the same manner.

6. Place the second Collar piece right side down on top, and stitch both long seams (**Figure M**), leaving the short ends opened and unstitched. Remove the pins, and turn the collar right side out. Press the seam allowances on both ends toward the inside.

7. To make the casing for the ribbon tie (**Figure N**), stitch down the length of the collar about 2 inches from one edge. Stitch again, about 2 inches from the opposite edge, as shown. The casing should be about 1¼ inches wide to accommodate the 1-inch-wide ribbon.

8. Thread the ribbon through the casing. Trim the ends of the ribbon at an angle. Gather the collar along the ribbon, and tie it around the goose's neck.

Figure J

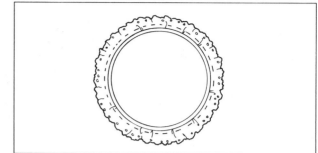

Figure K

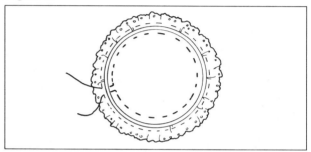

Figure L

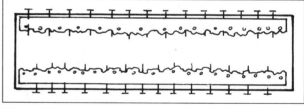

Figure M

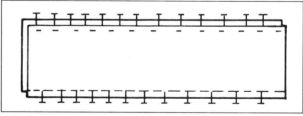

Figure N

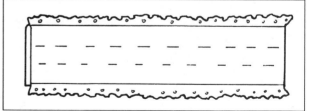

CELEBRATIONS OF CHRISTMAS

3 x 10-inch piece of pink felt for the ears

2 x 17-inch piece of white felt for the belt

3-inch square piece of brown felt for the belt buckle

15-inch-square piece of red calico (inner card holder)

15-inch-square piece of cream-colored calico for the outer card holder

15-inch-square piece of lightweight interlining

15-inch-square piece of 6-ply quilt batting

1 yard of 1-inch-wide red grosgrain ribbon

Two ½-inch-diameter black buttons for the eyes

14 yards of yarn for the pompom

One-half bag of polyester fiberfill

Heavy-duty flesh-tone thread; and regular thread to match the fabrics

Long sharp needle; and normal sewing needles

Hot-melt glue and a glue gun (or white glue); cosmetic cheek blusher; and a red felt-tip marker

A few pounds of marbles or clean pebbles for the beanbag weights

Elf Christmas Card Holder

This cute little elf will gladly hold all of your beautiful Christmas cards in his calico basket. The card holder basket can also be filled with pine cones, ornaments, or everyone's favorite, candy canes! The bulk of the elf's body is a simple beanbag that contains weights to keep the elf perched on the edge of a mantle or table. The elf is approximately 30 inches tall.

Materials

One leg from a pair of flesh-tone pantyhose

¾ yard of 44-inch red calico for the shirt and shoes

½ yard of 44-inch-wide green calico for the pants, hat, and collar

6 x 20-inch piece of unbleached muslin for the hands

½ yard of felt for the beanbag

Cutting the Pieces

1. Scale drawings are provided on pages 155-156 for the Collar, Hat, Pants, Shoe, Sleeve, Shirt, Beanbag, Beanbag Bottom, Card Holder, Hand, Ear, and Buckle. Enlarge the drawings to make full-size paper patterns. (Refer to the Tips & Techniques section on enlarging scale drawings.)

2. Cut the pieces as listed in this step from the specified fabrics. Fold the fabric into a double thickness, so you can cut two of each piece at a time, and the resulting pieces will be matching pairs. Pay attention to the "place on fold" notations on the scale drawings. Transfer any placement markings or instructions to the fabric pieces.

Red calico: Shirt - cut two
              Shoe - cut four
              Sleeve - cut two

Green calico: Pants - cut two
               Collar - cut two
               Hat - cut one

Unbleached muslin: Hand - cut four

Felt: Beanbag - cut two
      Beanbag Bottom - cut one

Pink felt: Ear - cut two

Brown felt: Belt Buckle - cut one

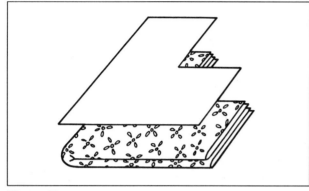

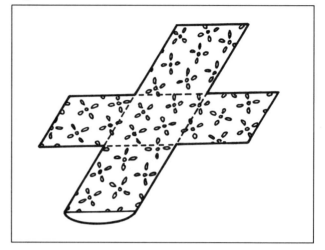

Figure B

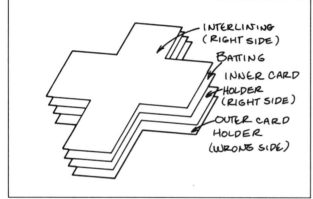

Figure C

LEAVE OPEN

Making the Card Holder

1. To cut the Outer Card Holder piece (**Figure A**), fold the 15-inch square of fabric in quarters and pin together so that it will not slip. Place the full-size basket pattern on top of the folded print square, making sure that the "place on fold" notations are on both folded edges of the fabric square. Pin the pattern to the fabric and cut it out.

2. Cut the Inner Card Holder, the Card Holder Interlining, and the Card Holder Batting, using the same pattern piece, and in the same manner as you did for the Outer Card Holder piece.

3. Stack the four Card Holder pieces (**Figure B**), in the following manner: Interlining (right side up), Batting, Inner Card Holder (right side up), and Outer Card Holder (right side down). Pin the four pieces together.

4. Stitch a ½-inch seam around the edges, sewing through all four layers. Leave one of the edges open and unstitched, as shown in **Figure C**. Turn the stack right side out, with the calico fabrics on the outside.

5. Topstitch the center square, as shown in **Figure D**, double stitching for strength.

6. Turn the remaining raw edges to the inside and whipstitch the opening edges together.

7. Fold up the four cardholder sides, and whipstitch the top edge of each corner, as shown in **Figure E**.

8. Cut the red grosgrain ribbon into four equal lengths, tie each in a bow, and tack one bow to each corner of the cardholder.

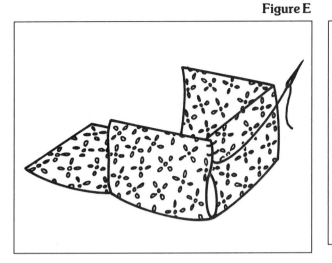

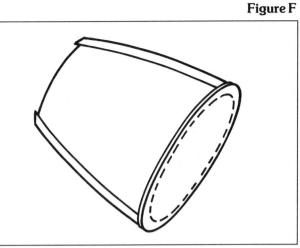

The Elf

The bulk of the elf's body is a simple beanbag that contains the weights. The head, legs and shoes, arms and hands, and shirt are made separately and glued or stitched to the weighted beanbag.

Making the Beanbag

1. Place the two Beanbag pieces right sides together and stitch the two curved side seams, leaving the straight upper and lower edges open and unstitched. Press the seams open, and leave the pieces turned wrong side out.

2. Place the Beanbag Bottom piece inside the lower (large) open edge of this assembly, and stitch it in place (**Figure F**). Turn the beanbag right side out.

3. Fill the beanbag about half full of marbles or whatever you have chosen for weights. Stuff the upper part with fiberfill.

Making the Legs and Feet

The elf really doesn't have legs — just stuffed pants!

1. Place two Pants pieces right sides together and stitch the side and inner leg seams (**Figure G**). Clip the curves and corner, and turn the pants right side out.

2. Place two Shoe pieces right sides together and stitch the seam all the way around the long, contoured edge (**Figure H**), leaving the top V-shaped edge open

Figure G

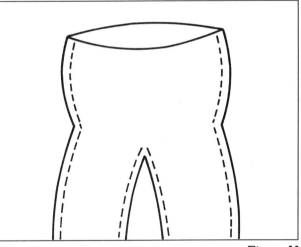

Figure H

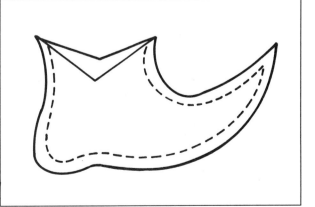

Figure I

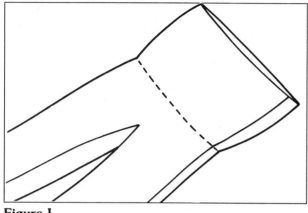

Figure J

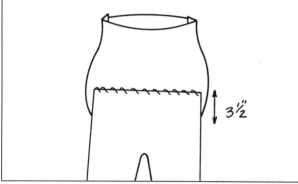

$3\frac{1}{2}''$

Figure K

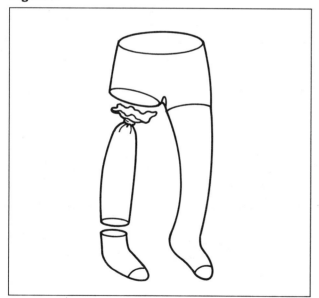

Figure L

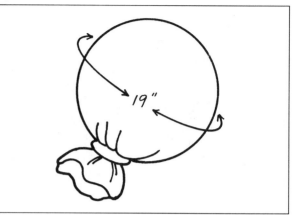

$19''$

and unstitched. Clip the curves and turn the shoe right side out. Stitch the second shoe in the same manner, using the remaining Shoe pieces. Stuff the shoes tightly with fiberfill.

3. Insert the lower end of one pant leg inside one shoe, and whipstitch together. Do the same with the remaining shoe and pant leg. Stuff fiberfill inside each pant leg up to the top of the legs only – do not stuff the top of the pants above the crotch.

4. Run a line of straight machine stitches across the pants, just above the crotch (**Figure I**), through both the front and back layers.

5. Whipstitch the aligned upper edges of the pants to the beanbag, about 3½ inches from the beanbag bottom (**Figure J**).

Making the Head

1. Tie a knot at the panty line on one pantyhose leg. Cut the hose 1 inch above the knot, and again 10 inches below the knot (**Figure K**). Turn the hose so the knot is on the inside.

2. Stuff the hose with generous amounts of fiberfill until the head is approximately 19 inches in circumference (**Figure L**). Tie the hose in a knot at the neck.

3. To sculpt the facial features, use heavy-duty thread and a long sharp needle, and follow the entry and exit points illustrated in **Figure M**.

    a. Enter at 1 at the knot, push the needle through the head, and exit at 2.

    b. To form the nose, sew a circle of basting stitches approximately 2½ inches in diameter, exiting at

3. Use the tip of the needle to lift the fiberfill within the circle. Pull the thread until the nose forms, and lock the stitch at 2.

c. To form the nostrils, reenter at 2, and exit at 4.

d. Enter ¼ inch directly above 4, and exit at 3.

e. Pull the thread until the nostril forms, reenter at 3, and exit at 5.

f. Enter ¼ inch directly above 5, and exit at 2. Pull the thread until the nostril forms, and lock the stitch at 2.

g. To form the eyes, reenter at 2, and exit at 6.

h. Pull the thread across the surface, enter at 2, and exit at 3.

i. Reenter at 3, and exit at 7.

j. Pull the thread across the surface, enter at 3, and exit at 2. Gently pull the thread until closed eyes appear, and lock the stitch at 2.

k. To form the mouth, reenter at 2 and, exit at 8.

l. Pull the thread across the surface, enter at 9, and exit at 3. Pull the thread until a lip line appears, and lock the stitch at 3.

m. To form the lower lip, reenter at 3, and exit at 10. Pull the thread across the surface, enter at 11, and exit at 2. Pull the thread until the lower lip forms, and lock the stitch at 2.

n. Reenter at 2, exit at 1, lock the stitch, and cut the thread.

4. **Figure N** shows the elf's completed face. (If you prefer, you can wait until after the head is attached to the body to complete the face.) Use a red felt-tip marker to draw lips along the lip lines. Glue two black buttons in place for the eyes. Glue the Ears in place along each side of the head. Glue strips of fake fur in place for the whiskers and eyebrows. Comb and trim the fake fur.

5. To give the elf a little color, brush cosmetic cheek blusher on the elf's cheeks and nose. Use the cheek blusher sparingly; you can always add more, but it's difficult to remove if you get too much.

Making The Hat

1. Fold the Hat piece in half, right sides together, and stitch the seam along the long straight edge. Leave the lower curved edge open and unstitched. Turn the hat right side out.

2. Fold under the seam allowance along the curved edge, and glue or whipstitch it in place.

3. To make a large pompom (**Figure O**), wrap yarn fifty times around a 5-inch piece of cardboard (or your

Figure M

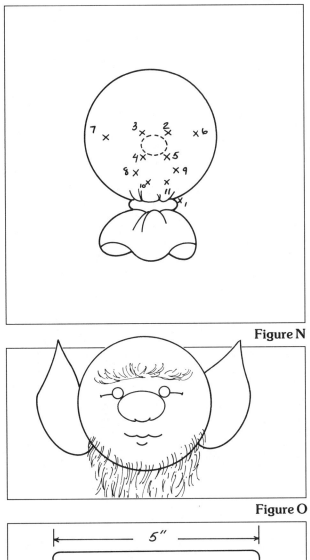

Figure N

Figure O

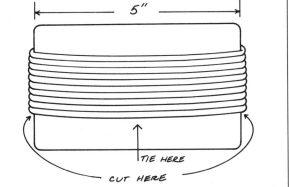

Figure P

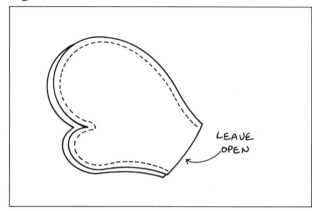

Figure Q

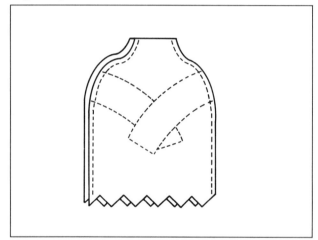

Figure R

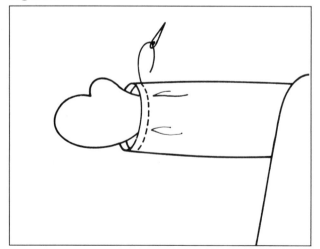

Figure S

thumb and index finger if you can stretch them 5 inches apart). Remove the cardboard, cut the strands at each end, and tie them together in the center. Tack the pom-pom to the tip of the hat. Place the hat on the elf's head, and arrange it to your liking. Glue or tack the hat to the top of the head.

Making the Hands, Shirt, and Collar

1. Place two Hand pieces together and stitch all the way around the contoured edge, leaving the wrist portion open and unstitched (**Figure P**). Clip the curves and corner, turn the hand right side out, and stuff the hand with fiberfill. Make another hand in the same manner, using the remaining two Hand pieces.

2. Fold one of the Sleeve pieces in half, placing right sides together. Stitch the seam along the edge opposite the fold, leaving both small ends open and unstitched. Press the seam open, and turn the sleeve right side out. Make the other sleeve in the same manner, using the remaining Sleeve piece.

3. To assemble the shirt and sleeves (**Figure Q**), place one of the Shirt pieces right side up on a flat surface. Place one sleeve on top, aligning the raw shoulder edge with the short edge of the sleeve. Place the other sleeve along the opposite edge in the same manner. Place the remaining Shirt piece on top. The sleeves should be sandwiched between the shirt pieces. Stitch the side seams, taking care not to catch any of the lower sleeve fabric in the seams. Clip the curves, and turn the shirt right side out.

4. Stuff one sleeve with fiberfill through the wrist opening. Turn under the seam allowance along the wrist, and run a line of basting stitches around the edge, securing the hem. Do not cut the thread.

5. To attach the hand (**Figure R**), insert the wrist edge of one hand inside the sleeve, making sure the thumb points upward. Pull the basting threads to gather the sleeve around the wrist. Whipstitch around the wrist to secure the hand.

6. Repeat the procedures in steps 4 and 5 for the remaining sleeve and hand.

7. To prevent the lower shirt edge from raveling, cut along the edge using pinking shears. Slip the shirt down over the top of the beanbag.

8. To make the collar (**Figure S**), place the Collar pieces right sides together, matching the points. Begin at the inner edge of the collar and stitch down the short straight seam, around the points, and back up the remaining short straight seam, as shown. Clip the corners, turn the collar right side out, and press.

9. Turn under the seam allowances around the circular neck edge. You will need to make short straight cuts in the seam allowance in order for fabric to lay flat (**Figure T**). Be very careful that you don't cut into the collar fabric beyond the seam allowance. Topstitch around the circular neck edge.

Attaching the Head, and Finishing

1. To attach the head (**Figure U**), insert the knotted neck on the head inside the neck opening on the shirt. Turn under a hem all the way around the neck edge of the shirt. Begin at the center back and whipstitch around the neck several times to secure the head.

2. Wrap the collar around the elf's neck, overlapping and glueing the ends at the center back.

3. Wrap the belt around the elf's waist, overlapping and glueing the ends together at the center front. Glue the buckle to the front of the belt.

4. Place the card holder on the elf's lap, and tack one hand to each upper corner, as shown in **Figure V**. Until those Christmas cards start coming in, you might like to fill the card holder with pine cones, Christmas ornaments, or everyone's favorite, candy canes!

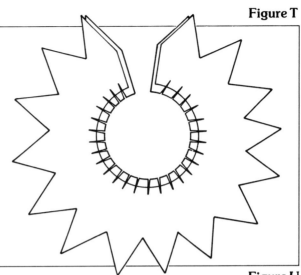

Figure T

Figure U

Figure V

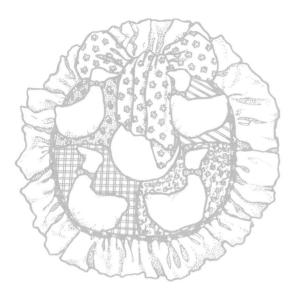

Stuffed Duck Wreath

You won't have to worry about these ducks flying south for the winter; they love the cold Christmas season. Four "quackers" play around the perimeter of this ruffled calico wreath. The wreath measures approximately 18 inches in diameter.

Materials

¼ yard of unbleached muslin for the ducks

Four different green calicos, 10-inch square of each

½ yard of 36-inch-wide red calico for the bow

Another ½ yard of red calico for the the border trim (optional), or 48-inch length of red edging trim

1½ yards of 36-inch-wide cotton fabric to coordinate with the green calico for the ruffle and wreath back (We used tan with green pin-dots.)

1 yard of ¼-inch-wide green grosgrain ribbon

One bag of polyester fiberfill

Thread to match the fabrics

A short length of florist's wire or string for a hanger

Figure A

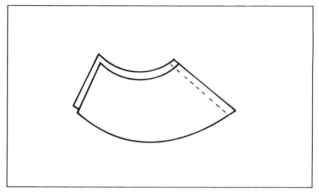

Cutting the Pieces

1. Scale drawings are provided on page 154 for the Duck and Wreath. Enlarge the drawings to make full-size paper patterns. (Refer to the Tips & Techniques section on enlarging scale drawings.)

2. Cut the pieces as listed in this step from the specified fabrics. Fold the fabric into a double thickness, so you can cut two of each piece at a time, and the resulting pieces will be matching pairs. Pay attention to the "place on fold" notations on the scale drawings and patterns. Transfer any placement markings or instructions to the fabric pieces.

Unbleached muslin: Duck - cut eight

Green calicos: Wreath section - cut one of each fabric

Cotton: Wreath section - cut four
      Ruffle - cut four, 9 x 36 inches

Red calico: Bow - cut two, 9 x 30 inches

Making the Wreath

1. Place the four green calico Wreath Sections in a circle on a flat surface until you find an arrangement that pleases you. When you decide on a pattern, place two Wreath Section pieces right sides together, and stitch the seam across the short straight edge, as shown in **Figure A**. Open out the two pieces, and press the seams open.

2. Attach the third and fourth Wreath Sections in the same manner, leaving one section unstitched, as shown in **Figure B**.

3. Assemble the coordinating cotton Wreath Back Sections in the same manner.

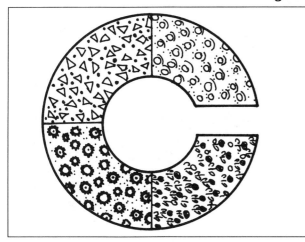

Figure B

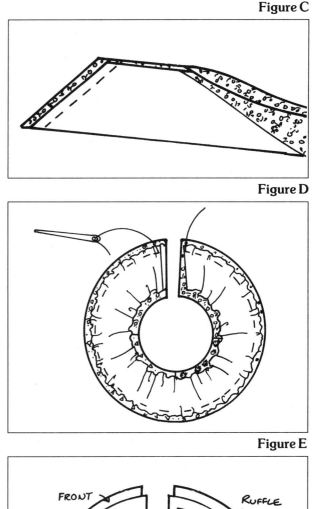

Figure C

Figure D

Figure E

4. To make the Ruffle, place two Ruffle pieces right sides together, and stitch across one short end. Open out the pieces, and attach the remaining Ruffle pieces in the same manner, until you have one continuous piece that measures 9 x 144 inches. Press the seams.

5. Fold one end of the Ruffle right sides together, and stitch across the short end (**Figure C**). Clip the corners and turn right side out. Repeat the procedure for the opposite end of the Ruffle.

6. With wrong sides still together, fold the Ruffle in half lengthwise. Run a line of basting stitches through both layers along the length of the raw edges. Pull the basting threads to gather the ruffle until it is the same length as the perimeter of the wreath.

7. Place the assembled wreath front right side up on a flat surface. Place the ruffle on top with the raw edge of the ruffle around the outer raw edge of the wreath, as shown in **Figure D**. Baste the ruffle in place.

8. Place the assembled wreath back right side down on top, matching inner and outer raw edges. The ruffle should be sandwiched between the wreath layers. Stitch the seams around the inner and outer curved edges (**Figure E**), taking care not to catch any of the ruffle in the inner edge seam. Do not stitch the short straight open ends. Remove the basting threads, clip the curves, and turn the wreath tube right side out through one of the open ends. Stuff the wreath tube firmly with fiberfill, right up to the open edges. Press the raw edges along the open ends to the inside, and whipstitch the edges together. (This seam will be covered by the bow.)

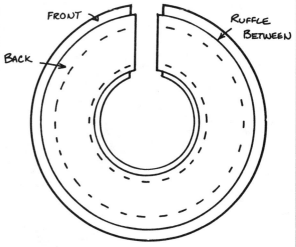

Figure F

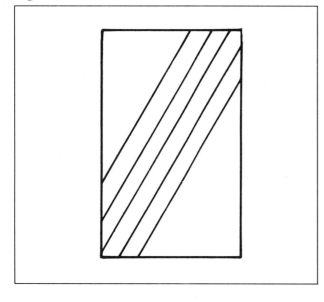

Figure H

Figure G

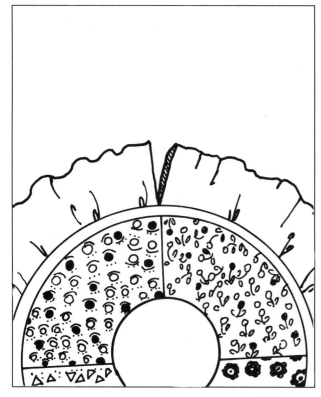

Note: If you are using purchased red edging trim, skip steps 9 and 10, and continue with step 11.

9. To make the red border trim around the wreath, as shown in the illustration, first cut several 1-inch-wide strips on the bias from the red calico fabric (**Figure F**). Stitch the bias strips end to end until they form one continuous strip that measures about 48 inches long. Check the length of the strip against the outer perimeter of the wreath to make sure it is long enough.

10. Fold the strip in half lengthwise, placing right sides together. Stitch a narrow seam along the long straight edge, leaving the short ends open. Trim the seam allowance, and turn the tube right side out. (A long knitting needle or Loop Turner will help in turning the tube right side out.) Turn the raw edges on the short ends to the inside.

11. To attach the border trim (**Figure G**), tack one end to the outer edge of the wreath at the whipstitched seam. Continue tacking the trim all the way around the perimeter of the wreath along the edge of the ruffle. When the border trim meets the beginning point, cut off any excess, turn the raw edges to the inside, and tack the end in place.

Making the Ducks

1. Place two Duck pieces right sides together and sew

Figure I

Figure J

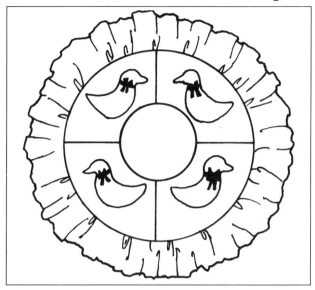

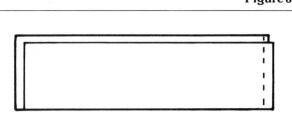

Figure K

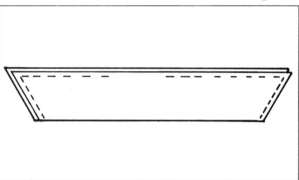

Figure L

a ¼-inch seam all the way around, leaving an opening on the lower edge (**Figure H**). Clip the curves, turn the duck right side out, and stuff with fiberfill. Turn the raw edges to the inside, and whipstitch the edges together.

2. Repeat the procedures to make three more ducks in the same manner.

3. Cut the green grosgrain ribbon into four equal lengths. Tie one ribbon around each duck's neck. Place the ducks on the wreath, positioning them as shown in **Figure I**. Whipstitch each duck to the wreath.

Making the Bow

1. To make the bow (**Figure J**), first place two Bow pieces right sides together, and stitch across one short end so you will have a 9 x 60-inch strip.

2. Fold the strip lengthwise with right sides together, and cut the ends at an angle (**Figure K**). Begin at one end and stitch across the angled edge, the long straight edge, and the opposite angled edge, leaving a space about 4 inches long unstitched in the middle for turning. Clip the corners, and turn the bow right side out. Press the seam allowances to the inside, and whipstitch the opening edges together. Press the finished bow.

3. Wrap the bow around the wreath, hiding the whipstitched seam (**Figure L**). Tie a big bow on the front of the wreath.

4. To make a hanger, simply insert a piece of florist's wire or string under the bow and twist (or tie) the ends.

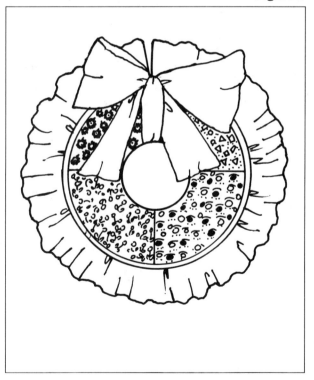

Joy Pillows

Three beautiful pillows that spell "Joy" will add just the right decorative touch to your home for the holidays. Each pillow measures approximately 22 inches square.

Materials

1¼ yards of 44-inch-wide green calico fabric for the "J" and pillow backs
2 yards of 44-inch-wide red cotton fabric for the pillow fronts and ruffle
½ yard of 44-inch-wide cream-colored cotton fabric for the "O" and top borders
½ yard of 44-inch-wide green cotton fabric for the "Y" and lower borders
⅜ yard of 44-inch-wide red calico for the side borders
Three 20-inch-square pillow forms or four bags of polyester fiberfill
Thread to match the fabrics
12-inch length of 1-inch-wide green ribbon

Cutting the Pieces

1. Scale drawings are provided on page 157 for the "J," "O," and "Y." Enlarge the drawings to make full-size paper patterns. (Refer to the Tips & Techniques section on enlarging scale drawings.)

2. Cut the pieces as listed in this step from the specified fabrics.

Green calico:
Pillow Back - cut three, 21 inches square
"J" - cut one

Red cotton:
Pillow Front - cut three, 13 inches square
Ruffle - cut five, 9 x 44 inches

Cream-colored cotton:
"O" - cut one
Top Border - cut three, 5 x 21 inches

Green cotton:
"Y" - cut one
Lower Border - cut three, 5 x 21 inches

Red calico:
Side Border - cut six, 5 x 13 inches

Making the Pillow Fronts

Note: All seam allowances are ½ inch unless otherwise specified in the instructions.

1. To assemble the "O" pillow, begin by placing one Pillow Front right side up on a flat surface. Place one Side Border piece right side down on top, aligning the raw edges, as shown in **Figure A**. Stitch the seam and press the seam allowance open. Attach the remaining side border in the same manner.

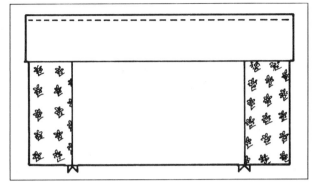

Figure C

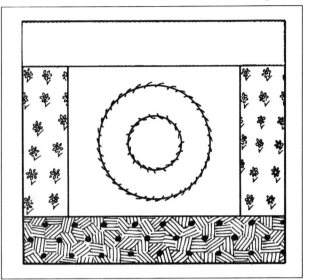

2. Place one Top Border piece right side down on top of the assembly, aligning the raw edges, as shown in **Figure B**. Stitch the seam, and press the seam allowance open.

3. Attach the Lower Border piece in the same manner. Press all seams open.

4. To applique the "O" (**Figure C**), first pin it to the center of the solid-color section. Use a closely spaced zigzag stitch setting on your machine and stitch around the outside and inside of the "O." (Refer to the Tips & Techniques section on applique, if necessary.)

5. Repeat steps 1 through 4 for the "J" pillow and the "Y" pillow, using the remaining Pillow Front and Border pieces.

Making the Ruffle

1. To make the ruffle (**Figure D**), place two Ruffle pieces right sides together, and stitch across one short end. Open out the pieces and attach the remaining Ruffle pieces in the same manner, until you have one continuous piece that measures 9 x 216 inches. Press the seams open. Turn the raw edges along the short ends to the inside and press.

2. Fold the ruffle lengthwise, placing wrong sides together. We hand-pleated the ruffle around the perimeter of the pillow, but you might prefer to gather the ruffle instead of hand-pleating. Steps 3 through 5 explain the hand-pleating method. Steps 6 and 7 explain the gathered method.

3. To hand-pleat, begin by pinning one end of the ruffle to one corner of the pillow front, placing the raw edges of the ruffle along the raw edge of the pillow front with right sides together (**Figure E**). The folded edge of the ruffle should be toward the center.

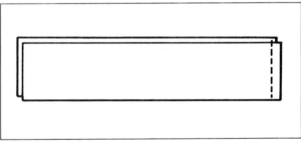

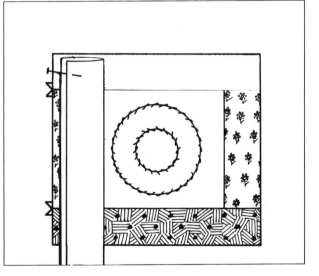

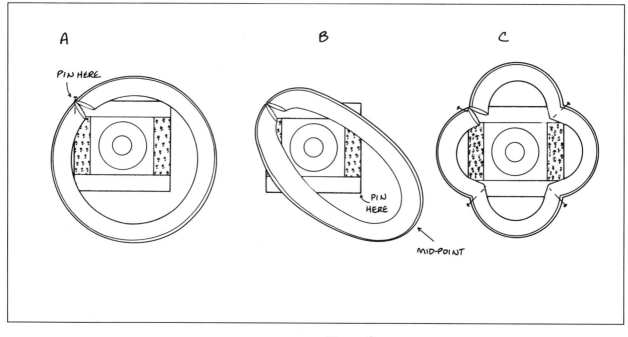

4. Loop the opposite end of the ruffle around the pillow front (make sure it is not twisted), and pin it to the same corner (**Figure F**, step a). Stretch out the ruffle loop until you find the mid-point, and pin it to the opposite corner (step b). Find and pin the mid-point for the remaining two corners in the same manner (step c). With the ruffle evenly divided around the perimeter of the pillow, you can more easily hand-pleat one side at a time. If you find it difficult to judge the number of pleats that should be one side, pin the mid-point of the ruffle to the pillow front in as many places as needed.

5. Pleat and baste the ruffle to the pillow front. To do this, simply make small folds in the ruffle as you baste the seam, as shown in (**Figure G**). Allow a little extra fabric at each corner so when the ruffle is opened out it will lie flat.

6. To gather the ruffle, run a line of basting stitches through both layers along the length of the raw edges. Pull the basting threads to gather the ruffle until it is the same length as the perimeter of the pillow. It should be about 84 inches long.

7. Place the pillow front right side up on a flat surface. Place the gathered ruffle on top with the raw edge of the ruffle around the outer raw edge of the pillow, as shown in **Figure H**. Baste the ruffle in place.

Figure G

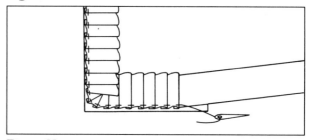

Figure H

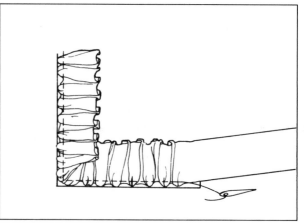

Assembling the Pillow

1. Place the Pillow Back right side down on top of the pillow front and ruffle, matching the raw edges on all four sides. The pillow front and back should be right sides together with the ruffle sandwiched between them, as shown in **Figure I**.

2. Stitch the seam around the pillow, leaving an opening for turning and stuffing, as shown. (If you are going to insert a pillow form, you will need to leave a much larger opening than if you plan to stuff the pillow using fiberfill.) Remove the basting threads, turn the pillow right side out, and insert the stuffing. Turn the seam allowances to the inside along the opening edges, and whipstitch or blind stitch the edges together.

3. Tie the green ribbon into a bow and tack it to the top of the "O," as shown in **Figure J**.

4. Repeat the procedures to assemble and stuff the "J" and "Y" pillows in the same manner.

Figure I

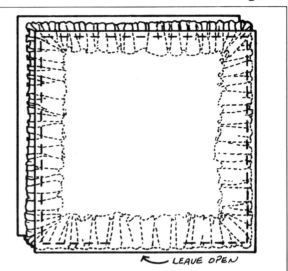

LEAVE OPEN

Figure J

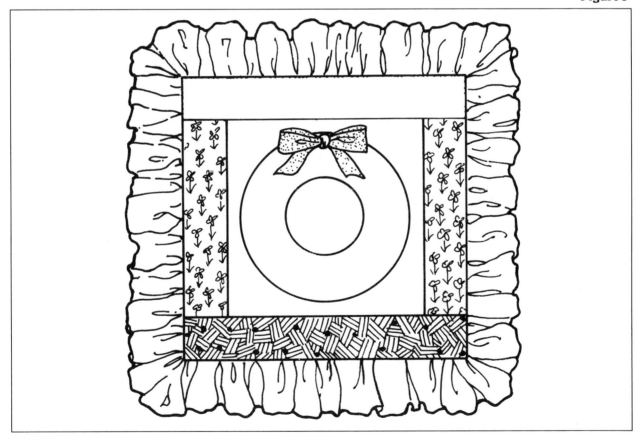

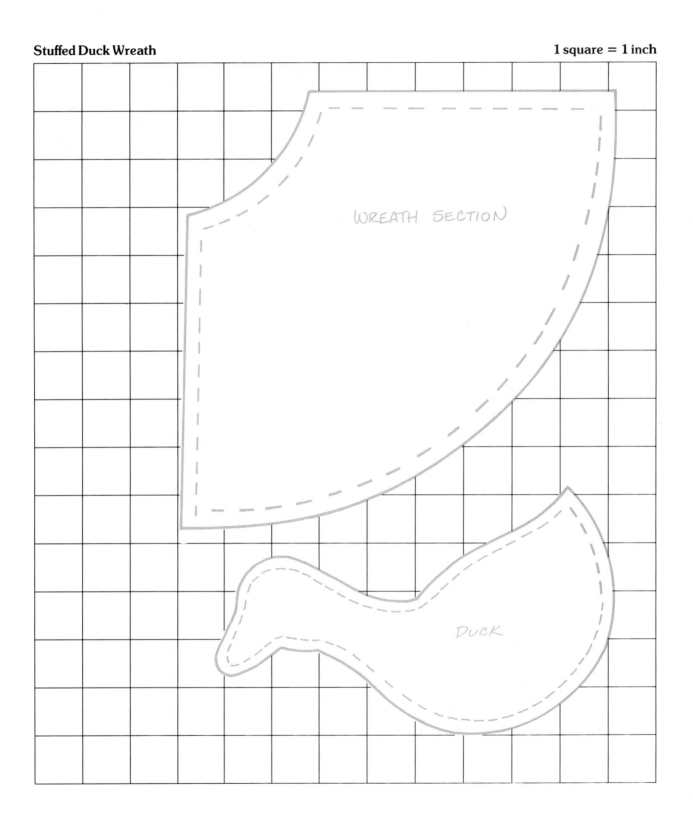

WREATH SECTION

DUCK

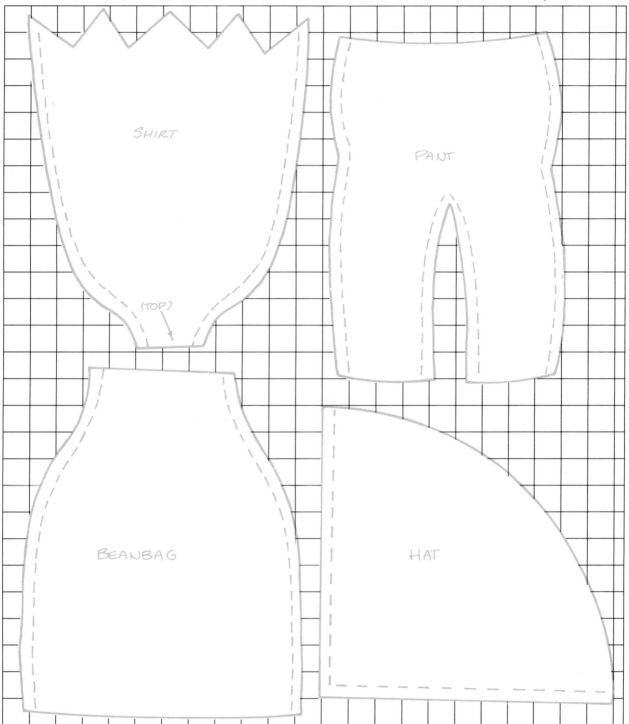

SHIRT

(TOP)

PANT

BEANBAG

HAT

Elf Christmas Card Holder

COLLAR

CUT LINE

PLACE ON FOLD

SLEEVE

SHOE

BUCKLE

HAND

EAR

PLACE ON FOLD

CARD HOLDER
(1/4 PATTERN)

PLACE ON FOLD

BEANBAG
BOTTOM

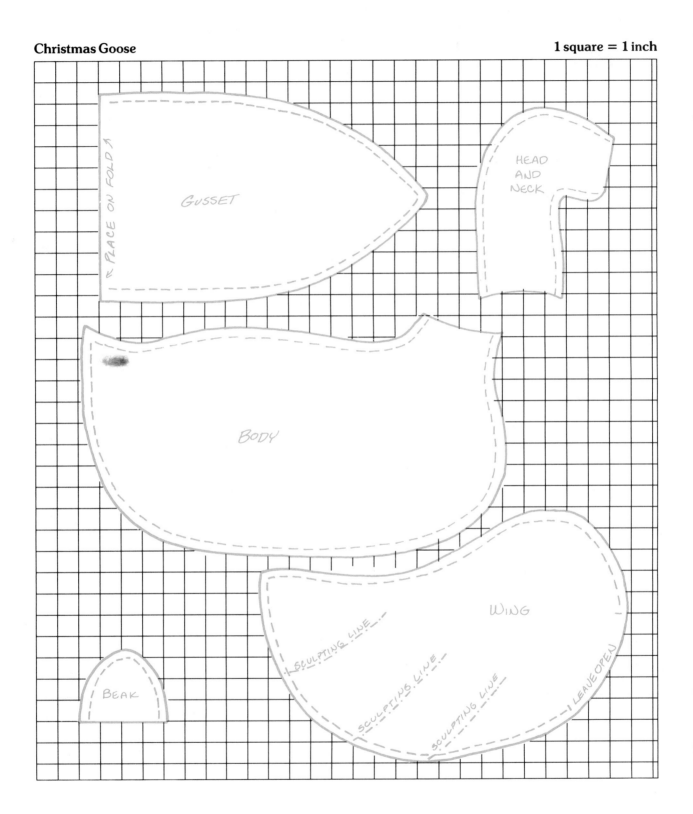

GUSSET

PLACE ON FOLD

HEAD
AND
NECK

BODY

WING

SCULPTING LINE

SCULPTING LINE

SCULPTING LINE

SCULPTING LINE

LEAVE OPEN

BEAK

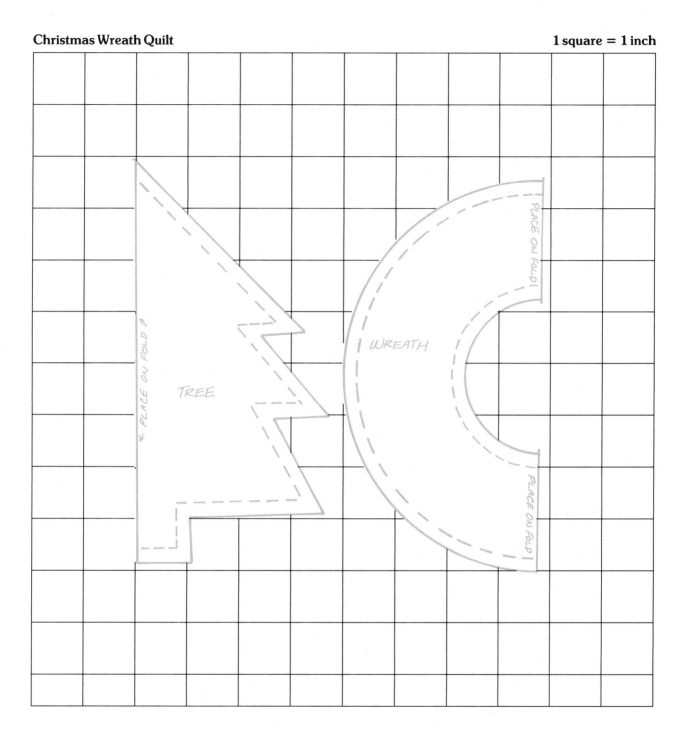

TREE

PLACE ON FOLD

WREATH

PLACE ON FOLD!

PLACE ON FOLD!

A City Christmas

The Victorians gave Christmas a glow and country traditions gave it a twinkle, but urban dwellers give it sparkle! Christmas in the city is bright and shiny, and all wrapped up in slick paper. The intensity of the season can be seen in the hustle of shoppers scurrying in and out of stores carrying gaily wrapped bundles, the jingle of bells, and the "Ho-ho-ho's" of the legions of "Santa's helpers" in every department store and shopping mall.

To make room for everything in a city Christmas, the original twelve days have been extended to forty-one, stretching the season from Thanksgiving to New Year's Day. Many stores report that one of their busiest days is the first day *after* Christmas when everyone exchanges the gifts purchased *before* Christmas.

A city celebration isn't just buying and exchanging gifts. It is also tree-lighting ceremonies, the traditional performances of "The Nutcracker Suite" and Handel's "Messiah," parades, and an extensive round of parties.

The myriad of nationalities and cultures that inhabit the concrete environment of the city require an equally varied selection of projects. There is a warm stadium blanket and tote, which can be customized with your team's initials. In keeping with the modern craze of physical fitness, we designed a special slim and trim Santa. Two stuffed educational toys for the kids to enjoy, and two adorable draftstoppers round out this section.

City Christmas

Stadium Blanket & Tote

Changeable Charlie

CELEBRATIONS OF CHRISTMAS

Slim Santa

Ballerina Draft Stopper

Clown Draft Stopper

Dress-Me Bears

CELEBRATIONS OF CHRISTMAS

Menus and Melodies

A City Menu

Perhaps no where is the season celebrated with parties, social functions, and gatherings of friends and acquaintances more than in the city. The streets are decorated with thousands of colorful lights, store windows are lavish displays of holiday decorations blended with luxurious items offered for sale, and everywhere can be heard recorded renditions of the songs of the season.

Dining in the city can be as homey as a small town in the corn belt or as sophisticated as the haute cuisine offered in the finest (and most expensive) restaurant. The variety and selection are practically endless. Combining the best of both, a menu for Christmas dinner might be:

Consomme and Melba Toast
Celery Curls and Olives
Roast Turkey
Oyster Dressing
Cranberry Relish
Sweet Potato Soufflé
Broccoli with Hollandaise Sauce
Green Salad Bowl with French Dressing
Individual Plum Puddings with Brandy Hard Sauce
Coffee and Tea

Oyster Dressing

Saltine Crackers crushed (not too fine), about one package	Butter - lots! Canned Oysters - 2 cans
½ pt. heavy cream	

Grease a casserole pan. Put in alternate layers of crushed crackers, oysters, and pats of butter. Final layer should be crackers and then pats of butter. Pour cream down sides and over top. Use fork to let cream down into layers. Bake 350° for 45 minutes or until brown.

Sweet Potato Soufflé

1 cup milk	3 Tbsp. butter
1 tsp. nutmeg	2 cups mashed
2 eggs, separated	sweet potatoes
½ cup sugar	½ cup each
Marshmallows	pecans and raisins

Scald milk and add sugar, salt, butter, nutmeg, and potatoes; beat until fluffy. Beat egg yolks and add to potatoes. Add raisins and pecans. Beat egg whites stiff, fold into potatoes and pour into greased baking dish. Bake in 350° oven 50 to 60 minutes or until firm. Top with marshmallows and brown. Serves 8.

Brandy Hard Sauce

⅓ cup butter	¾ cup powdered
2 Tbsp. brandy	sugar

Cream butter and sugar, and add the brandy gradually, beating until smooth. Chill. Makes ¾ cup sauce.

Broccoli with Hollandaise Sauce

2½ pounds fresh broccoli	Boiling water 1 tsp. salt

Wash broccoli and split thick heads. Place broccoli in boiling salted water, with ends down and head out of water. Cook uncovered 10 to 20 minutes. Turn broccoli so all of it is under water and cook 5 minutes longer. Drain. Makes about 4 cups.

Hollandaise Sauce

(There are two methods of preparing this sauce. Hollandaise purists use only the freshest ingredients.)

½ cup butter	2 egg yolks, well beaten
¼ tsp. salt	

Dash cayenne pepper
1 Tbsp. lemon juice

Method One:

Divide butter into three portions. Place egg yolks with ⅓ of the butter in top of double boiler over hot (not boiling) water. Beat constantly with wire whisk; when butter melts add another portion, and as mixture thickens add remaining butter, beating constantly. As soon as mixture is thickened, remove from heat and add seasonings and lemon juice. If sauce separates, beat in 2 tablespoons boiling water, drop by drop. Makes ¾ cup.

Method Two:

Melt all of the butter in top of double boiler. Add to egg yolks gradually, stirring constantly. Return to double boiler and cook over hot water until thickened, stirring constantly. Remove from heat and stir in seasonings and lemon juice. Sauce may be prepared 30 to 45 minutes in advance, and kept hot by covering and placing pan in hot (not boiling) water. Makes ¾ cup.

For the numerous rounds of parties, try some of the following party punches and goodies.

Wassail

(This is a modern version of the age-old holiday drink.)

1 gallon apple cider	2 tsp. whole allspice
2 tsp. whole cloves	Two 3-inch sticks
Orange slices,	cinnamon
studded with cloves	⅔ cup sugar

In large pan, combine all ingredients (except oranges), and heat until mixture comes to boiling point. Reduce heat. Cover and simmer 20 minutes. Strain punch and pour into heatproof punch bowl. Float orange slices in bowl. Makes about 32 ½ cup servings.

Hot Cinnamon Cider

3 quarts apple cider
⅓ cup red cinnamon candies
1 Tbsp. whole allspice
3 Tbsp. honey

Heat cider, cinnamon candies and allspice to boiling; reduce heat. Cover and simmer 5 minutes. Remove allspice; stir in honey. Makes about 24 ½ cup servings.

Chicken Livers en Brochette

8 chicken livers	8 slices bacon
Salt	Pepper

Cut each liver into four pieces, and each slice of bacon into five pieces. Season with salt and pepper. Alternate four pieces of liver and five pieces of bacon on each skewer. Bake in 425° oven until bacon is crisp and livers are cooked. Serve hot. Serves 8.

Roquefort Puffs

1 egg white
2 oz. Roquefort cheese
8 crackers or 2-inch bread rounds
Paprika

Beat egg whites until stiff; cream the cheese, fold in beaten egg white, and heap on crackers. Bake in 300° oven 15 minutes or until brown. Garnish with paprika. Makes 8 puffs.

Sugar Plum Tree

(You might want to try this one just for fun.)

1 large pineapple
½ pound sweet cherries

Cut a 1-inch slice from top of pineapple, keeping all the spiny leaves intact. Wash leaves thoroughly and wipe dry. Press leaves outward, curving them to represent branches of a tree. Set upright on the cut surface, and stick cherries on ends of leaves. Use as the centerpiece of a large salad plate or hors d' oeuvres server. For a children's party, use various colored gumdrops or tiny animal crackers instead of cherries.

Music to Enjoy

The following recorded albums include many favorite modern Christmas songs.

Merry Christmas
Andy Williams
Columbia Records #CS-9220
This record presents such recent favorites as "Silver Bells," "Let it Snow," and "Have Yourself a Merry Little Christmas."

Christmas Album
Lynn Anderson
Columbia Records #C-30957
Here are offered modern urban selections such as "Rockin' Around the Christmas Tree," "I Saw Mommy Kissing Santa Claus," "Jingle Bell Rock," and "Frosty the Snowman."

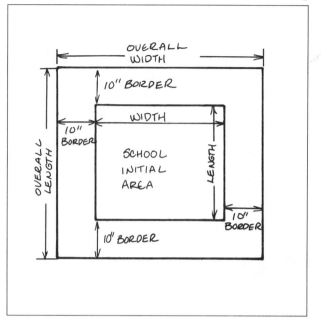

Stadium Blanket & Tote

In just one or two pleasurable afternoons you can whip up a warm stadium blanket and matching tote bag for those cold autumn football games. The blanket will display your team's colors and school initials in the bargain! The handy tote is a real cinch to make, and features outer pockets for an umbrella and a flask of hot toddies, coffee, or cocoa.

Designing the Blanket

Because your blanket will be a custom design, to display your school's initials and colors, you'll have to create your design and do a bit of figuring before you go to the fabric store. Follow the steps in this section to design your blanket and come up with a list of materials to purchase. You'll need several sheets of graph paper with a grid of ¼-inch squares, and a pencil.

1. First, decide on an approximate overall finished size for your blanket. It may have to be adjusted slightly when you work out the school initials, but you want a general size to aim for. We made ours 54 inches wide and 49 inches long; wide enough to cover two people's laps, but not so large that it becomes unwieldy. Deduct 20 inches from both the width and length, to allow for borders, and you will have the finished size of the area that will comprise the school initials (**Figure A**).

2. Draw the outline of the school initials area on a piece of graph paper, using a scale of ¼ inch to 1 inch. (If you have never used graph paper or scale drawings before, just pretend that each ¼-inch square on the graph paper is actually a 1-inch square, and you won't go wrong.) If a single sheet of graph paper is not large enough to draw the outline, cut off the borders from a second sheet and tape it to the first one, carefully aligning the graph lines.

3. Draw the school initials inside the outline, creating large block letters and using the graph lines as the edges. We have provided a block-letter alphabet in

Figure B

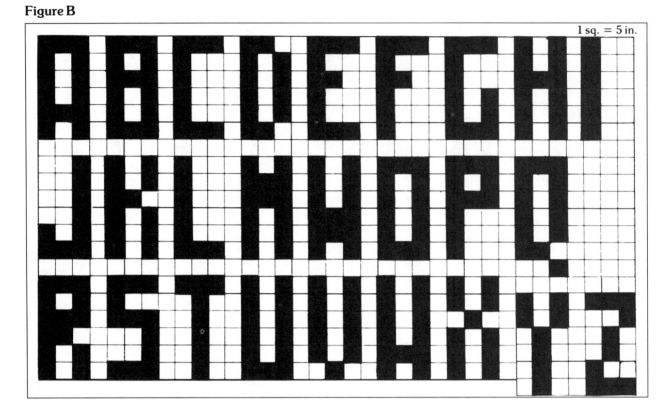

1 sq. = 5 in.

Figure B, in case you need help with the letters. Being Oklahomans ourselves, we used the initials OU. Our example is shown in **Figure C**, along with another example for the mythical All Fools University, so you can see how it's done. Note that the strokes of the letters all are of a uniform width, and the vertical outside lines of the first and last letters run along the vertical outside outlines of the initials area. You may discover that the overall size of the area is not quite right; if so, complete the letters as you want them to appear. The borders can be adjusted to accommodate the initials section, and the overall size of the blanket can be adjusted, if necessary. When you have finished the graph, shade in the letters so you won't get confused in the next step.

4. The fabric initials section will be composed of vertical strips string-quilted together. Each strip is either a solid color or a combination of colors, which form the initials when sewn together. Use a pen or pencil of a different color to mark off the vertical strips on the graph that you created in step 3. Our example is shown in **Figure D**; note that the vertical dividing lines run along the

edges of the block-letter outlines.

5. We used red and white, the OU school colors. On our blanket, vertical strip #1 (**Figure D**) is solid red. Vertical strip #2 consists of a red section at the top, a white section in the middle, and another red section at the bottom. Strip #3 is solid red. Strip #4 is solid white, and serves to separate the "O" from the "U." Strips #5 and #7 are each solid red, and strip #6 is primarily white with a short red portion at the bottom. Count the graph squares on your diagram to determine the finished size of each strip that is a solid color, and make a list of these pieces. For each strip that is composed of two colors, count the graph squares to determine the finished size of each section of the strip, and make a list of these pieces as well. Remember that you are working to scale, so if the strip is four squares wide, that translates to 4 inches finished size. Be sure to indicate on your list the color of each solid strip and of each section of the strips that are two-colored.

6. Make a second, larger graph to illustrate the finished blanket with borders. You need not draw in the

Figure C

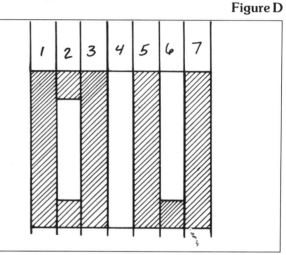

school initials; just draw the outline of the initials section, and then add one or more borders along each edge to achieve the desired finished size of the blanket. Our example is shown in **Figure E**. We made each border strip the same width as the strokes that comprise the school initials, and used a double border along each edge. Make a list of the border strips for your blanket, indicating finished size and color for each one.

7. The cutting size for each piece must be slightly larger than the finished size, to allow for seams, so you need to make one more list. We used a ½-inch-wide seam allowance. To begin, work from the list you made in step 5. Each solid strip and each section of a two-colored strip must be cut 1 inch longer and 1 inch wider than the finished dimensions noted on your original list. Make a list of the cutting dimensions of each piece from step 5. Now move on to the list you made in step 6. In our example, border strips 1, 2, 3, and 4 also must be cut 1 inch wider and 1 inch longer than the finished dimensions. The outermost borders (5, 6, 7, and 8) must be cut a bit differently: Strips 5 and 6 should be cut 1 inch longer but only ½ inch wider than the finished size. Strips 7 and 8 must be cut ½ inch wider but the same length as the finished dimensions. Add to your list the color and cutting dimensions of each border strip.

8. The edges of the blanket are finished with binding strips. Each binding strip should be cut 4 inches wide. The strips that are used to bind the upper and lower edges should be cut the same length as the finished width of the blanket, and the strips that are used to bind the side edges should each be cut 2 inches longer than the finished length of the blanket. Count the graph squares to determine the length of each of these strips, and add them to the list you made in step 7, indicating color as well.

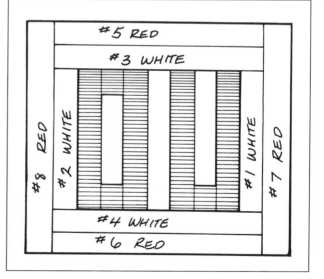

Figure F

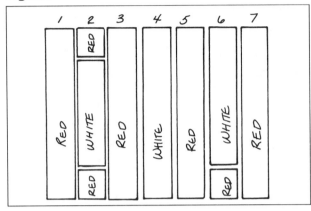

9. You now have a list of all the pieces required to make the blanket. We made our blanket reversible, using a quick-quilting technique that combines piecing and quilting procedures all in one. In order to make the blanket in this manner, you'll need to purchase enough fabric to cut two of each piece on your list, except for the final binding strips. Make a note of this fact on the list from step 7.

10. The tote that we made should be large enough to accommodate your blanket, unless it is significantly larger than ours. You will need the following amounts of fabric to make the tote: a 22 x 32-inch piece of fabric for the body of the tote (we used white), and a 16 x 32-inch piece of fabric for the straps, handle, and pockets (we used red). Add these amounts to your list from step 7, indicating what color each piece should be.

11. You now should have a list of all the fabric pieces required to make the blanket and tote. The list should indicate the color of each piece as well. Work from the list to determine how many yards of each color fabric you will need, or simply take the list with you to the fabric store and ask for help from a salesperson. (Do not discard the list of pieces, as you will need it later when you cut the fabrics.) We chose medium-weight tight-weave woolen fabric, so the blanket would be warm but not bulky. Quilt batting is not required inside the blanket if you use woolen fabric. If you choose a fabric that is not as warm as wool, purchase a package of bonded quilt batting as well. You'll also need sewing thread of an appropriate weight and fiber content for the fabric, a 4-foot length of ⅛-inch-diameter satin-finish cord for the tote, and a 1-foot length of nylon fastener tape in a color that matches the tote pocket fabric.

THE BLANKET

Assembling the School Initials

Note: All seam allowances are ½ inch wide unless otherwise specified in the instructions. We have included instructions for sewing batting strips into the blanket, but if you are not using batting simply ignore the references to it. The construction techniques are the same with or without batting.

1. Refer to your list of pieces for the blanket, and cut two of each piece from the specified color. Do not cut any pieces for the tote just yet, but cut all of the pieces for the school initials, border strips, and binding strips. Remember that you need to cut only one of each binding strip.

2. The first step in assembling the school initials section is to piece together the shorter strips that form each of the two-colored vertical strokes. We suggest that you begin by laying out all of the pieces for the blanket front initials section. Use the graph of the initials section that you made earlier, as a guide to place the pieces properly. In our example of the initials section, shown in **Figure F**, strokes #2 and #6 are the only two-colored strokes. To piece together the strips that form stroke #6, place the two strips right sides together, aligning one end of the red strip with one end of the white strip. Stitch the seam along the aligned ends and press the seam open. Replace the assembled stroke where it belongs in the arrangement. Follow the same procedures to piece together each stroke that contains more than one color, and replace each one in the arrangement. Now lay out the identical pieces that will form the blanket back initials section, and piece together the strips for each two-colored stroke in the same manner.

3. To prevent mistakes in string-quilting the strokes, we suggest that you label each one with a number inside the seam allowance at the upper end of the stroke, so you'll be able to tell at a glance which stroke you are looking at and which end is the top. Because you want the initials to read correctly on both the front and back of the blanket, the numbers should be reversed for the strokes of the blanket back initials section. The numbering system we used for the blanket front section is shown in **Figure F**. For the blanket back section simply reverse the order: stroke #1 for the blanket front is numbered as stroke #7 (or whatever number corresponds with the last stroke in your arrangement) for the blanket back, etc.

4. If your blanket requires quilt batting, cut one strip of batting to match each stroke in the initials section.

5. To begin string-quilting, place stroke #1 from the blanket back section wrong side up on a flat surface. Place stroke 1 from the blanket front section right side up on top, so the fabrics are wrong sides together. Make sure that both strokes are turned the same way end for end, so the upper ends are aligned at the top. Place a strip of batting between the two strokes. Baste the layers together ½ inch from the aligned long right-hand edges (**Figure G**). Trim the batting seam allowance close to the basting line.

6. In order to cut down on the number of words you have to read, from now on we will refer to strokes taken from the blanket front initials section as "front strokes;" those taken from the blanket back section will be called "back strokes." Place back stroke #2 right side up on a flat surface, with the upper end at the top. Place the assembly from step 5 on top, so that the basted edge is aligned with the long right-hand edge of back stroke #2. Place front stroke #2 wrong side up on top of the stack, and place a batting strip on top of that. The upper ends of all the strokes should be aligned. Pin the layers together along the long right-hand edge and stitch the seam through all thicknesses. Trim the batting seam allowance close to the stitching line.

7. Turn the batting strip, front stroke #2, and back stroke #2 outward, so that the strokes are wrong sides together with the batting between. The assembly should now look like our example in **Figure H**. Press the fabrics along the seam line. Baste together the two #2 strokes ½ inch from the aligned long right-hand edges, and trim the batting seam allowance.

8. Place back stroke #3 right side up underneath the #2 strokes of the assembly from step 7. Place front stroke #3 right side down on top, and place a batting strip on top of that. Make certain that all upper ends are aligned, and stitch the seam along the aligned right-hand edges. Trim the batting seam allowance and turn the #3 strokes and batting outward. Baste the #3 strokes together ½ inch from the aligned long right-hand edges, and trim the batting seam allowance.

9. Continue to add the successive strokes in this manner until the entire initials section is complete. If your numbering was correct, the initials should read correctly on both the front and back of the assembled section. Baste the layers together ½ inch from each side edge of the assembly, as shown in **Figure I**. Trim the batting seam allowances close to each basting line.

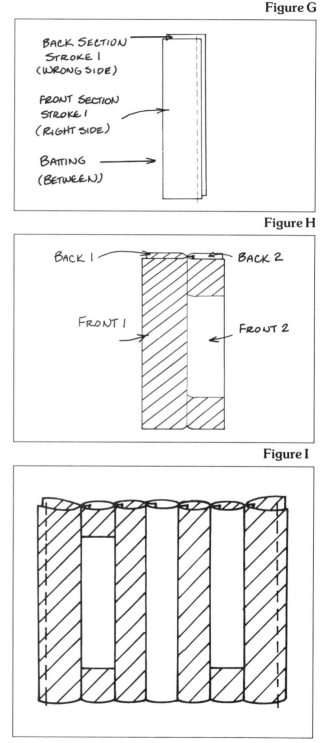

Figure G

BACK SECTION STROKE 1 (WRONG SIDE)

FRONT SECTION STROKE 1 (RIGHT SIDE)

BATTING (BETWEEN)

Figure H

BACK 1   BACK 2

FRONT 1   FRONT 2

Figure I

Figure J

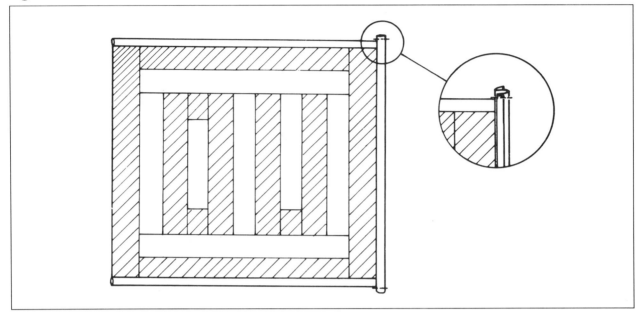

Adding the Borders

1. Refer back to **Figure E**, and number each of the border strips for the blanket front and back. There's no need to designate which end is which, and the border strips for the front and back of the blanket should be numbered identically.

2. Place the assembled initials section on a flat surface. Place a #1 border strip right side up underneath the initials section, aligning the long right-hand edge of the border strip with the right-hand edge of the initials section. Place the remaining #1 border strip right side down on top, aligning the long right-hand edge of the border strip with the right-hand edge of the initials section. Stack a batting strip on top, and stitch the seam along the aligned right-hand edges. Trim the batting seam allowance, and turn the borders and batting outward. Baste ½ inch from the aligned right-hand edges.

3. Follow the same procedures to stitch the two #2 border strips to the left-hand edge of the initials section.

4. Follow the same procedures to stitch the two #3 border strips to the upper edges of the initials section and previous border strips.

5. Stitch the two #4 border strips to the lower edges of the initials section and previous border strips in the same manner.

6. You now should have a front and back border strip attached to each edge of the initials section. Follow the same procedures to attach any remaining border strips that you have included in your design, working in numerical order. On our blanket, border strips #5, 6, 7, and 8 comprise the second layer of borders. When all remaining borders have been attached and turned outward, baste the free edges together all the way around the blanket and trim the batting seam allowances.

7. To encase the raw upper edge of the blanket, use one of the binding strips that matches the length of the upper edge. Place it right side down on top of the blanket, aligning the long upper edge of the binding strip with the raw upper edge of the blanket. Stitch a 1-inch-wide seam along the aligned upper edges, and then turn the binding strip upward. Press the seam allowances toward the strip, and press a 1-inch-wide allowance to the wrong side of the binding strip along the free long edge. Fold the strip in half lengthwise, placing wrong sides together so that it encases the raw upper edge of the blanket, and whipstitch the pressed edge to the back of the blanket.

8. Follow the same procedures to bind the lower edge of the blanket, using the remaining binding strip that matches the length of the edge.

9. To bind one side edge of the blanket, use one of

the longer binding strips. Place it right side down on top of the blanket, aligning one long edge of the binding strip with one raw side edge of the blanket. The strip should extend 1 inch beyond the bound upper and lower edges of the blanket. Stitch a 1-inch-wide seam along the aligned edges, and turn the binding strip outward. Press the seam allowances toward the binding strip, and press a 1-inch-wide allowance to the wrong side of the strip along the free long edge. Now fold the strip in half lengthwise, placing RIGHT sides together. Stitch a seam across the upper end of the strip, ¼ inch outside the bound upper edge of the blanket (**Figure J**). Stitch a seam across the lower end of the strip, ¼ inch outside the bound lower edge of the blanket. Trim these seam allowances very close to the stitching lines. Turn the binding strip right side out, so that it encases the raw edge of the blanket, and whipstitch the pressed edge to the back of the blanket.

10. Bind the opposite side edge of the blanket in the same manner, using the remaining binding strip.

THE TOTE

Cutting the Pieces

1. Cut a 22 x 32-inch piece from the desired fabric color for the basic Tote piece.

2. Cut from the contrasting fabric the pieces listed in this step.

Strap – cut two, 2⅛ x 32 inches
Handle – cut one, 3½ x 10½ inches
Umbrella Pocket – cut one, 11 x 19 inches
Flask Pocket – cut one, 7¾ x 12½ inches

Assembling the Tote

1. To prepare the Tote piece, press a ¼-inch-wide hem to the wrong side of the fabric along each 22-inch edge. Turn each of these edges under again, forming a ¾-inch-wide hem, and machine stitch each hem close to the pressed edge.

2. Repeat the procedures described in step 1 to hem each of the longer edges of the Tote piece.

3. To prepare one of the Strap pieces, press a ¼-inch-wide hem to the wrong side of the fabric along each long edge. Prepare the remaining Strap piece in the same manner.

4. Figure K shows one of the straps stitched to the Tote piece. Place the Tote piece right side up on a flat surface. Place one of the straps right side up on top, 4½

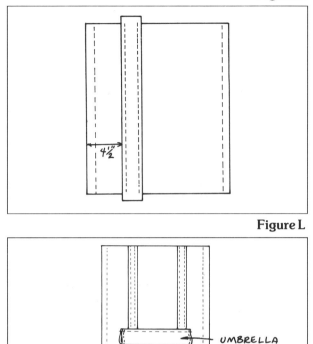

Figure K

Figure L

UMBRELLA POCKET

inches from one long edge of the Tote piece. The strap should extend equally beyond each end of the Tote. Topstitch the strap in place, ¼ inch inside each long edge. Follow the same procedures to topstitch the remaining strap to the Tote piece, 4½ inches from the opposite long edge.

5. Fold the ends of each strap to the wrong side of the Tote piece, and tack them in place.

6. To prepare the Umbrella Pocket piece, fold it in half lengthwise, placing right sides together. Stitch a ½-inch- wide seam along the aligned 19-inch edges, leaving both ends open. Press the seam open, and finish the raw edges of the seam allowances by zigzag stitching over them. Press a ½-inch-wide hem to the wrong side of the fabric around each open end. Turn each of these edges under again, to form a double-turned hem, and machine stitch each hem. Turn the assembled pocket right side out.

7. Flatten the pocket so that the lengthwise seam runs along one edge, and place the pocket on top of the Tote piece, as shown in **Figure L**. Topstitch through

Figure M

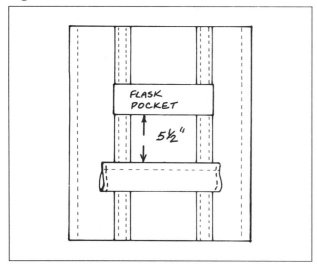

Figure N

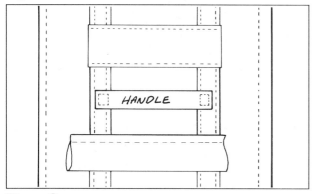

Figure O

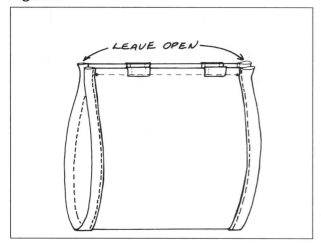

all thicknesses close to the seamed edge of the pocket.

8. To prepare the Flask Pocket piece, turn and machine stitch a double ½-inch-wide hem to the wrong side of the fabric along each edge. Cut a 5-inch length of nylon fastener tape, and separate the halves. Stitch or glue one of the halves to the wrong side of the hemmed flask pocket along one short end. Cut another 5-inch length of tape, separate the halves, and stitch or glue one half to the wrong side of the flask pocket along the opposite end.

9. Place the flask pocket right side up on top of the tote (**Figure M**). It should be 5½ inches from the umbrella pocket, and the flask pocket should lie along the outer edges of the straps. Mark the placement of the flask pocket on the tote, and remove it. Stitch or glue the unused halves of the nylon fastener strips to the tote straps, so that they will match the halves that are sewn to the pocket. Replace the pocket, and topstitch through all layers close to each long edge.

10. To prepare the Handle piece, fold it in half lengthwise, placing right sides together. Stitch a ½-inch-wide seam along the aligned long edges and across one end, leaving the remaining end open. Clip the corners, and turn the handle right side out. Press the seam allowance to the inside of the handle around the open end and press the handle flat, adjusting it so that the lengthwise seam runs along one edge. Whipstitch the opening edges together.

11. Place the assembled handle across the tote, midway between the umbrella and flask pockets. Adjust it so that the ends overlap the straps evenly, and topstitch in a rectangular pattern to attach each end of the handle to the strap and tote (**Figure N**).

12. Fold the entire tote assembly in half widthwise, placing right sides together. Stitch the seam across the aligned ends of the tote, just below the hem that runs across each end, but do not stitch across the hem that runs along each side edge (**Figure O**). You may wish to double stitch this seam for extra strength. Turn the tote right side out.

13. Cut the length of satin-finish cord in half, and tie a small knot near each end of each resulting piece. Thread one cord through the casing formed by the hem around one open end of the tote. Pull up the ends of the cord as you push the fabric toward the center, to gather the ends. Tie the ends of the cord in a half-knot and bow, and then knot the bow. Use the remaining length of cord to close the opposite end of the tote in the same manner.

Changeable Charlie

Charlie is a quick-change artist, with interchangeable felt facial features. He is also a teaching toy, who can help youngsters learn to zip, button, and tie.

Materials

½ yard of lightweight denim for the torso, legs, and pocket (We used a railroader's striped denim.)

½ yard of red calico fabric for the shirt

¼ yard of lightweight fusible lining fabric

⅜ yard of red felt for the shoes and hat

½ yard of flesh-tone fleece for the head, ears, and hands

Scraps of felt in white, black, red, and pink for the facial features

5 yards of black rug yarn for the hair

One 7-inch non-metal zipper

One pair of white shoelaces (or two 12-inch lengths of ¼-inch-wide ribbon or cotton cord)

Two 1-inch buttons

One bag of polyester fiberfill

Twenty-six small nylon fastener spots or about 13 inches of nylon fastener strip

Long sharp needle; heavy-duty flesh-tone thread; and regular thread to match the fabrics

Hot-melt glue and a glue gun (or white glue); non-toxic black felt-tip marker

Cutting the Pieces

1. Full-size patterns are provided on page 241 for the Ear, Eyelid, Noses, Eyes, Irises, Eyebrows, Mouths, and Mustaches. Trace the patterns onto tracing paper or dressmaker's paper.

2. Scale drawings are provided on page 240 for the Hat, Hat Bill, Hand, Torso, Sleeve/Leg, Shoe, Shirt Front Applique, Head, and Strap. Enlarge the drawings to make full-size paper patterns. (Refer to the Tips & Techniques section.)

3. Cut the pieces as listed in this step, from the specified fabrics. Fold the fabric into a double thickness, so you can cut two of each piece at a time, and the resulting pieces will be matching pairs. Pay attention to the "place on fold" notations on the scale drawings or patterns. Transfer any placement markings or instructions to the fabric pieces.

Note: The facial features (Eyes, Eyebrows, Noses, Mouths, and Mustaches) will be cut later.

Denim: Torso - cut two
Upper Pocket - cut one, 2½ x 8 inches
Lower Pocket - cut one, 4½ x 8 inches
Strap - cut two
Leg - cut two
Red calico: Sleeve - cut four
Shirt Front Applique - cut one
Red felt: Shoe - cut four
Hat - cut two
Hat Bill - cut one
Fleece: Head - cut two
Ear - cut four
Hand - cut four
Fusible lining: Shirt Front Applique - cut one

Making the Pocket and Shirt Front

Note: All seam allowances are ½ inch unless otherwise specified in the instructions. Charlie's clothing also serves as his body.

1. Choose one of the Torso pieces for the front, and place it right side up on a flat surface. Place the fusible Shirt Front Applique piece on top, aligning the shoulder edges, and then place the calico Shirt Front Applique right side up on top. Trim away any excess fusible lining material. Follow the manufacturer's instructions that

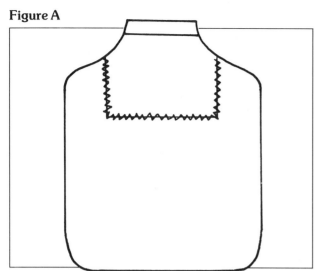

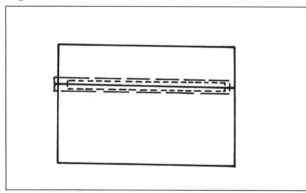

Figure C

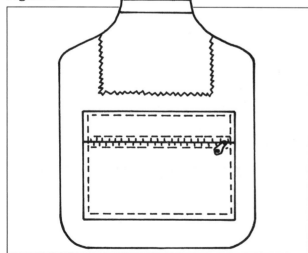

Figure D

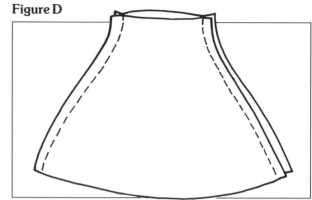

came with the fusible lining fabric.

2. Adjust your sewing machine to a closely spaced zigzag setting, and stitch over the side and lower edges of the applique to secure it (**Figure A**). If you prefer, this can be done by hand, using a closely spaced blanket stitch. (Refer to the Tips & Techniques section.)

3. To create the zipper pocket, first press a ½-inch hem to the wrong side along all edges of the Upper and Lower Pocket pieces.

4. Cut the zipper to 6 inches in length. (Refer to the Tips & Techniques section.) Place the shortened zipper right side up on a flat surface. Place the Upper and Lower Pocket pieces on top (**Figure B**). The pressed edges of the Pocket pieces should meet (but not overlap) along the center of the zipper. Topstitch close to each edge of the zipper.

5. Place the front torso/shirt assembly right side up on a flat surface. Pin the zipper pocket right side up on top, placing the upper edge of the pocket about ¾ inch below the shirt applique (**Figure C**). Topstitch the pocket to the Torso piece, ¼ inch from each outer edge, as shown.

Making the Sleeves and Straps

1. To make one sleeve, place two Sleeve pieces right sides together, and stitch the seam along each side edge (**Figure D**). (Disregard the lettered dots; they will be used later for the legs.) Clip the curves, press the seams, and turn the sleeve right side out.

2. Repeat step 1 to make a second sleeve in the same manner, using the two remaining Sleeve pieces.

3. To make one strap, fold one Strap piece in half lengthwise, placing right sides together. Stitch the seam along the straight short and long edges, leaving the an-

Figure E

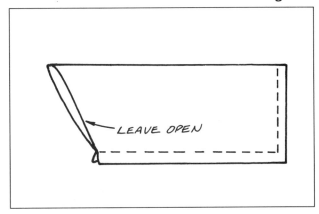

Figure F

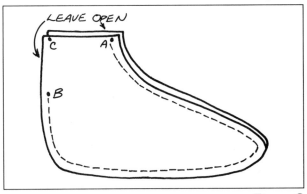

Figure G

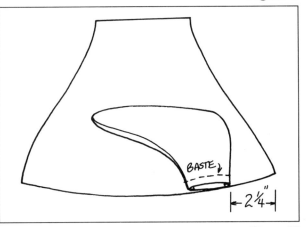

Figure H

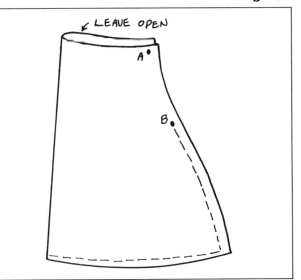

gled short edge open and unstitched (**Figure E**). Clip the corners, turn the strap right side out, and press.

4. Work a 1-inch buttonhole across the strap, about 1 inch above the straight lower edge. (Refer to the Tips & Techniques section on buttonholes, if necessary.)

5. Repeat steps 3 and 4 to make a second strap in the same manner, using the remaining Strap piece.

Making the Legs and Shoes

1. Place two Shoe pieces right sides together, and stitch the seam along the contoured edge (**Figure F**), beginning at point A and ending at point B. Leave the seam open between points B and C, and leave the straight upper edge open, as shown. Clip the curves, and turn the shoe right side out. Press the seam allowances to the inside between B and C.

2. Repeat step 1 to make a second shoe in the same manner, using the remaining two Shoe pieces.

3. Place one Leg piece right side up on a flat surface. Place one shoe on top (**Figure G**), aligning the upper edge of the shoe with the lower edge of the Leg. The toe of the shoe should point toward the left, and the upper edge of the shoe should be placed about 2¼ inches from the right-hand edge of the Leg. Baste the shoe to the Leg along the seamline.

4. Temporarily fold the toe of the shoe, and pin it in place so it will be out of the way of the Leg side seams. Fold the Leg in half lengthwise, placing right sides together. The shoe will be sandwiched between the two layers of the Leg. Stitch the seam along the lower edge, from the fold to the corner, then turn the corner and stitch the side seam to point B (**Figure H**). Leave the

Figure I

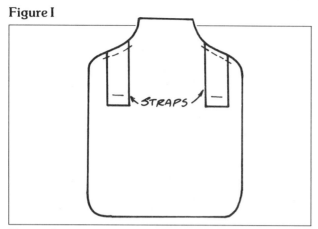

Figure J

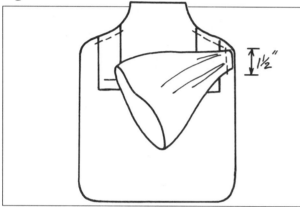

Figure K

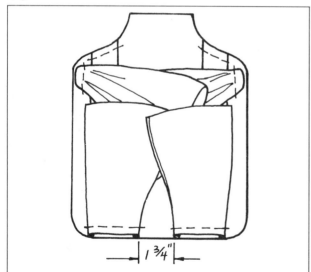

Figure L

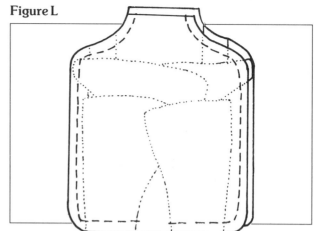

seam open between points A and B, and leave the upper edge open, as shown. Clip the corners, turn the leg right side out, and press the seam allowances to the inside between points A and B.

5. Repeat steps 3 and 4 to make a second leg/shoe assembly, using the remaining Leg piece and the second assembled shoe. Make this assembly a mirror image of the first, placing the shoe 2¼ inches from the left-hand side of the Leg, with the toe pointing to the right side.

Assembling the Body

1. Place the back Torso piece (the one without the applique and pocket) right side up on a flat surface. Place the straps on top, aligning the angled edge of each strap with an angled shoulder edge, as shown in **Figure I**. Baste the straps in place along the seamlines.

2. Place one of the stitched sleeves on top of this assembly, as shown in **Figure J**, aligning the upper edge of the sleeve with the side edge of the Torso. Neatly fold the upper edge of the sleeve to form small pleats so that the edge measures 1½ inches wide. Pin the sleeve to the Torso close to the aligned edges, and baste it in place, as shown.

3. Repeat step 2 to baste the remaining sleeve to the opposite edge of the Torso.

4. Place one leg/shoe assembly on top of the Torso, as shown in **Figure K**, and pin the upper edge of the leg to the lower edge of the Torso close to one side. Pin the second leg/shoe assembly on top in the same manner, close to the opposite edge. Be sure the folded side of each leg faces outward. There should be about 1¾ inches between the upper ends of the legs. The shoes should still be folded and pinned to the legs to keep them out of the way of the Torso seams, but if they were unfolded, the toe of each shoe should point outward. Baste the upper ends of the legs to the Torso piece.

5. Pin the front torso/shirt assembly right side down on top of the back Torso piece. The sleeves, straps, and legs will be sandwiched between the two Torso pieces. Stitch a continuous seam along each shoulder, side, and lower edge, as shown in **Figure L**. Leave open the neck edge, and the lower seam between the legs. Clip the corners and curves, and turn the torso right side out. Press the seam allowances to the inside along the opening between the legs, and around the open neck edge.

6. Bring the straps to the front of the torso, and sew a button to the front torso/shirt assembly underneath each buttonhole. Button the straps.

7. Stuff the torso with fiberfill, and whipstitch the opening edges together between the legs. Be sure the neck is stuffed firmly, right up to the pressed edge, but do not stitch the neck closed. Stuff each leg through the opening in the inner seam, and whipstitch the opening edges together. Stuff each shoe through the opening near the top of the back seam, and whipstitch the edges together. Do not stuff the sleeves.

8. Fold in half one of the shoelaces (or lengths of ribbon or cord). Tack the folded center of the lace to the top of one shoe, as shown in **Figure M**. Tie the shoelace in a bow.

Adding the Hands

1. Place two Hand pieces right sides together. Stitch the seam all the way around the long contoured edge, as shown in **Figure N**. Leave the wrist edge open. Clip the curves, and turn the hand right side out. Stuff the hand lightly, and baste the wrist edges together.

2. To soft-sculpt the fingers, use heavy-duty thread and a long sharp needle, and follow the entry and exit points illustrated in **Figure O**.

    a. Enter at 1 on the palm side of the hand, push the needle through the hand, and exit directly opposite 1 on the back of the hand.

    b. To form the first finger, stitch up and down through the hand along the dotted line, and exit at point 2 at the end of the finger.

    c. Reenter at 2, push the needle through the hand, and exit at point 3 on the palm.

    d. Reenter at 3 on the palm, and exit at 3 on the back of the hand.

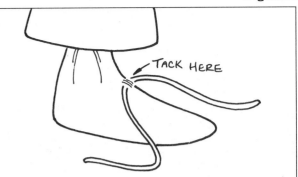

Figure M

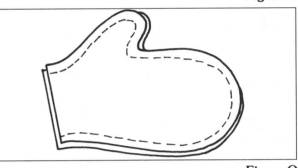

Figure N

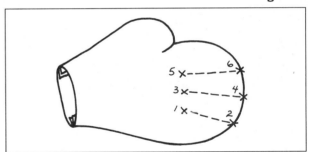

Figure O

    e. Repeat steps b through d at points 3 and 5 to form the remaining fingers. Lock the stitch at 6, and cut the thread.

3. Repeat steps 1 and 2 to make the second hand, using the two remaining Hand pieces.

4. Press the open edge of one sleeve to the wrong side of the fabric. Run a line of basting stitches around the pressed edge of the sleeve. Do not cut the thread.

5. Insert the wrist edge of one hand inside the end of the sleeve, making sure the thumb points upward. Pull the basting threads to gather the sleeve around the

Figure P

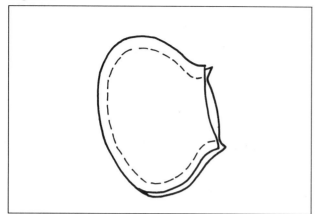

Figure Q

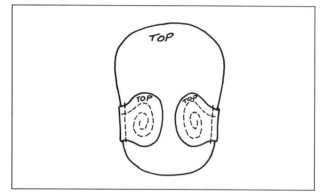

Figure R

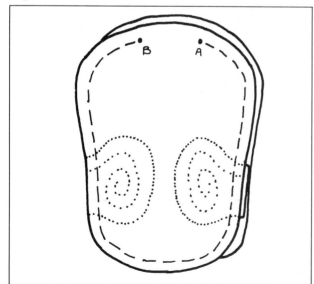

wrist. Tie off the thread, and whipstitch around the wrist several times to secure the hand to the sleeve.

6. Repeat steps 4 and 5 to attach the remaining hand.

Making the Head

1. To make one ear, place two Ear pieces right sides together, and stitch the seam along the contoured edge, as shown in **Figure P**. Leave the short straight edge open. Clip the curves, and turn the ear right side out. Do not stuff the ear.

2. To soft-sculpt the ear, topstitch (by hand or machine) through both layers, following the spiral stitching line provided on the Ear pattern.

3. Repeat steps 1 and 2 to make a second ear in the same manner, using the remaining Ear pieces.

4. Place one Head piece right side up on a flat surface, and baste the stitched ears on top, as shown in **Figure Q**. Be sure the top of the ear points toward the top of the Head.

5. Place the remaining Head piece right side down on top and stitch the contoured seam, beginning at point A and ending at point B (**Figure R**). Leave the seam open between A and B. Clip the curve, turn the head right side out, and press the seam allowances to the inside between A and B.

6. Stuff the head firmly, and whipstitch the opening edges together.

7. To make Charlie's hair, wrap the rug yarn into a 9-inch-long continuous loop. Gather the yarn loop at the center, and stitch the center of the yarn to the top center of Charlie's head, over the whipstitched seam, as shown in **Figure S**. Pull down the ends of the loops on each side, and stitch or glue them to Charlie's head.

8. Place the head over the open neck edge of the body, as shown in **Figure T**. The neck should be about 2½ inches above the chin, and the chin should point in the same direction as the front of the torso. Carefully bend Charlie's head downward so his chin rests on his shirt. (You will have to tuck the neck edge under a bit at the front to get this right.) Whipstitch around the neck several times to secure the head. You may wish to tack the underside of the chin to the shirt just below the neck, to keep Charlie's head from wobbling.

Making the Hat

1. Place the Hat Bill and one of the Hat pieces right sides together, aligning the shorter curved edges. Stitch

CELEBRATIONS OF CHRISTMAS

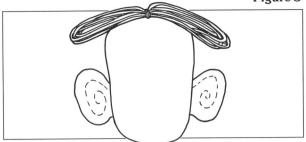

the seam along this edge only (**Figure U**). Open the two pieces, clip the curve, and press the seam allowances toward the Hat.

2. Place the remaining Hat piece against the front Hat piece, right sides together, aligning the long curved edges (**Figure V**). Trim the lower edge of the back Hat so it does not extend past the seam that joins the front piece to the bill. Stitch the seam along the long curved edge. Clip the curve, turn the hat right side out, and press the hat.

The Facial Features

1. Use the full-size patterns provided, and cut the facial features from felt. We cut the Eyes from white, the Mouths from red, the Irises, Mustaches, and Eyebrows from black, and the Noses from pink. Cut one Eye piece for each Iris.

2. Assemble matching pairs of Eye/Iris combinations, using glue to adhere the felt layers.

3. We used a non-toxic black marker to draw a smile line on the long oval-shaped mouth. For the one with teeth showing, we cut the teeth from white felt, and glued them to the mouth. For the one with the tongue sticking out, we cut a tongue from pink felt, and glued it onto the mouth. Use your imagination for variations, and for additional facial features.

4. Cut six small squares or circles of nylon fastener strip. Separate the halves, and glue one half of each to the face at the placement markings indicated for the facial features (mouth/mustache, nose, eyes, and eyebrows). Glue the matching half of each fastener strip to the back of a facial feature. Be sure to use the proper halves on each piece, or they will not stick together. Cut additional fastener squares or spots, and glue the proper half of each to the back of an extra facial feature.

5. Stick a set of facial features on Charlie's face, and tuck the rest into his bib pocket for safe keeping.

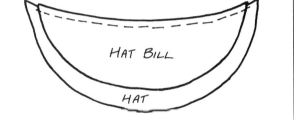

HAT BILL

HAT

Figure V

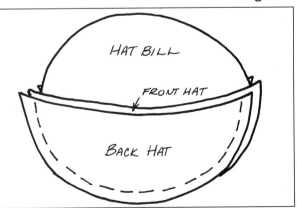

HAT BILL

FRONT HAT

BACK HAT

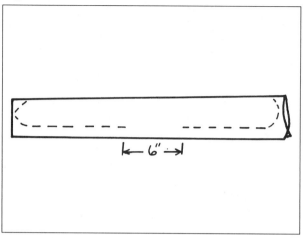

Ballerina & Clown Draft Stoppers

Do you use rolled-up towels to stop the cold winter winds that whistle under your doors? Now you can stitch up one of our adorable draft stoppers to handle the task efficiently and beautifully. The ballerina will be perfect for a little girl's room, and the clown will fit anywhere there are cold people who need a warm chuckle.

Materials

For the ballerina:

One leg of regular flesh-tone pantyhose
6½ x 45-inch piece of muslin for the legs
8 x 8-inch piece of black felt
2 yards of 4-inch-wide gathered white eyelet trim
23-inch length of ⅜-inch-wide pink satin ribbon
24 yards of yarn for the hair (We used dark brown.)
1¼ yards of ½-inch-wide black seam tape, grosgrain, or satin ribbon for the shoe ties
3 x 36-inch piece of nylon net
Three pink pinwheel beads
Heavy-duty flesh-tone thread; a long sharp needle; and thread to match the fabric

For the clown:

One leg of white pantyhose
14 x 45-inch rectangle of fabric for the legs and hat (We used a heavy cotton duck fabric in a multi-colored stripe.)
Four pieces of red felt, each 5 x 9 inches; and one piece of red felt, 2 x 2 inches
Two 10-inch squares of yellow flannel
½ skein of red rug yarn for the hair
Several long craft pipe cleaners of any color
Nine 1-inch-diameter red pompoms for the hat and ankles
Two yards of double-fold bias tape in a color that coordinates with the clown's leg fabric
Heavy-duty white thread; a long sharp needle; and thread to match the fabrics

You will also need:

A bag of polyester fiberfill
Cosmetic cheek blusher
Black and red felt-tip pens or fabric marking pens
Hot-melt glue and a glue gun (or white glue)

THE BALLERINA

The ballerina's legs form the actual draft stopper. Her head is made separately, and then stitched to the legs. An eyelet collar covers the neck seam. To fit the draft stopper to a particular door or window, measure the length of the area you wish to cover, and alter the length of the muslin rectangle to fit. It should be 6½ inches wide, and about 1 inch longer than the door.

Cutting the Pieces

1. A full-size pattern for the Eyelash, and scale drawings for the Ballet Shoe, Clown Shoe, and Clown Hat are provided on page 239. Trace the full-size pattern onto tracing paper or dressmaker's paper. Enlarge the drawings to make full-size paper patterns. (Refer to the Tips & Techniques section on enlarging scale drawings if necessary.)

2. Cut the pieces listed in this step from the specified fabrics. Fold the fabric into a double thickness, so you can cut two of each piece at a time, and the resulting pieces will be matching pairs. Pay attention to the "place on fold" notations on the scale drawings and patterns. Transfer any placement markings or instructions to the fabric pieces.

> Black felt: Ballet Shoe - cut four
> Eyelash - cut two
>
> Red felt: Clown Shoe - cut four
>
> Striped cotton: Clown Hat - cut one

Making the Legs

Note: All seam allowances are ½ inch unless otherwise specified in the instructions.

1. Fold the muslin rectangle in half lengthwise with right sides together. Stitch a straight seam along the long edge, leaving a 6-inch opening at the center, and stitch a curved seam across each short end, as shown in **Figure A**. Trim the excess seam allowances along the curved ends. Clip the curves.

2. Turn the tube right side out, bringing the ends through the opening. Stuff the tube with fiberfill, using the blunt end of a pencil or long knitting needle to push the fiberfill into the ends. Press the seam allowances to the inside along the edges of the opening, and whipstitch the opening edges together.

3. Place two Ballet Shoe pieces together and stitch the seam all the way along the long curved edge. Leave the straight, angled edge open and unstitched (**Figure B**). Trim the seam allowances to ¼ inch, clip the curve, and turn the shoe right side out.

4. Cut two 10-inch lengths of black seam binding, grosgrain, or satin ribbon. Stitch one length to the wrong side of the fabric on each side of the shoe, as shown in **Figure B**.

5. Repeat the procedures in steps 4 and 5 to make the second shoe, using the two remaining Ballet Shoe pieces and two lengths of seam tape or ribbon.

Figure B

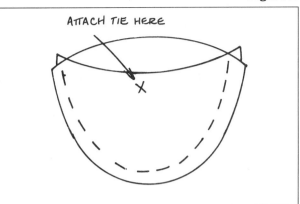

ATTACH TIE HERE

Figure C

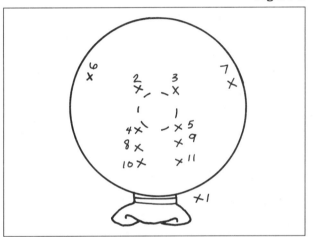

6. Slip one of the shoes over one end of the leg tube, and wrap the two ribbons around the leg in a criss-cross pattern. Tie the ends in a bow or knot. Install the remaining shoe on the other foot in the same manner.

Making the Head

1. Tie a knot in one leg of regular-weave pantyhose near the panty line. Cut across the hose about 1 inch above the knot, and about 10 inches below the knot. Turn the hose so the knot is on the inside, and stuff with fiberfill until the head is approximately 5 inches in diameter. Tie the hose in a knot at the neck and trim off the excess hose below the knot.

2. Follow the entry and exit points illustrated in **Figure C** to sculpt the facial features, using a long sharp

Figure D

Figure E

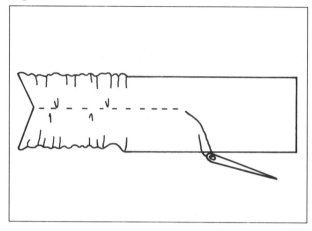

needle and heavy-duty flesh-tone thread.

  a. Enter at 1, push the needle through the center of the head, and exit at 2. To form the nose, sew a circle of basting stitches about the size of a silver dollar, and exit at 3.

  b. Use the tip of the needle to carefully lift fiberfill within the circle, and gently pull the thread until a little round nose appears. Lock the stitch, reenter at 3, and exit at point 2.

  c. To form the nostrils, reenter at 2, and exit at 4.

  d. Enter ¼ inch above 4 and exit at 3.

  e. Reenter at 3 and exit at 5.

  f. Enter about ¼ inch above 5 and exit at 2. Pull the thread and lock the stitch at point 2.

  g. To form the eye lines, pull the thread across the surface, enter at 6, and exit at 3.

  h. Pull the thread across the surface, enter at 9, and exit at 2. Pull gently to form the mouth line and lock the stitch at 2.

  i. To form the mouth, reenter at 2, and exit at 8.

  j. Pull the thread across the surface, enter at 9, and exit at 10. Pull the thread across the surface, enter at 11, and exit at 2. Pull gently to

form the lower lip, and lock the stitch at 2.

  k. To form the lower lip, reenter at 2, and exit at point 10.

  l. Reenter at point 2 and exit at 1. Lock the stitch and cut the thread.

  3. Cut two Eyelashes, and glue them to the eye lines.

  4. Place the head at the center of the leg tube, so that the leg seam runs along the bottom. Whipstitch around the head several times to secure it to the tube; the collar will cover the stitches.

  5. To make the ballerina's hair, cut twenty-four strands of yarn, each 1 yard long. Gather the strands into an even pile and wrap a piece of thread around the center of the strands. Stitch the center to the top of the ballerina's head, as shown in **Figure D**. At each side, about where the bottom of the ear would be if she had one, stitch the yarn to the head as shown. Braid the yarn below these stitches on each side, and secure by tying a short length of yarn around each braid near the end. We rolled up each braid into a knot, and secured the knotted braid with a few stitches.

  6. Run a line of basting stitches along the center length of the nylon net rectangle, as shown in **Figure E**. Gather the net tightly and lock the stitch, but do not cut the thread. Continue working with the same thread to tack the gathered-net bow to the top center of the head, over the hair. Tack the pinwheel beads to the center of the net bow.

  7. To finish the ballerina's face, draw eyebrows, using the black marker or pen. Use the red marker to draw an upper lip above the mouth stitches, and a lower lip between the two mouth stitches, as shown in

Figure F. Brush cosmetic blusher across the cheeks.

Making the Collar

1. Run a line of long basting stitches close to the bound edge of the gathered eyelet trim. Pull up the basting stitches to gather the trim even more, and place it around the ballerina's neck. Adjust the gathers so the ends overlap at the back. Tack the collar to the neck.

2. Wrap the length of pink satin ribbon around the ballerina's neck and tie it in a bow at the front.

THE CLOWN

The clown draft stopper consists of a leg tube with a shoe on each end. A ruffled flannel collar covers the neck seam, and a conical clown's hat perches on top of a red rug yarn wig.

Making the Legs

1. Measure the width of the door or window along which you plan to use the clown. Cut a rectangle from the fabric you have chosen for the clown, 6½ inches wide and 1 inch *shorter* than the measured width, to allow for his big feet.

2. Fold the rectangle in half lengthwise, placing right sides together, and stitch the seam along the long edge only. Do not stitch across the ends.

3. Turn the tube right side out, and press the seam allowance to the inside around each open end. Stuff the tube tightly with fiberfill.

4. Place two Clown Shoe pieces right sides together and stitch the seam all the way around the outer edge, leaving a 3-inch opening on one side (**Figure G**). Clip the curves, turn the shoe right side out, and press the seam allowances to the inside along the opening edges. Stuff the shoe firmly with fiberfill, and whipstitch the opening edges together.

5. Repeat the procedures in step 4 to make a second shoe, using the remaining two Clown Shoe pieces.

6. Place the leg tube on a flat surface so that the seam is on the bottom. Place one shoe against one open end of the leg tube with the toe end pointing upward, and whipstitch it securely in place, as shown in (**Figure H**). Glue four small red pompoms around the ankle to cover the whipstitches.

7. Repeat the procedures in step 6 to attach the remaining shoe to the opposite end of the leg tube, making sure that both feet point in the same direction.

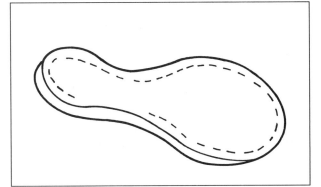

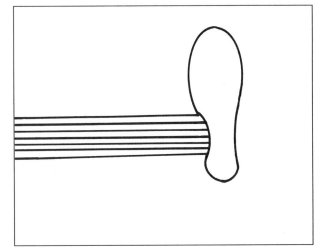

Figure I

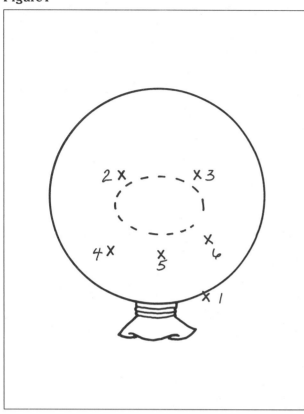

Figure J

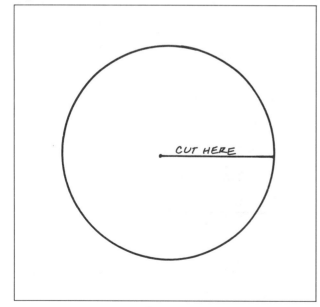

Making the Head

1. Tie a knot in the white pantyhose near the panty line. Cut off the leg about 1 inch above the knot, and about 10 inches below the knot. Turn the hose so the knot is on the inside. Stuff with fiberfill until the head is about 5 inches in diameter. Tie the hose in a knot at the neck and trim the excess hose below the knot.

2. Follow the entry and exit points illustrated in **Figure I** as you sculpt the facial features, using a long sharp needle and heavy-duty thread.

    a. Enter at 1, push the needle through the center of the head, and exit at 2. To form the nose, sew a circle of basting stitches 2 inches in diameter, and exit at 3.

    b. Use the tip of the needle to carefully lift fiberfill within the circle, and pull the thread gently until the nose appears. Lock the stitch, reenter at 3, and exit at 2.

    c. To form the mouth, reenter at 2, and exit at 4.

    d. Pull the thread across the surface, enter at 5, and exit at 6. Pull the thread across the surface, enter at 5, and exit at 2. Gently pull the thread until a smile appears. Lock the stitch at point 2, and cut the thread.

3. Use the black marker or pen to draw the lip line. Draw his big nose, using the red marker. In addition, draw two red cheek circles, and when the ink is dry, brush cheek blusher across the clown's cheeks. The eye area will be hidden by hair, so there's no need to draw or sculpt eyes.

4. Fold the Hat piece along the "place on fold" line with right sides together, and stitch the seam along the long straight edge only. Turn the hat right side out and press the seam allowance to the inside around the circular lower edge. Stitch a red pompom to the point of the hat.

5. To make the clown's hair, wrap the half skein of rug yarn into a continuous loop about 8 inches in diameter. Gather and tie the loop at the center so that it forms a figure eight. Cut the ends of the loops on each side. Whipstitch the tied center of the yarn to the top of the clown's head at the pantyhose knot, and spread the hair out around the top of the head. Trim the ends if the hair is too long.

6. Glue or whipstitch the hat to the clown's hair and head. Do not attach the head to the leg tube just yet.

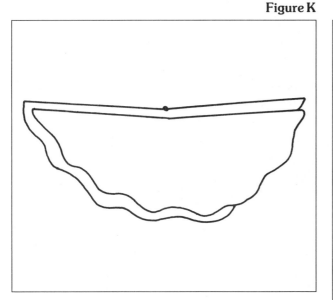

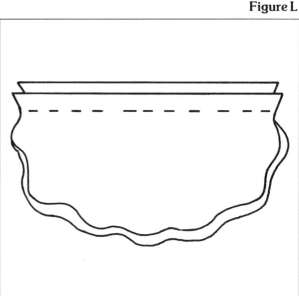

Making the Collar

1. Cut a 10-inch-diameter circle from each of the squares of yellow flannel. Cut along the radius of each circle, from the outer edge straight in to the center of the circle (**Figure J**).

2. Place the two flannel circles together, aligning the radius cuts. Grasp the corners formed by the radius cuts and pull them outward until the two edges of each cut form a straight line (**Figure K**). Stitch a seam through both flannel layers along the radius cut edge, as shown in **Figure L**. Open out the two layers of flannel, and press the seam open.

3. Use the double-fold bias tape to encase the entire outer raw edge of the collar and form a casing, as shown in **Figure M**. Leave the ends open.

4. Twist the pipe cleaners together end to end so you have one long piece, and thread it through the casing around the outer edge of the collar. Cut off any excess pipe cleaner that extends beyond the ends of the casing, and stitch across the ends so the pipe cleaner can't work its way out. Bend the pipe cleaner inside the casing so the collar has a ruffled look.

5. Place the leg tube on a flat surface, with the toes pointing upward. Place the collar on top, at the center of the tube. Place the clown's head on top of the collar, at the center. Whipstitch around the neck, through the collar, and into the leg tube, to secure the assembly.

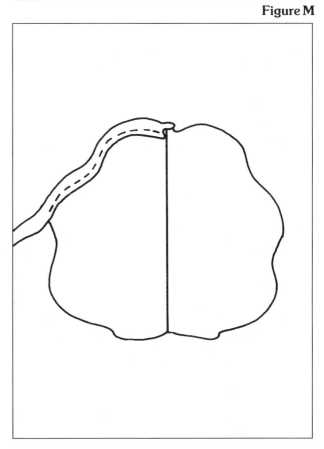

Dress-Me Bears

Make these squeezably soft bears and watch your children delight in learning the button, tie, hook, and zip skills necessary to dress themselves. The boy bear wears overalls, and the girl bear wears a frilly gingham dress. They make quite a pair to find under the Christmas tree.

Materials

¾ yard of off-white velour knit fabric
⅜ yard of blue gingham for the dress
¼ yard of red gingham for the shirt
⅜ yard of blue broadcloth for the overalls
8 x 16-inch piece of fusible interfacing
Felt: Small piece of pink; 10 x 22-inch piece of black; and an 8 x 22-inch piece of brown
14-inch length of 4-inch white gathered eyelet trim
White lace: 1⅛ yards of ¼-inch-wide, and 1 yard of ½-inch-wide
Satin ribbon: 10-inch length of ¼-inch red, 15-inch length of ¾-inch blue, and a 16-inch length of ¼-inch white
24-inch length of ¼-inch-wide black velvet ribbon
24-inch length of ¼-inch-wide brown grosgrain ribbon

½-inch-wide single-fold bias tape: 1⅛ yards of white, and ¼ yard of red
1½ yards of ¼-inch-wide elastic
One 7-inch neckline zipper, and one small hook-and-eye closure
Buttons: Two ¼-inch-diameter white; two ¾-inch-diameter white; and three ⅜-inch-diameter white
One-pound bag of polyester fiberfill
Embroidery hoop; needle; and red, black, blue, and white floss
Long sharp needle; heavy-duty white thread, and regular sewing thread to match the fabrics
Two 4-inch lengths of ¼-inch wooden dowel rod
Hot-melt glue and a glue gun (or white glue)

Cutting the Pieces

1. Scale drawings are provided on pages 247-248 for the Torso, Head, Arm, Leg, Bodice Back, Bodice Front, Dress Sleeve, Overalls, Shirt Back, Shirt Front, Shirt Sleeve, Collar, Ear, Boy Shoe, and Girl Shoe. Enlarge the drawings to make full-size paper patterns. (Refer to the Tips & Techniques section on enlarging scale drawings.)

2. Cut the pieces in this step from the specified fabrics. Pay attention to the "place on fold" notations. Fold the fabric into a double thickness, so you can cut two of each piece at a time, and the resulting pieces will be matching pairs. Transfer any placement markings or instructions to the fabric pieces.

Off-white velour: Arm - cut four
 Leg - cut four
 Torso - cut two
 Head - cut two
 Ear - cut four

Fusible interfacing: Head - cut one

Black felt: Nose - cut one, ½ x 1-inch triangle

Pink felt: Cheek - cut two, 1-inch-diameter circle

Note: The instructions for cutting the body pieces are listed for ONE bear. Both bodies are identical, so you will need to repeat the instructions to cut the pieces for the second bear.

3. Cut the pieces for the girl bear's clothing.

Blue gingham: Bodice Front - cut one
 Bodice Back - cut two
 Skirt - cut one, 5 x 23½ inches
 Sleeve - cut two

Black felt: Shoe - cut four

4. Cut the pieces for the boy bear's clothing.

Red gingham: Shirt Sleeve - cut two
  Collar - cut two
  Shirt Front - cut two
  Shirt Back - cut one
Blue broadcloth: Overalls - cut four
  Strap - cut two, 2½ x 8 inches
Brown felt: Shoe - cut four
  Shoe Tongue - cut four, 1¾ x 2-inches

Making the Body and Head

1. Pin two Arm pieces right sides together. Stitch the seam from point A to point B (**Figure A**). Clip the curves, turn right side out, and press the seam allowances to the inside. Baste the straight edges across the end of the arm. Make a second arm.

2. Assemble each leg in the same manner as the arms. Fold the leg so the seams match in the center (**Figure B**), and baste the straight edges across the end of the leg.

3. Place the Torso pieces right sides together with the arms and legs sandwiched between (**Figure C**). Stitch the seam around the edges, leaving an opening for turning and stuffing. Clip the curves and corners, turn the assembly right side out through the opening, and press the seam allowances to the inside along the opening edges. Stuff the torso firmly, inserting one of the short dowel rods vertically into the neck to make it rigid. Whipstitch the opening edges together. Do not stitch the openings in the arms and legs.

4. Stuff each arm firmly, starting with the hand and working up to 1 inch below the elbow. Stitch across the elbow stitching line, and then stuff the upper arm lightly. Whipstitch the opening edges together.

5. Stuff each leg firmly, starting with the foot and working up to 1 inch below the knee. Thread a long sharp needle with heavy-duty white thread, and take one stitch all the way through the leg at each knee dot (**Figure D**). Pull the thread tightly to form the indentations, lock the stitch, and cut the thread. Stuff the upper leg lightly, and whipstitch the opening edges together.

6. Adhere the fusible-interfacing Head piece to the wrong side of one of the velour Head pieces, following the manufacturer's instructions. Place this Head piece in an embroidery hoop, and use three strands of embroidery floss as you work the facial features (**Figure**

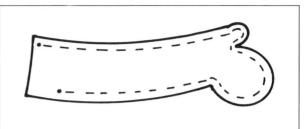

Figure A

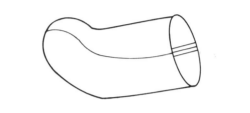

Figure B

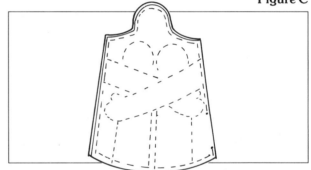

Figure C

E). The list indicates the color and the stitches needed. (See the Tips & Techniques section if you are unsure how to make these stitches.)

  Blue eyes - Satin stitch
  Black upper eyelids - Outline stitch
  Blue lower eyelids - Backstitch
  Black eyelashes - Two backstitches (girl), one backstitch (boy)
  White eye highlight - French knot
  Black eyebrow - Outline stitch
  Red mouth - Backstitch, French knot (girl only)
  Black vertical mouth line - Backstitch

7. Glue the Nose piece and the two Cheek pieces to the face. For washable bears, you may prefer to embroider the nose and cheek spots.

8. Place two Ear pieces right sides together, and stitch

Figure D

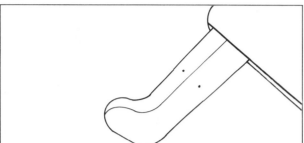

Figure E

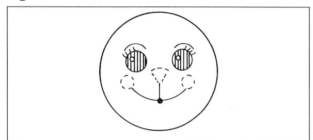

Figure F

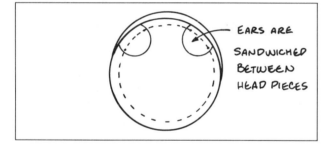

EARS ARE SANDWICHED BETWEEN HEAD PIECES

Figure G

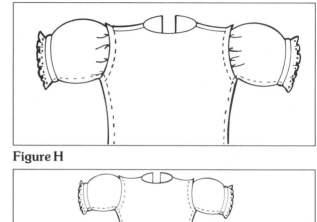

Figure H

and add stuffing around the opening if needed. Whipstitch around the opening twice to secure the head to the body.

Making the Girl Bear's Clothing

1. Place the Front Bodice and the two Back Bodices right sides together, and stitch the shoulder seams. Press the seams open.

2. Gather each Sleeve cap to fit each armhole opening on the bodice assembly. Stitch the seams, and press the seam allowances toward the sleeves.

3. Hem the lower edge of each sleeve. Trim the edge with ¼-inch white lace trim.

4. Make a casing on each sleeve for the elastic, using white bias tape. Stitch close to each long edge of the tape, leaving the short edges open. Thread narrow elastic through the casing, and adjust the elastic so the sleeve fits snugly around the bear's arm. Secure the ends of the elastic.

5. Fold the bodice-and-sleeve assembly right sides together, and stitch the underarm and side seams (**Figure G**). Press the seams, and turn the assembly right side out.

6. Fold the Skirt piece in half with right sides together. Stitch a 2-inch back seam. Stitch a narrow hem around

the seam all the way around the long curved edge, leaving the short straight edge open. Clip the curves, turn right side out, and stuff lightly. Topstitch ¼ inch from the curved edge, and then baste the straight raw edges together. Make a second ear.

9. Place the Head pieces right sides together, sandwiching the ears between (**Figure F**). Stitch the seam all the way around the outer edge. Clip the back Head piece only (the one that's not embroidered) along the clip lines indicated on the pattern. Clip the curves, and turn the head right side out. Fold the flaps formed by the clips to the inside of the head.

10. Stuff the head tightly. Push one or two of your fingers into the opening to make room for the neck. Insert the neck portion of the body into the head opening,

Figure I

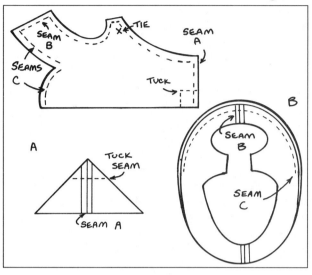

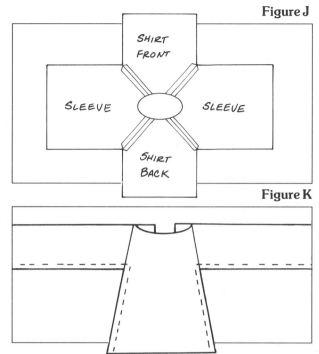

the lower edge. Trim it with ½-inch-wide lace trim.

7. Gather the raw edge of the skirt to fit the bodice assembly. Pin the skirt to the bodice (**Figure H**), placing right sides together. Stitch the seam and press.

8. Stitch a narrow hem around the neckline of the dress. Trim with ½-inch-wide lace.

9. Press the seam allowances to the wrong side of the fabric along each side of the center back dress opening. Install the zipper, following the "centered application" instructions on the zipper package. Sew the hook-and-eye to the back opening. (You may omit the zipper and use snaps or hooks-and-eyes.)

10. Tie the length of red ribbon in a bow and tack it to the top center front of the dress. Sew white ¼-inch buttons to the center front of the bodice. Tie the length of blue ribbon in a bow, and tack it to the head at the edge of one ear.

11. The length of 4-inch-wide gathered eyelet trim will serve as the apron. Stitch hems along each short edge. Cut two 8-inch lengths of narrow white ribbon, and stitch one length to the upper corner on each side of the apron for the ties.

Making the Shoes

Two of the pieces will be Outer Shoe pieces and two will be Shoe Lining pieces. Refer to **Figure I**.

1. Fold one Outer shoe piece right sides together, and stitch seam **A**. Refold the piece so the seam is flat,

and sew across the tuck line indicated on the pattern (step a).

2. Refold the piece as it was before you stitched the tuck, and stitch seam B. Refold the piece still with right sides together, aligning the top and bottom seams, and stitch seam C (step b).

3. Repeat steps 1 and 2 to assemble the second outer shoe, and the shoe linings, using the remaining three Shoe pieces. You should have four identical assemblies. Turn both outer shoes right side out, and leave both lining shoes wrong side out.

4. Slip the shoe linings inside the outer shoes. They should now be wrong sides together. Stitch the two layers together all the way around and close to the upper edge. Cut two 6-inch lengths of black velvet ribbon. Stitch one ribbon to each side of the shoe.

Making the Boy Bear's Clothing

1. Stitch the Sleeves to the Shirt Front and Shirt Back pieces (**Figure J**). Press the seams open.

2. Fold the shirt assembly right sides together, and stitch a continuous underarm and side seam on each side (**Figure K**). Hem the lower edge of the shirt, and both sleeves.

Figure L

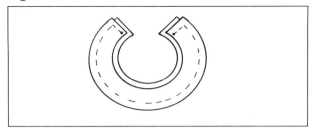

Figure M

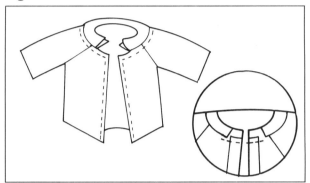

Figure N

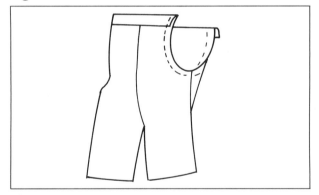

3. Place the Collar pieces right sides together, and stitch a continuous seam from dot to dot (**Figure L**). Leave the inner curved edge unstitched. Clip the outer curve and corners, turn right side out, and press. Baste the inner raw edges together.

4. Place the collar against the right side of the shirt. Adjust the collar so the raw neck edges are even, pin the collar, and stitch the seam.

5. Press open the red bias tape. Place it right side down around the neckline, with one long edge of the tape even with the raw edges of the neckline. Stitch the tape to the collar and shirt, over the existing seam line.

6. Fold each shirt front facing along the fold line indicated on the pattern, placing right sides together. Stitch through all layers along the neck seam line (**Figure M**, inset). Turn each corner right side out, and press. Topstitch ⅛ inch from the folded edge all the way around the front and the collar (**Figure M**). Turn the collar upward so the seam allowances and the bias tape are flat against the wrong side of the shirt.

7. Work three buttonholes down the left shirt front, and sew three buttons to the right shirt front. If you prefer, substitute snaps, and sew the buttons over them.

8. Place two Overalls pieces right sides together, and stitch the center seam only. The inner leg seam is not a portion of the center seam, and should not be stitched at this time. Clip the curves, and press the seam allowances open. Repeat the procedures, using the remaining two Overalls pieces.

9. Place the overalls assemblies right sides together, and stitch the side seams and the inner leg seams. Hem the lower edge of each leg.

10. To finish the armholes (**Figure N**), fold the upper straight edges to the right side of the fabric, and stitch all the way around the armholes. Clip the curves, turn the folded upper corners right side out, and press.

11. Stitch narrow hems along both long edges of each Strap piece. Fold each Strap piece in half lengthwise, placing wrong sides together, and stitch close to the hemmed edges.

12. Fold one end of the strap under, and work a buttonhole across the end. It should be large enough to accommodate a ¾-inch-diameter button. Sew a button to each side of the overalls front. Button the straps onto the overalls and place them on the bear. Adjust the straps to fit, crossing them at the back and pinning the free ends to the wrong side. Remove the overalls and stitch the straps in place on the back.

13. The boy bear's shoes are almost identical to the girl bear's, except that they have tongues. Assemble the shoes, following the instructions for the girl bear's shoes. Round off one end of each Tongue piece, and stitch them together in pairs. Place the straight edges underneath the curved opening and hand-stitch in place. Cut four 6-inch lengths of brown grosgrain ribbon, and stitch one length of ribbon to each side of the shoe for the ties.

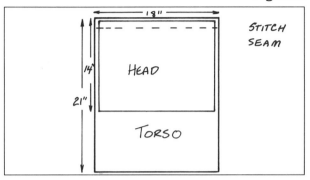

STITCH SEAM

18"

HEAD

14"

21"

TORSO

Slim Santa

The physical fitness craze surely has gone too far when it reaches the North Pole! It must have taken Santa a full year of hearty workouts to lose all those excess pounds, but it will take you only a few hours to assemble his 4½-foot tall likeness.

Materials

1¼ yards of 45-inch-wide red double-knit (stretchy) fabric
½ yard of flesh-tone double-knit (stretchy) fabric, at least 36 inches wide
⅜ yard of 36-inch-wide medium-weight black fabric for the boots and mittens (We used polished cotton.)
2½ x 18-inch strip of black vinyl fabric for the belt
½ yard of 36-inch-wide white or off-white furry fabric for the suit and hat trim
Small scraps of white and black felt
One skein of white or off-white rug yarn
Three black buttons, ⅞ or 1 inch in diameter
One holly sprig

Two bags of polyester fiberfill
White glue or hot-melt glue and a glue gun
Heavy-duty thread to match the fabrics

Cutting the Pieces

There are no patterns required for Slim Santa, because he is constructed primarily of stuffed tubes made from simple fabric rectangles. Cut from the specified fabrics the pieces listed in this section, and label each one. The only non-rectangular pieces are the Bottom and Pompom, which are circular.

Description	Dimensions	Quantity
Red fabric:		
Arm	9½ x 14 inches	2
Torso	18 x 21 inches	1
Bottom (circular)	6¾-inch diameter	1
Leg	9½ x 25 inches	2
Hat	15 x 18 inches	1
Flesh-tone fabric:		
Head	14 x 18 inches	1
Nose	5 x 7 inches	1
Black fabric:		
Boot	8 x 9½ inches	2
Mitten	7¾ x 9½ inches	2
Fur fabric:		
Suit Trim	7 x 22 inches	1
Hat Trim	7 x 22 inches	1
Pompom (circular)	12-inch diameter	1

Torso, Arms, and Legs

Note: All seams are ½-inch wide.

1. Place the Torso and Head pieces right sides to-

Figure B

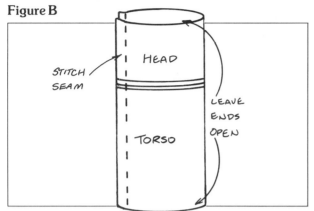

Figure C

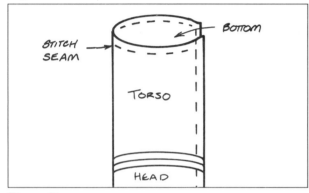

Figure D

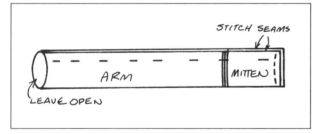

curves and turn the tube right side out.

4. Stuff the tube firmly with fiberfill, up to a few inches of the top of the head. We made our Slim Santa very straight, with no body contours. Gather together the fabric at the top of the head and wrap it with thread to close it off. Santa's hat and facial features will be added later.

5. Place one Arm piece and one Mitten piece right sides together, aligning 9½-inch edges. Stitch the seam along the aligned edges and press open.

6. Fold the arm-mitten assembly in half lengthwise, placing right sides together. Stitch the seam along the long edge and the mitten end (**Figure D**), leaving the arm end open. Clip the corner and turn right side out. Stuff the mitten and arm firmly, to within 1 inch of the open end. Pin the open end closed for the time being.

7. Assemble and stuff a second arm in the same manner, using the remaining Arm and Mitten pieces.

8. Assemble and stuff two separate leg tubes, as described for the arms in steps 5 and 6, using one Leg and one Boot piece for each. Close off the boot end of the tube as you did the mitten end of the arm in step 6.

Body Assembly

1. Unpin the open end of each arm and press the seam allowance to the inside. Pin the open end to the torso, just below the horizontal head-torso seam. The vertical seam in the head-torso tube should run straight up the center back, between the arms. Each arm should be turned so that its long seam faces the body. Whipstitch around the top of each arm several times, to secure it to the torso.

2. The legs are sewn to the front of the torso, just above the torso-to-bottom seam. Each leg should be turned with its long seam running along the outside (like the side seams of a pair of trousers). Whipstitch the legs to the torso, as you did the arms.

3. Fold the fur Suit Trim piece in half lengthwise, placing right sides together, and stitch the seam along the long edge only. Turn right side out and press flat. Wrap the suit trim around Santa's body, covering the tops of the legs at the front. Overlap the ends at the back and glue or whipstitch in place.

4. Wrap the black vinyl belt strip around Santa's body about 6 inches above the fur trim. Overlap the ends at the back and glue in place. Sew the buttons to the torso front between the head and belt.

gether, aligning an 18-inch edge of the Torso with an 18-inch edge of the Head. Stitch the seam along the aligned edges (**Figure A**), and press open.

2. Fold the torso-head assembly in half lengthwise, placing right sides together. Stitch the seam along the long edge only, leaving both ends open (**Figure B**), and press.

3. To close off the lower end of the torso-head tube, insert the circular Bottom piece, placing right sides together. Stitch the seam as shown in **Figure C**. Clip the

5. To make each boot bend in a more foot-like shape, first create a crease line by hand stitching up and down through the boot about 5 inches from the toe end, as shown in diagram 1, **Figure E**. Bend the toe end of the boot upward along the crease line, forming a right angle, as shown in diagram 2. Whipstitch the two sections of the boot along the fold line, as shown.

Hat and Face

1. Fold the Hat piece in half widthwise, placing right sides together. Stitch a curved seam along the aligned 15-inch edges (**Figure F**), beginning about ½ inch inside the lower corner and curving up to about 3 inches from the long folded edge, as shown. Trim the seam allowances to ½ inch, clip the curve, and press.

2. Run a line of basting stitches around the top of the hat (the smaller open end), and gather to close. Turn right side out.

3. To make the pompom, run a line of basting stitches close to the edge of the circular Pompom piece. Pull up the basting threads to gather the fabric around a handful of fiberfill, and tie off.

4. Fold the Hat Trim piece in half lengthwise, placing right sides together, and stitch the seam along the long edge only. Turn right side out and press flat.

5. Santa's completed head is shown in **Figure G**. Glue or baste the hat and fur hat trim to the head. Fold the tip of the hat downward, and glue it to the trim. Glue the gathered side of the pompom to the hat tip and trim, as shown. Glue the holly sprig to the trim, just in front of the hat tip.

6. To create Santa's eyes, cut two semi-circular white felt Eye pieces, each about 1¼ inches across the straight lower edge and 1 inch long. Cut two black felt Iris pieces slightly smaller than the Eyes (**Figure G**). Glue or whipstitch the two white Eyes to Santa's face, leaving a 1½-inch space between them, as shown. Attach a black Iris to each Eye.

7. Contour the Nose piece by tapering one end to about 3 inches wide and rounding off the corners. Baste ¼ inch from the edge, all the way around. Manipulate a wad of fiberfill into the general shape of the Nose piece, and gather the fabric around the fiberfill.

8. Place the gathered side of the nose against Santa's face (**Figure G**), with the smaller end between the eyes, and whipstitch in place.

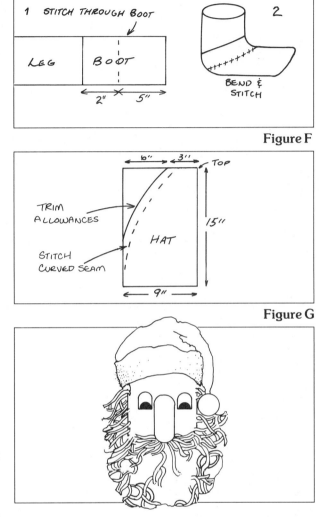

9. Santa's whiskers are composed of several yarn bunches. To make one bunch, cut about twenty-five 4-inch lengths of rug yarn and tie a short length of yarn around the center. Make ten additional yarn bunches in the same manner.

10. To form the beard (**Figure G**), glue or stitch ten yarn bunches to Santa's face along the beard line, allowing about 1 inch between bunches. The beard should extend upward to the hat. Fluff and spread the strands to fill in the gaps between bunches, glueing where necessary. Attach the final bunch just below the nose, as the mustache.

A South-of-the-Border Christmas

I n the North American view, a celebration south of the border is epitomized by warm hospitality and climate, spicy and delicious food, and unique holiday decorations that span a rainbow of bright colors.

In a way, Christmas traditions south of the border have remained timeless. The Nativity scene is the center of the celebration. Its origins as a traditional motif date from the thirteenth century when the Franciscans, looking for a way to meld religious significance into the seasonal celebration, created a life-size crèche in the church in Greccio. A living Nativity is still a popular Christmas custom and many people crowd the streets to march in the procession.

In this section, we feature the colors and sights that reflect the traditions of our neighbors to the south...with a few North American touches. Our Super Crepe Crèche is made from a modern product that resembles corn husk; and the bright-yellow, reusable piñata is also made in a new non-traditional manner. The festive caftan shines in the brilliant hues of the southern sky, and the rainbow wreath and stocking live up to their names. This section wouldn't be complete without our beautiful little doll, Priscilla. She would be welcome under a Christmas tree on either side of the border.

South-of-the-Border Christmas

Super Crepe Crèche

Festive Caftan

CELEBRATIONS OF CHRISTMAS

Pinata, Rainbow Wreath & Stocking

Priscilla

Menus and Melodies

South of the Border

We owe many holiday traditions to our neighbors south of the border, among which are chocolate, poinsettias, and the turkey. The turkey was popular in Mexico long before the Mayflower landed in Massachusetts. Today, whether north or south of the border, Christmas dinner would not be complete if it didn't feature a turkey roasted to a golden brown.

The most popular adjective for Mexican and Spanish foods would have to be "hot." But this is not necessarily a true description of the spicy and delicious dishes. While many foods traditionally contain chilies, peppers, garlic, and onion, the combination can be as hot, and conversely, as mild as taste dictates.

Corn (maize), tomatoes, and beans are staples in the Mexican diet. Two items freshly prepared for every meal are tortillas and a bowl of salsa. Salsa, a relish-type dish containing chopped onions, chilies, peppers, garlic, tomatoes, and any other type of chopped vegetable you prefer, can be mild or as hot as fire. If you prefer hot salsa, use jalapeños and other hot peppers and chilies; for mild salsa, use bell peppers and fewer (or milder) chilies.

Wheat flour, sugar, butter, and cream were not available in old Mexico in great quantities, so sweet, rich desserts such as pies, cakes, and puddings were replaced in the Mexican diet by fresh fruits. Today, sweet desserts are still not as popular in Mexico as they are in North America and Europe.

A Mexican Menu

Roast Turkey with Dressing
Chicken with Squash (Pollo con Calabaza)
Christmas Eve Salad (Ensalada de Nochebuena)
Spanish Rice
Tamales
Potatoes with Cheese (Papas con Queso)
Buñuelos (Fried Pastry)
Tortillas
Bread Pudding (Capirotada)
Rompope (Rum Eggnog)
Cafe de Olla (Clay Pot Coffee)

Ensalada de Nochebuena

Fresh fruits: oranges, apples, bananas, pomegranate seeds
3 small beets; cooked, peeled, and thinly sliced
Lime or lemon juice
Unsalted peanuts
Pine nuts, pecans, or sunflower seeds
Lettuce or romaine leaves

Dressing

2 Tbsp. sugar
¼ tsp. salt
3 Tbsp. white vinegar

Line salad bowl with lettuce or romaine leaves. Peel bananas and oranges and cut into thin slices. Slice apple into thin small wedges, and dip into lemon or lime juice to prevent discoloration. Arrange apple, orange, beet, and banana slices on top of lettuce. Sprinkle nuts and pomegranate seeds over top. Combine sugar, salt, and vinegar and blend until sugar is dissolved. Pour over salad.

Pollo con Calabaza

(You can use any type of squash for this dish; and pork can be substituted for chicken.)

1 chicken	2 to 4 squash
Onion, chopped	1 or 2 tomatoes,
Cilantro	chopped
Whole pepper corns	Garlic
1 can whole corn	Cumin

Cut chicken in pieces, remove skin and fat. Place about ¼ cup water in heavy frying pan. Cook chicken until browned. Combine squash, onion, tomatoes, spices, and corn with chicken. Do not add any more water. Cover and let steam until squash and vegetables are tender.

Spanish Rice

(You can use instant or regular rice.)

Put a small amount of shortening or lard in a large frying pan. Add enough rice for number of people to be served, and fry until rice is toasted and brown. Grind together garlic, cilantro, peppers, and chilies, and place in pan. Add one chopped tomato, or 1 can tomato sauce to rice. Add enough water to cover rice. Cover, and cook over low heat until water is cooked down (if rice is not done, add a little more water and cook a little longer). Do not stir rice during cooking.

Flour Tortillas

(An old saying goes; "Never count the tortillas, for if you do, you will not have enough.")

Tortillas are turned one time only during the cooking process. Traditionally, tortillas are freshly prepared for every meal; however, they can be wrapped in foil and stored in the refrigerator for two or three days.

3 cups sifted flour
3 Tbsp. shortening or lard
1 tsp. salt
2 tsp. baking powder

Mix all ingredients together. Add enough water to form a stiff dough. Roll dough in balls about the size of a large lemon. Roll one dough-ball into a 6- to 8-inch circle. Cook on an ungreased, hot griddle until done, turning once. A properly cooked tortilla should be white with brown spots, not brown all over.

Capirotada

Stale bread,	Pecans
any type	Apples, bananas,
Cinnamon (optional)	and raisins
Milk	Brown sugar
White cheese, grated	

Tear bread into chunks, place in casserole dish and cover with milk to soak. Add the chopped apples, bananas, and pecans. Add raisins, cinnamon, and brown sugar. Stir. Cover with grated cheese. Bake at 350° for 30 minutes, or until cheese has browned slightly and liquid is reduced.

Migas

(Recipe by Rosa Maria Caravazos Roffe. While not a dish to serve with Christmas dinner, migas make a quick-and-easy and delicious breakfast.)

Place a small amount of cooking oil in a heavy frying pan. Tear flour tortillas into bit-sized chunks, and fry until slightly brown and crispy. Drain tortillas on paper towel. Chop one onion, two cloves garlic, one tomato, bell pepper (optional), celery (optional), and two cayenne or jalapeño peppers. Combine everything, except tomatoes, in frying pan and stir. Allow two eggs for each person and beat as you would scrambled eggs. Pour into mixture in frying pan and cook until eggs are done. Add tomatoes, and salt and pepper to taste. Serve with an accompanying bowl of salsa.

Music to Enjoy

The following recorded albums contain a wealth of favorite Christmas carols and songs in both English and Spanish.

Feliz Navidad
Organo Melodico, Juan Torres
Musart Records #1601

Christmas in Mexico
Zavala Hermanos
Capitol Records #SM-10488

CELEBRATIONS OF CHRISTMAS

Priscilla

This beautiful little doll, dressed in a frilly gown and bonnet, will delight your little doll on Christmas morning. Priscilla has a soft huggable body, sculpted facial features, and stands about 22 inches tall.

Materials

1 yard of 44-inch ivory-color polyester jersey knit for the body

4 x 36-inch piece of white eyelet fabric for the bonnet

1 yard of sheer white handkerchief or blouse-weight cotton for the gown

2¾ x 15-inch piece of 11-count white aida cloth

1½ yards of 1-inch white eyelet trim

15-inch length of gathered 4-inch white eyelet trim (or a 30-inch length of ungathered eyelet trim)

1½ yards of 2-inch white flat finishing lace

2 yards of 1-inch gathered lace

2¼ yards of 1-inch white satin ribbon

2¼ yards of 1-inch double-fold white seam binding

Two skeins of light ivory-colored rug yarn for the hair

Four ⅜-inch-diameter two-hole buttons

Four baby buttons

Two snaps, buttons, or ties

One bag of polyester fiberfill

Embroidery floss in pink, lilac, blue, and green

Long sharp needle; heavy-duty ivory thread; and regular thread to match the fabrics

Cosmetic cheek blusher

Acrylic paints in red and black, and a fine-tipped artist's brush (or fine-point felt-tip markers in red and black)

Cutting the Pieces

1. Scale drawings are provided on page 235 for the Head, Arm, Nose, Body, Sleeve, Leg, Yoke Front, and Yoke Back. Enlarge the drawings to make full-size paper patterns. (Refer to the Tips & Techniques section on enlarging scale drawings.)

2. Cut the pieces as listed in this step from the specified fabrics. Fold the fabric into a double thickness, so you can cut two of each piece at a time, and the resulting pieces will be matching pairs. Pay attention to the "place on fold" notations on the scale drawings and patterns. Transfer any placement markings or instructions to the fabric pieces.

Jersey knit: Head - cut two
Body - cut two
Arm - cut four
Leg - cut four
Nose - cut one

White cotton: Yoke Front - cut one
Yoke Back - cut two
Sleeve - cut two
Skirt - cut two, 14 x 45 inches

Making the Head

Note: All seam allowances are ⅜ inch unless otherwise specified in the instructions

1. Place the Head pieces right sides together and stitch the seam (**Figure A**), leaving the neck edge open and unstitched. Clip the curve and turn the head right side out.

2. Stuff the head and neck with fiberfill, smoothing out the wrinkles along the curves.

3. To soft-sculpt the facial features, use a long sharp needle and heavy-duty thread, and follow the entry

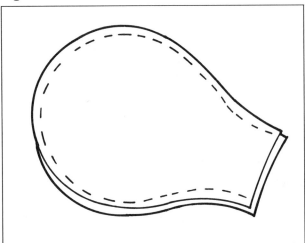

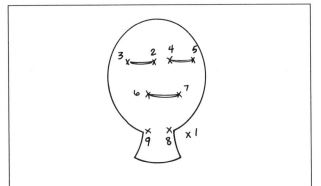

Figure C

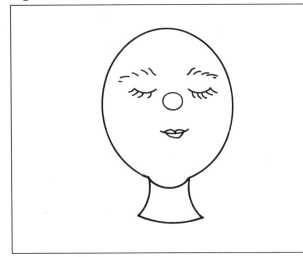

and exit points illustrated in **Figure B**.

    a. To make the eyes, enter at point 1 on the neck, push the needle through the head, and exit at point 2.

    b. Reenter at 2 and exit at 3.

    c. Pull the thread across the surface, enter at 2, and exit at 4.

    d. Pull the thread across the surface, enter at 5, and exit at 4. Gently pull the thread until the eye lines appear. Lock the stitch at 4.

    e. To form the mouth, reenter at 4, and exit at 6.

    f. Pull the thread across the surface, enter at 7, and exit at 2. Gently pull the thread until the mouth line appears, lock the stitch at 2, and cut the thread.

    g. To form the chin, enter at 1, and exit at 8.

    h. Pull the thread across the surface, enter at 9, and exit at 8. Gently pull the thread until the chin appears, lock the stitch at point 8, and cut the thread.

4. To make the nose, run a line of basting stitches around the perimeter of the Nose piece, close to the edge. Do not cut the thread. Place a small ball of fiberfill in the center, and pull the basting threads to gather the nose around the fiberfill. Knot the thread to secure the gathers. Do not cut the thread.

5. Place the nose on Priscilla's face in the proper location. Take very small whipstitches or blind stitches to secure the nose to the face.

6. To finish the face, refer to **Figure C** as you paint or draw the eyelids, eyebrows, and lips. To give her a little color, rub a small amount of cheek blusher across her cheeks and chin, and put a little dab on the tip of her nose.

Making the Body

1. Pin the two Body pieces right sides together and stitch the seams, as shown in **Figure D**. Leave the seams unstitched on the back and neck, as indicated on the scale drawings. Clip the curves and turn the body right side out. Don't stuff the body just yet.

2. Slip the neck through the opening in the top of the body, aligning the front body seam with the center of the face. The head seams will be on the sides. Whipstitch the neck to the body through the opening in the back of the body, as shown in **Figure E**.

3. Stuff the body through the same opening, and then whipstitch the opening edges together.

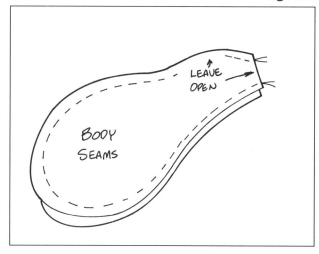

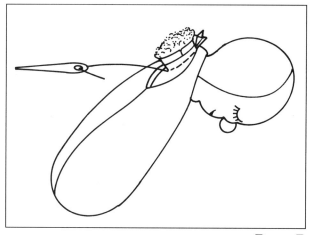

Making the Arms and Legs

1. Place two Arm pieces right sides together and stitch the seams (**Figure F**), leaving an opening at the shoulder. Clip the curves and turn the arm right side out. Press the seam allowances along the opening to the inside. Stuff the arm with fiberfill, and whipstitch the opening edges together.

2. Make a second arm in the same manner, using the remaining Arm pieces.

3. To soft-sculpt the elbow, use a long sharp needle and heavy-duty thread, and follow the entry and exit points illustrated in **Figure G**.

    a. Enter at point 1 on the inside of the elbow, push the needle through the arm, and exit directly opposite 1 on the outside of the elbow.

    b. Wrap the thread around the front of the elbow, enter at 1, push the needle through the arm, and exit opposite 1 on the other side of the arm.

    c. Wrap the thread around the front of the arm again, lock the stitch at 1, and cut the thread.

4. Repeat the procedures in step 3 to soft-sculpt the elbow on the second arm.

5. Place two Leg pieces right sides together and stitch the long contoured seam (**Figure H**), leaving an opening at the upper end. Press the seam allowances along the opening to the inside. Clip the curves and turn the leg right side out. Stuff the leg with fiberfill, and whipstitch the opening edges together.

6. Make a second leg in the same manner, using the remaining Leg pieces.

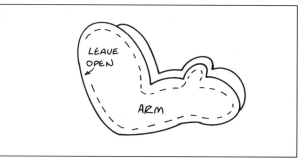

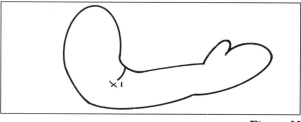

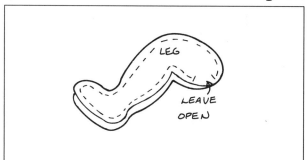

Figure I

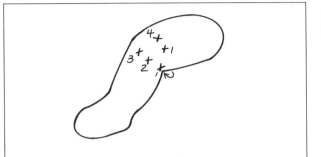

Figure J

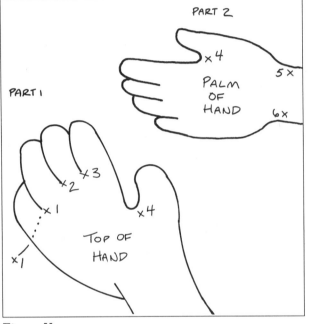

Figure K

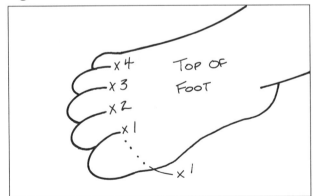

7. To soft-sculpt the knees, use a long sharp needle and heavy-duty thread. Follow the entry and exit points illustrated in **Figure I**.

    a. Enter at point 1 on the inside of the knee, push the needle through the leg, and exit directly opposite 1 on the outside of the knee.

    b. Pull the thread across the surface, enter at 2, and exit at 3.

    c. Pull the thread across the surface, enter at 4, and exit at 1 on the outside of the knee. Gently pull the thread until the knee forms.

    d. Repeat sub-steps a through c, and lock the stitch at point 1.

8. Repeat the procedures in step 7 to soft-sculpt the second knee.

Sculpting the Fingers and Toes

1. To soft-sculpt the fingers, use a long sharp needle and heavy-duty thread. Follow the entry and exit points illustrated in **Figure J**, part 1.

    a. To form the base of the first finger, enter at point 1 on the palm, push the needle through the hand, and exit directly opposite 1 on the top of the hand.

    b. Wrap the thread around the end of the hand, reenter at 1 on the palm, and exit at 1 on the top. Pull the thread tightly to form the first finger, and lock the stitch at 1.

    c. To form the second finger, reenter at 1, push the needle underneath the surface, and exit at 2 on the top.

    d. Repeat sub-steps b and c at point 2 and then at point 3 to form the remaining fingers. Lock the stitch at 3.

    e. To form the wrist (**Figure J**, part 2), reenter at 3, push the needle underneath the surface, and exit at 4 on the palm side of the hand.

    f. Reenter at 4 and exit at 5. Pull the thread across the surface, enter at 6, and exit at 4. Gently pull the thread until the wrist forms, lock the stitch, and cut the thread.

2. Repeat the procedures in step 1 to soft-sculpt the second hand.

3. To soft-sculpt the toes, use a long sharp needle and heavy-duty thread. Follow the entry and exit points illustrated in **Figure K**.

CELEBRATIONS OF CHRISTMAS

Figure L   **Figure M**

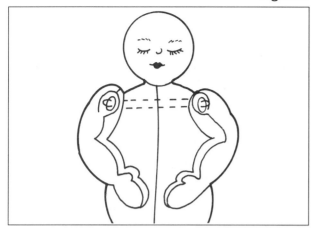

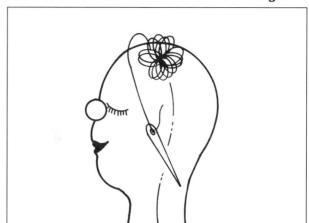

a. To form the base of the big toe, enter at point 1 on the sole, push the needle through the foot, and exit at point 1 on the top of the foot.

b. Wrap the thread around the end of the foot, enter at 1 on the sole, and exit at 1 on the top. Pull the thread until the toe forms, and lock the stitch at point 1.

c. To form the second toe, reenter at 1 on the top, push the needle underneath the surface, and exit at 2 on the top of the foot.

d. Repeat sub-steps b and c at points 2, 3, and 4 to form the remaining toes. Lock the stitch at point 4, and cut the thread.

4. Repeat the procedures in step 3 to form the toes on the second foot.

Attaching the Arms and Legs

The arms and legs are attached to the body using heavy-duty thread that is stitched through a button located inside each arm and leg. With the arms and legs attached in this manner, they can move as if jointed.

1. Work through the shoulder opening, and stitch a ⅜-inch two-hole button inside the arm, as shown in **Figure L**. Attach a button to the opposite arm in the same manner.

2. Place an arm on each side of the body, as shown in **Figure L**. Use heavy-duty thread and a long sharp needle, and enter one arm through the shoulder opening. Sew through one of the buttons and push the needle straight through the body to enter the second arm. Stitch through the button on the opposite arm in the

same manner. Gently pull the thread until the arms are snug against the body. Reverse the procedure, passing the needle through the body, and securing the buttons in both arms.

3. Repeat the procedures in step 2 until the arms are securely attached to the body. Don't attach the arms so tightly that they restrict movement. Lock the last stitch inside one arm and cut the thread.

4. Add a little more fiberfill to make the shoulders plump, then whipstitch (or blind stitch) the opening in each arm.

5. Work through the leg opening, and stitch a ⅜-inch two-hole button inside each leg. Place a leg on each side of the lower portion of the body, and stitch them in place in the same manner that you did for the arms.

Making the Hair

1. Use a long piece of heavy-duty thread, and tack one end of the yarn skein to the top of the forehead. Leave the needle and thread hanging from this point for the moment.

2. To make one curl (**Figure M**), wrap the yarn around a pencil twenty times. Take up your threaded needle, and pass it between the yarn loops and the pencil. Remove the pencil while holding the loops together, and tack the yarn curl to the head, as shown. Do not cut the thread or the yarn.

3. Continue with the same yarn and thread, and repeat the procedures in step 2 until the head is completely covered with curls. When the thread becomes too short, lock the stitch and rethread the needle. Use

Figure N

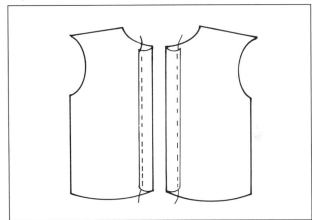

Figure O

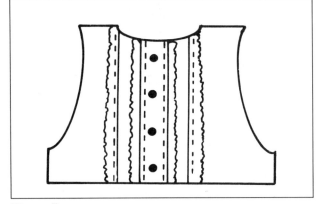

Figure P

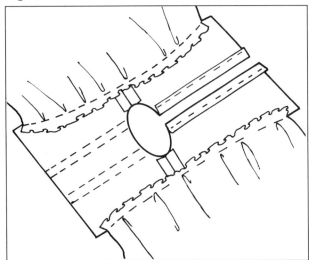

both skeins of yarn, if necessary.

4. When the last curl is in place, lock the stitch, cut the yarn, and tuck the end underneath a curl.

Making the Gown

1. On each Yoke Back, press and then stitch a ½-inch hem to the wrong side of the fabric along the center back (**Figure N**).

2. One of the Skirt pieces will be the outer skirt and one will be the underskirt. Press and stitch a ¼-inch hem to the wrong side of the fabric along one long edge of each Skirt piece. These will be the lower edges. Press and stitch a 1-inch hem to the wrong side of the fabric along both short edges of each Skirt piece. These will be the back opening edges. Stack the Skirt pieces evenly, placing both pieces right side up. Run a line of basting stitches through both layers close to the upper edge. This will be gathered later to fit the gown bodice.

3. To form two pleats in the Yoke Front, fold and stitch along the lines indicated on the pattern, stitching a length of 1-inch-wide gathered lace in each pleat (**Figure O**). Topstitch another length of lace ½ inch from each pleat, and sew the four baby buttons along the center.

4. Pin the yokes right sides together along the shoulder seams (**Figure P**). Stitch the seams and press.

5. On one Sleeve, press and stitch a ¼-inch hem to the wrong side of the fabric along the lower edge. Topstitch lace trim over the hemmed edge. Gather the upper end of the sleeve, ¼ inch from the raw edge.

6. Pin the gathered edge of the sleeve to one armhole edge of the yoke assembly, placing right sides together (**Figure P**). Adjust the gathers and stitch the seams.

7. Repeat steps 5 and 6 to form and attach another sleeve to the opposite side in the same manner.

8. Fold the bodice assembly right sides together, and stitch the underarm and side seams. Press the seam.

9. Place the gathered skirt right side up on a flat surface. Pull up the basting threads until the upper edge of the skirt is the same width as the lower edge of the bodice assembly. Place a length of 1-inch gathered lace on top so the edge of the lace is even with the edge of the skirt. Baste the lace in place. With right sides together, pin the upper edge of the skirt around the lower edge of the bodice, aligning the back opening edges

(**Figure Q**). The lace will be sandwiched between the skirt and bodice. Stitch through all thicknesses along the gathering line. Press the seam allowances toward the bodice.

10. To finish the gown, turn under and topstitch a ¼-inch hem around the neckline. Topstitch 2-inch-wide flat finishing lace around the lower edge of the outer skirt. Topstitch 1-inch-wide gathered lace along the lower edge of the underskirt.

11. Run basting stitches around the lower edge of each sleeve. Dress Priscilla in her gown, and adjust the sleeves to fit her arms. Secure the gathers. Tack the back open edges of the gown, or join them using a hook-and-eye closure or snap at the neckline and skirt line. Use scrap fabric and a safety pin to diaper Priscilla.

Making the Bonnet

1. Refer to the cross-stitch graph on page 123. (If you have never done this type of needlework before see the Tips & Techniques section on cross-stitch.)

2. Work the design in the center of the aida cloth strip. Staystitch ¼ inch from all outer edges to keep the edges from raveling.

Assembling the Bonnet Front

1. Cut a 15-inch length of narrow eyelet trim. Pin it to the aida cloth, placing right sides together. The bound edge of the eyelet should be ¼ inch from one long raw edge of the cloth (**Figure R**). The scalloped edge of the eyelet should extend in toward the center of the strip. Baste along the seam line.

2. Pin the pregathered eyelet trim over the narrow eyelet and aida cloth, following the procedures described in step 1. Stitch along the seam line through all thicknesses. Turn the eyelet trims outward, and press the seam allowances toward the aida cloth.

3. Repeat step 1 to baste another 15-inch length of narrow eyelet trim to the opposite long edge of the aida cloth in the same manner.

4. Run a line of basting stitches just inside the seam line on one long edge of the piece of eyelet fabric. Pull up the threads to form even gathers, until the edge measures 15 inches long.

5. Pin the gathered fabric to the aida cloth, over the eyelet previously attached. Place the gathered edge of the fabric even with the raw edge of the aida cloth strip,

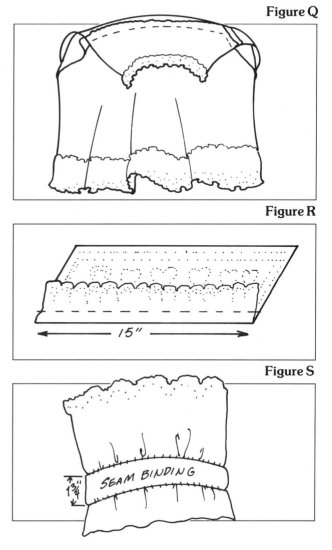

Figure Q

Figure R

15"

Figure S

SEAM BINDING

1¾"

right sides together. Stitch along the seam line. Turn the eyelet trim and fabric outward. Press all seam allowances toward the aida cloth.

6. A length of seam binding will cover all of the raw edges and seam allowances that have been turned to the wrong side of the aida cloth. Cut a 15-inch length of seam binding and press it open. Press a hem allowance to the wrong side of the binding along each long edge, so that it is 1¾ inches wide. Pin the binding to the aida cloth assembly, placing wrong sides together, so that the pressed edges of the binding lie along the stitched seams on each long edge of the aida cloth. Whipstitch the long edges of the binding (**Figure S**).

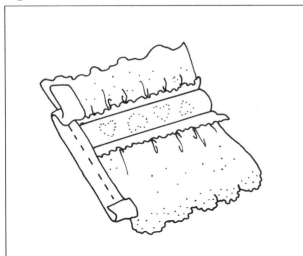

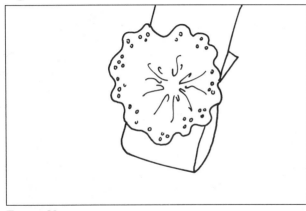

Figure V

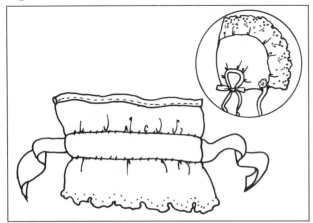

Finishing the Edges

1. Cut a length of seam binding as long as one side edge of the assembled bonnet. Press the binding open, and press a ¼-inch hem to the wrong side on each short end.

2. With the right sides together, pin the binding along one side edge of the bonnet (from the front of the wide eyelet trim to the end of the eyelet fabric), placing the center line of the binding along the seam line (**Figure T**). Stitch along the seam line, being careful to keep the eyelet trims flat as you stitch over them.

3. Refold the binding along the seam line, and press the binding and seam allowance to the wrong side of the bonnet.

4. Whipstitch the binding to the bonnet edges.

5. Cut an 8-inch length of narrow eyelet trim and a 21-inch length of satin ribbon. The ribbon will serve as a tie. The eyelet will be gathered into a circle to look like a flower, and will be used to anchor the tie to one end of the aida cloth strip.

6. Press a narrow allowance to the wrong side on each short raw end of the eyelet. Run a line of basting stitches along the bound edge of the eyelet, and pull up tight gathers so that the eyelet forms a circle with the gathered edge in the center. Take a few stitches to secure the circle.

7. Fold a 1½-inch allowance to the wrong side on one end of the ribbon. Pin the folded end of the ribbon to the right side of the aida cloth strip on the bonnet near one side seam, and pin the eyelet flower on top (**Figure U**). The center of the eyelet flower should be approximately 1 inch from the side edge. Take several hand stitches through all thicknesses at the center of the flower, using pink embroidery floss. Cut the opposite end of the ribbon at an angle.

8. Repeat all of the procedures in this section to finish the opposite side of the bonnet.

9. To finish the back edge, fold under a ½-inch casing and stitch close to the edge (**Figure V**). Cut both ends of the remaining length of satin ribbon at an angle. Thread the ribbon through the casing, gathering the fabric as you go. When you reach the end, pull the ribbon through until the ends are an equal length. Pull up the ribbon ends to gather the back of the bonnet (**Figure V**, inset), and tie them in a bow.

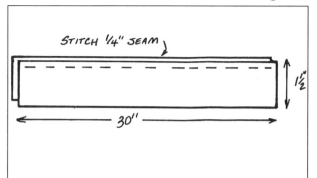

Stitch ¼" seam

1½"

30"

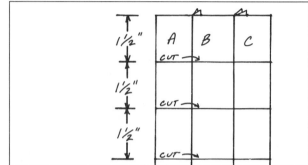

Figure B

A   B   C

1½"   CUT →

1½"   CUT →

1½"   CUT →

Festive Caftan & Hat

Bright colors, geometric patch-work, and a one-size-fits-all feature make these items a must on your gift list. Don't forget to make a set for yourself, as well! The cool and com-fortable caftan simply can't be beat for lounging or receiving visitors. Don the festive hat, with matching patchwork band, and you're all set for springtime gardening.

Materials

3⅛ yards of 44- or 45-inch-wide cotton fabric in a solid color, for the body of the caftan (We chose tur-quoise. **Note:** If you are making the caftan for some-one taller than about 5½ feet, purchase 3⅝ yards.)

⅛ yard each of three different solid-color cotton fabrics, at least 36 inches wide, for the patchwork (We used turquoise, bright yellow, and bright red. Purchase twice as much of each fabric if you wish to use more patchwork on the caftan than we did.)

A straw hat with brim

One ¾-inch-diameter spherical button, of a color that coordinates with the fabrics, for the hatband

Thread to match the caftan fabric

Assembling the Patchwork

Note: All patchwork seams are ¼ inch wide.

1. Cut a 1½ x 30-inch straight strip from each of the three patchwork fabrics. Let's call them A, B, and C, so we won't get bogged down in the diagrams and instruc-tions that follow. (In our color scheme, A was turquoise, B was yellow, and C was red.)

2. Pin the A and B strips right sides together, aligning them evenly, and stitch the seam along one long edge only (**Figure A**). Open them out and press both seam allowances in the same direction.

3. Place C on top of B with right sides together. Ad-just them evenly, aligning one long edge of C with the free long edge of B. Stitch the seam along the aligned long edges. Open out C and press both seam allow-ances in the same direction. The assembly should now look like the one shown in **Figure B**.

Figure C

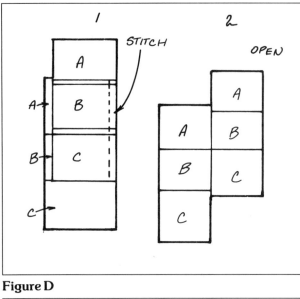

Figure D

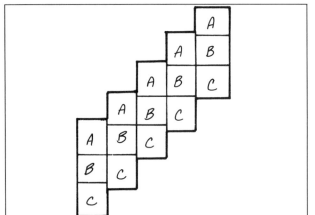

Figure E

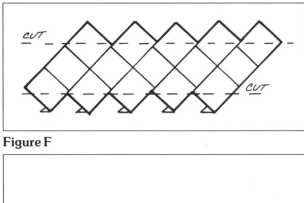

Figure F

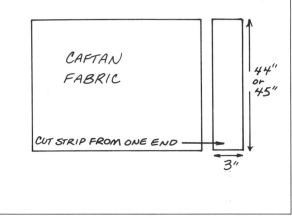

all of the remaining multicolored strips (one at a time) to the patchwork assembly, offsetting in the same direction and keeping the color progression the same. **Figure D** shows five of the strips sewn together; you want to keep on going until all twenty multicolored strips are sewn together in this manner.

7. Mark two straight cutting lines along the patchwork assembly (**Figure E**), as far from the center squares as the corners of the outer squares will allow. Run a line of short machine stitches just inside each marked line, to help keep the seams from coming undone. Cut along each marked line.

8. The patchwork that you just completed will be used for the caftan. Repeat steps 1 through 7 to create a second identical patchwork assembly, which will also be used for the caftan.

9. To make the patchwork for the hatband, follow the same procedures, with the following exceptions: In step 1, cut the strips 1½ x 36 inches, not 1½ x 30 in-

4. To create short multicolored strips, cut across the A-B-C assembly at 1½-inch intervals, as shown in **Figure B**. You should be able to get twenty multicolored strips from the assembly.

5. Place two of the multicolored strips right sides together. Adjust them so that they are offset by one square (**Figure C**), making sure that the A squares are at the same end, and stitch the seam along one long edge. When the strips are opened out and pressed, the assembly should look like the second diagram in **Figure C**.

6. Repeat the procedures described in step 5 to stitch

ches. In step 4, you should be able to get twenty-four multicolored strips from the **A-B-C** assembly. In step 6, sew together all twenty-four of the multicolored strips.

Making the Caftan

1. Cut a 3-inch-wide strip from one end of the caftan fabric (**Figure F**). Set aside the strip for use in the hatband assembly – the remaining bulk of the fabric will be used for the one-piece caftan.

2. Fold the caftan fabric in half widthwise and then again lengthwise; it should now be folded in quarters, as shown in **Figure G**. Smooth and even out the layers. To mark the cutting lines for the rectangular neck opening, measure from the folded center point 2¼ inches along the short folded edges and 5½ inches along the long folded edges, as shown. Cut through all layers of fabric to form the neck opening. Mark a curved cutting line along the lower outside corners, as shown, and cut through all four layers along the line.

3. Open out the caftan and place it wrong side up on a flat surface. Make a straight clip, about ¼ inch long, at each corner of the neck opening, as shown in **Figure H**. Leave the caftan wrong side up.

4. Square off the ends of the two caftan patchwork assemblies. Cut from each one a 13-inch length and a 10-inch length. Place one of the 13-inch patchwork strips wrong side up on top of the caftan, aligning a long edge of the patchwork with a long edge of the neck opening, as shown in **Figure H**. Adjust it so that the strip extends equally beyond each end of the neck opening. Stitch a ¼-inch-wide seam, as shown, stopping it ¼ inch beyond each end of the neck opening.

5. Turn the patchwork strip right side up along the seam line and press the seam. Turn the strip through the neck opening, so that it lies right side up against the right side of the caftan, and press again. Press under the seam allowance along the unstitched portions of the seamed edge. Press a ¼-inch seam allowance to the wrong side of the patchwork along the free long edge.

6. Repeat steps 4 and 5 to stitch the second 13-inch patchwork strip to the opposite long edge of the neck opening. **Note:** Check the color arrangement on the first strip – either the **A** or **C** color triangles will be closest to the neckline. Place the second 13-inch strip against the caftan so that the same color triangles are aligned with the neckline edge.

7. Repeat steps 4 and 5 to stitch a 10-inch patchwork

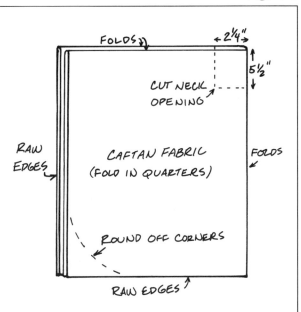

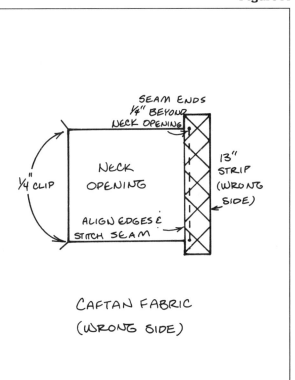

Figure I

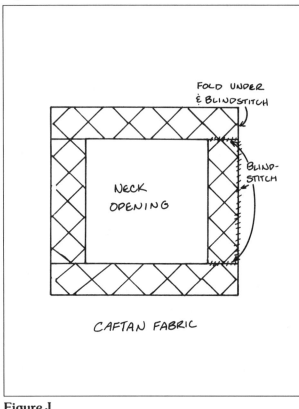

FOLD UNDER
& BLINDSTITCH

BLIND-
STITCH

NECK
OPENING

CAFTAN FABRIC

Figure J

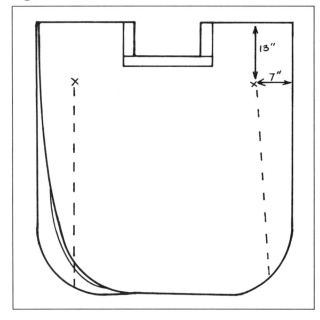

13"

7"

strip to each short edge of the neck opening. Be sure to place them so that the color arrangement is the same as for the longer strips.

8. On the right side of the caftan, fold under both ends of each 10-inch patchwork strip, so they are even with the outer edges of the other strips (**Figure I**). Note that the end strips cover the side strips. Blindstitch all free edges in place, as shown. Press the assembly.

9. Slip the caftan over your head, adjust it so that it hangs evenly, and mark the hemline at the front and back. Trim the ends, if necessary, so the hem won't be very wide. Double-turn and press a narrow hem to the wrong side of the caftan, all the way around the entire outer edge. Machine stitch the hem.

10. Fold the caftan in half widthwise with wrong sides together, and place it on a flat surface. Smooth and even out the layers. The side seams are simply sewn through both layers, as shown in **Figure J**. Measure 13 inches down from the folded shoulder line, and 7 inches in from one side edge, and mark this point. Repeat to mark the upper end of the second side seam, as shown. Pin the layers together and run a straight line of machine stitches from each marked point to the adjacent lower corner, as shown.

11. For a more colorful caftan, assemble additional patchwork strips and use them to trim the armhole openings. You may also wish to make a couple of patch pockets and trim them with patchwork.

Making the Hatband

1. To determine the length of the basic hatband piece, measure around the hat crown just above the brim, and add 3 inches. Trim the length of the hatband patchwork to this measurement, squaring off the ends.

2. Cut a hatband lining piece from the 3-inch-wide strip of caftan fabric that you set aside earlier, making it the same size as the trimmed patchwork.

3. Place the patchwork and lining strips right sides together. Stitch a narrow seam along both long edges and one end, leaving the other end open. Clip the corners, turn the assembly right side out, and press.

4. Press the seam allowances to the inside at the open end of the hatband, and blindstitch.

5. Wrap the hatband around the hat crown (patchwork side out, of course), and overlap the ends at the center back. Tack the ends together, and stitch the spherical button over the tacking stitches.

Rainbow Wreath & Stocking

Seven brilliant colors of fringed felt give this easy-to-make wreath and stocking the look of raffia. It will take only a couple of enjoyable hours to put them together and jazz up your south-of-the-border decor.

Materials

72-inch-wide felt: ⅞ yard of red; and ⅛ yard each of pink, orange, bright yellow, light green, turquoise, and dark blue

17-inch-diameter wreath form (either polystyrene foam or straw)

Dried wheat-grass ornaments: On the wreath we used an 8-inch-tall angel and three 2½-inch-diameter stars; on the stocking we used a 6-inch-long spray and one 5-inch-diameter star

Hot-melt glue and a glue gun, or white glue

½ yard of clear thin fishing line or nylon thread

Cutting the Felt

1. A scale drawing for the Stocking pattern is provided on page 82. Enlarge the drawing to make a full-size pattern.

2. Cut from the specified colors of felt the pieces listed in this step; most are simple rectangles except the Stocking, for which you made a pattern, and the Wreath Cover, which is a circle. (See Tips & Techniques, if necessary, for methods of drawing large circles.) Label each piece for reference during assembly.

Description	Dimensions	Quantity
Red:		
Wreath Cover (circular)	30-inch diameter	1
Wreath Strip	8 x 30 inches	1
Stocking	use pattern	2
Stocking Strip	5 x 8 inches	1
Stocking Strip	3 x 8 inches	2
Hanger	½ x 6 inches	1
Pink:		
Wreath Strip	3 x 36 inches	1
Stocking Strip	3 x 8 inches	3
Orange:		
Wreath Strip	3 x 40 inches	1
Stocking Strip	3 x 8 inches	3
Yellow:		
Wreath Strip	3 x 46 inches	1
Stocking Strip	3 x 8 inches	3
Green:		
Wreath Strip	3 x 50 inches	1
Stocking Strip	3 x 10 inches	2
Turquoise:		
Wreath Strip	3 x 54 inches	1
Stocking Strip	3 x 9 inches	2
Blue:		
Wreath Strip	3 x 54 inches	1
Stocking Strip	3 x 10 inches	1
Stocking Strip	3 x 8 inches	1

Making the Wreath

1. Place the wreath form in the center of the red felt Wreath Cover piece (**Figure A**). Cut four slits across the center of the felt, as shown, so that you can wrap the felt around the inside curve of the wreath. Wrap the

Figure A

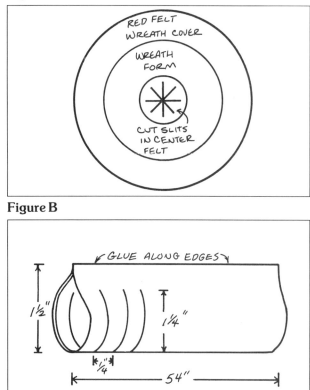

Figure B

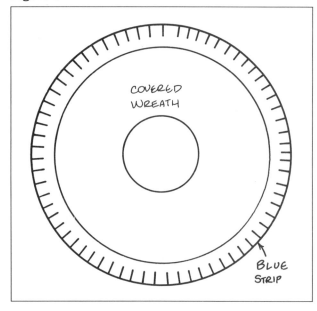

Figure C

Figure D

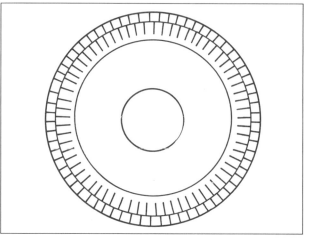

center fabric up and over the wreath form, all the way around the inside edge, and glue it in place on the top surface. This will be the back of the finished wreath, so don't worry too much about making it extra-neat. The inside edge will be covered by fringe, so it doesn't matter if the form shows through the slits in places.

2. Wrap the outer felt up and over the wreath form, all the way around the outside edge, folding it into pleats and trimming where necessary. Glue it to the back of the form, over the center fabric. As you work, check the front to make sure the fabric is relatively smooth – it will be covered by fringe strips, but you don't want to leave any large lumps or wrinkles.

3. To create the first layer of fringe, run a very narrow bead of glue close to one long edge of the blue Wreath Strip. Fold the Strip in half lengthwise and press together the aligned long edges (**Figure B**). Make straight clips at ¼-inch intervals along the folded long edge, as shown, from one end to the other. Each clip should be about 1¼ inches long.

4. Repeat step 3 to glue, fold, and clip each of the five remaining 3-inch-wide Wreath Strips. Follow the same procedures to glue, fold, and clip the wider red Wreath Strip, making the clips about 2½ inches long.

5. Wrap the fringed blue strip around the front of the wreath as shown in **Figure C**. Note that the uncut edges face inward and the clipped folded edge faces outward. The uncut edge should be placed at about the point where the wreath starts to curve around the outside edge. Glue the unclipped edge in place, overlapping the ends neatly.

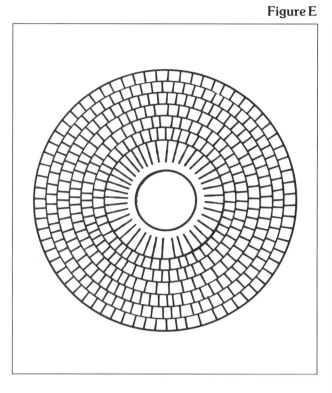

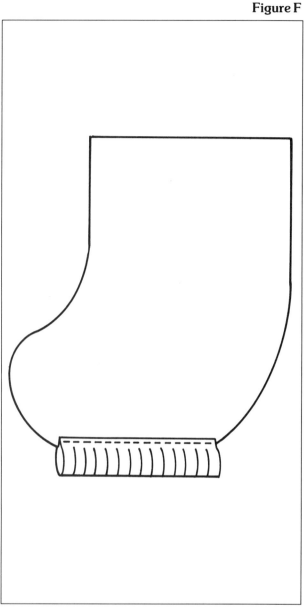

6. Wrap the fringed turquoise strip around the front of the wreath as shown in **Figure D**. It should be placed so that the clipped edge overlaps the blue strip by about ½ inch all the way around. Glue it in place.

7. Repeat step 6 to attach the fringed green strip, then the yellow one, then the orange one, and then the pink one. Each strip should be turned with its clipped edge facing outward, and each should overlap the previous strip by about ½ inch.

8. The final fringed strip is the wider red one. It is attached in the same manner but the unclipped long edge should be placed along the inside curve on the back of the wreath, so that the strip covers the entire inner edge of the wreath (**Figure E**). The fringed edge will lap over the previous pink strip on the front, as shown.

9. To hang the straw angel in the center of the wreath, use the fishing line or clear nylon thread to make a hanger loop. Insert the thread through one or two of the straw stalks at the back of the angel's head, pull through, and tie the ends in a knot. Tack the knotted end of the loop to the inside edge of the wreath.

10. Glue the three small straw stars to the front of the wreath, spacing them evenly around the upper half.

Making the Stocking

1. The stocking front is covered with overlapping fringe strips, just like the wreath. You should have eighteen felt Stocking Strip pieces, all 3 inches wide except for one wider red one. Glue, fold, and clip each of the 3-inch-wide Strips, as you did for the wreath. Re-

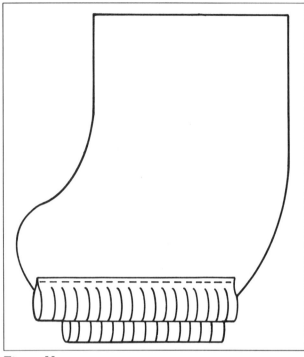

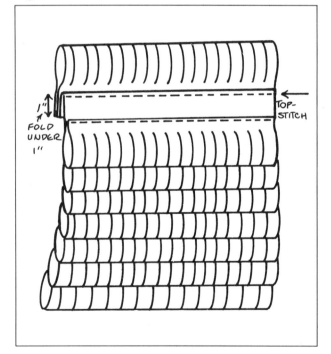

peat for the wider red Strip but make the clips only 1 inch long.

2. Topstitch the 8-inch-long blue fringe strip to one Stocking piece just above the lower edge, as shown in **Figure F**. Note that the clipped loops hang downward and the line of stitches is close to the unclipped edge of the fringe strip.

3. Topstitch the longer blue fringe strip in place (**Figure G**), so that it overlaps the first strip by about ¾ inch.

4. Topstitch a green fringe strip above the two blue ones, so that it overlaps the strip below by only ½ inch. Add the next green strip, overlapping the first green one by ¾ inch.

5. Add the two turquoise strips next, lapping the first one only ½ inch over the green strip below, and lapping the second one ¾ inch over the first turquoise one.

6. Continue working in this manner, adding two yellow strips next, then two orange ones, then the two narrow red ones, and then two pink ones. Overlap as described for the previous strips.

7. Topstitch a single orange strip above the two pink ones, overlapping by ½ inch. Add a single yellow strip next, and then a single pink strip, overlapping each by ½ inch. The upper edge of the top pink strip should be about 2 inches from the upper edge of the Stocking.

8. Place the wide red fringe strip on top of the Stocking piece, aligning the unclipped long edge of the strip with the top Stocking edge. The fringed edge should face the bottom of the Stocking piece. Topstitch ½ inch from the aligned upper edges.

9. Fold the top of the Stocking to the wrong side 1 inch from the edge – this will cause the loops of fringe to point upward, as shown in **Figure H**. Topstitch through all layers along the folded edge, as shown.

10. Fold the top fringe loops down over the topstitched upper edge, and press.

11. Place the second Stocking piece against the back of the fringe-covered stocking front, aligning it evenly along the side and lower edges. Trim the top of the back Stocking piece even with the front.

12. Fold the red felt Hanger piece in half widthwise. Place the aligned free ends between the two Stocking pieces at the upper back corner – the folded end should extend up above the stocking, forming a hanger loop. Glue together the two Stocking pieces around the outer edges, glueing the hanger in place at the top.

13. Glue or tack the large straw star to the front of the stocking near the top, and glue the straw spray to the center of the star.

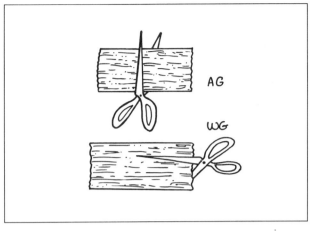

Super Crepe Crèche

This beautiful crèche features Mary, Joseph, Baby Jesus, the Three Wise Men, a shepherd, two sheep, the manger, and the stable. All are made easily and inexpensively from Super Crepe, a versatile product that resembles the texture of a corn husk. The stable is about 15 inches tall.

Materials

Cindus Super Crepe: three packages brown, three packages grasscloth, and one package gold

Eight hollow soft plastic eggs on craft stems, each about 2 x 2½ inches in diameter

Three 12-inch-long chenille stems (These will be covered with Super Crepe so color doesn't matter.)

One 9½ x 11-inch piece of 1-inch-thick polystyrene foam for the stable

One 12 x 15-inch piece of corrugated cardboard

4-inch length of ½-inch-diameter wooden dowel rod

One facial tissue

Hot-melt glue and a glue gun (or white glue)

Black felt-tip marker

General Directions

Cindus Super Crepe is a uniform crepe paper with a texture resembling that of a cornhusk. It is highly bleed- and fade-resistant.

Super Crepe has a definite grain line, much like wood. For that reason, the item will look different depending on whether a piece is cut across the grain or with the grain. Where instructions specify "AG," cut the paper across the grain line. Where instructions specify "WG," cut the paper with the grain line. **Figure A** shows these two methods of cutting the crepe.

Super Crepe is available in full packages only, and each sheet measures 20 x 36 inches, so you will have some left over. Either add some more figures to the crèche, or put the remainder aside for future use.

If you cannot find Cindus Super Crepe in your area, write to: Cindus Corporation, Attn: Craft Product Manager, Decorative Crepe Products Division, 515 Station Avenue, Cincinnati, Ohio, 45215.

Scale drawings are provided on pages 245-246 for the Cape, Cape Decoration, Turban, Burnoose, Beard for Joseph and First Wiseman, and Beard/Hair for Second Wiseman. Enlarge the drawings to make full-size paper patterns. (Refer to the Tips & Techniques section on enlarging scale drawings if necessary.)

Figure B

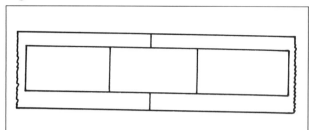

Figure C

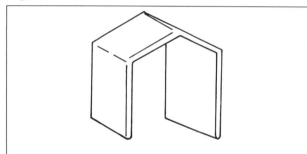

Figure D

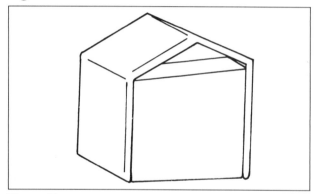

Figure E

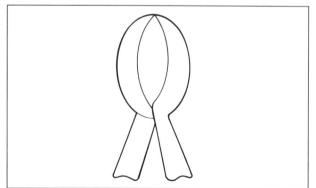

Making the Stable

1. To make the back of the stable, cut a piece of brown crepe, 12 inches AG x 20 inches WG. Cover the piece of polystyrene foam with the piece of brown crepe, wrapping the edges around to the back, and glue it in place.

2. To make the sides and roof of the stable (**Figure B**), cut two pieces of brown crepe, each 12 inches AG x 18 inches WG. Place these pieces on a flat surface, end to end. Cut the corrugated cardboard into three pieces, each 5 x 12 inches. Glue the three pieces of cardboard to the crepe pieces, end to end. Wrap the edges of the crepe around the cardboard, overlapping and glueing them down.

3. Before the glue dries completely, bend the middle cardboard piece along the center line to form the peak of the roof (**Figure C**). Let the glue dry thoroughly on all pieces.

4. Glue the stable back to the sides and roof, as shown in **Figure D**. The side walls should cover the edges of the back piece. Make sure that all lower edges are flush, or you'll end up with an unstable stable.

Making the Heads

The heads of all the figures are made in the same manner; only the hair and head coverings are different.

1. To make one head, cut three strips of grasscloth crepe, each 1 inch AG x 10 inches WG. Cover one plastic egg with glue. Place the middle of one crepe strip on top of the egg, and press the strip along the surface of the egg until you reach the stem (**Figure E**).

2. Glue the second and third strips to the egg in the same manner, overlapping each strip slightly to cover any remaining exposed surface.

3. Twist the ends of all the strips together at the base of the egg. Wrap and glue a narrow strip of crepe around the twisted ends to secure the twists and create a neck (**Figure F**).

4. Make five more heads in the same manner; four using grasscloth crepe, and one using brown crepe.

5. To make one nose, cut a strip of grasscloth crepe ¼ inch AG x 10 inches WG. Tie a half-knot in the middle of the strip (**Figure G, inset**). As you tighten the knot, you will notice that one side sticks out more than on the other. The side of the knot that sticks out forms the nose.

Figure I

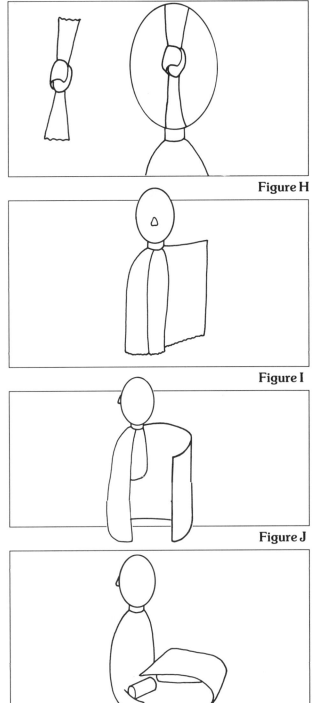

6. Glue the nose strip to the head, centering the knot, and placing the flat side of the strip toward the head (**Figure G**).

7. Make five more noses, four from grasscloth crepe, and one from brown crepe, and attach them to the heads in the same manner.

Mary

1. To make Mary's body, cut a piece of grasscloth crepe 17 inches AG x 4½ inches WG. Spread glue along one 17-inch edge. Wrap the glued edge around the neck (**Figure H**). Roll the lower portion of the crepe into a loose tube as you work around the neck.

2. To make Mary's robe, cut a piece of grasscloth crepe 6 inches AG x 15 inches WG. Spread glue along one 6-inch edge and wrap the glued edge around the neck (**Figure I**). Make sure the edge ends up on the back of the figure, and glue it in place.

3. Mary is shown kneeling before the manger. To create the kneeling position, slightly flatten the robe and carefully bend it toward the back at the knees. To keep the figure from falling forward, glue a 2¾-inch length of dowel rod to the inside of the robe, across the grain of the crepe. This added weight will help stabilize the figure. Refer to **Figure J** as you fold and glue the lower end of the robe in place.

4. To make Mary's hair, cut two pieces of brown crepe, each 1½ inches AG x 4 inches WG. Glue one

Figure K

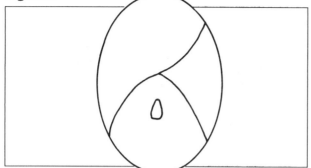

Figure L

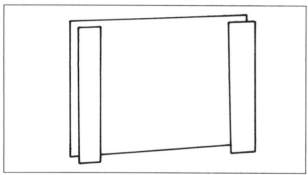

Figure M

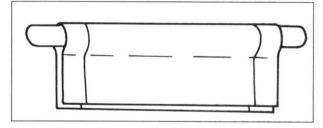

Figure N

strip to the surface of the head, angling it down across the left side of the face, as shown in **Figure K**. Overlap the first strip with the remaining one, angling it down across the right side of the face. The ends of the strips at the back of the neck will be covered by the sleeve.

5. To make the arms, cut a piece of grasscloth crepe 3 inches AG x 8 inches WG. Roll it into a tight tube that is 8 inches long. Set the arm tube aside for the moment.

6. To make the sleeves, cut a piece of grasscloth crepe 5 inches AG x 6¾ inches WG. In addition, cut a strip of brown crepe for each cuff, 5 inches AG x ¾ inch WG. Place the sleeve piece on a flat surface. Glue one cuff strip along each shorter edge of the sleeve piece (**Figure L**).

7. Turn the sleeve piece upside down and place the arm tube lengthwise along the center. Wrap the sleeve piece around the arm tube, and glue the two sides together from the arm to the edge (**Figure M**).

8. Center the arm and sleeve assembly across the back, just below the neck, and glue it in place so the arms extend forward (**Figure N**). When the glue has dried, trim the ends of the arm tube at an angle so they resemble hands.

9. To make the veil, cut a piece of grasscloth crepe 3 inches AG x 20 inches WG. Fold this piece in half widthwise, and cut a 2-inch triangular notch, 1 inch from the fold and 1½ inches from the front edge, as shown in **Figure O**. Fold under a ¼-inch hem along the unnotched edge.

10. Unfold the veil and center it across the top of the head with the notches at the back. Refer to **Figure P** as you wrap and glue the veil around the head. First glue Flap A to the back of the head. Bring the two Corners B together, overlapping them slightly at the center back. Glue the corners to the back of the veil. Glue the lower edges of the veil to the robe, and trim the excess crepe, as shown.

11. To make Mary's halo, cut a piece of gold crepe 3¼ inches AG x 6½ inches WG. Fold the crepe in half, placing white sides together, to form a 3¼-inch square. Glue the two halves together. Cut a 3-inch-diameter circle from the square using pinking shears. Glue the halo to the veil at the back of the head (**Figure Q**).

Joseph

1. To make Joseph's robe, cut a piece of grasscloth

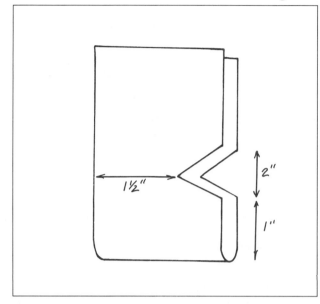

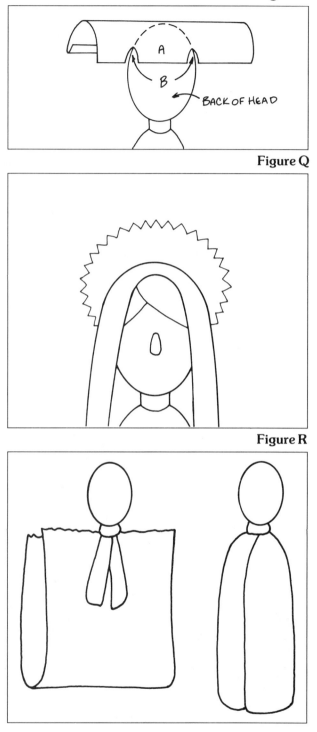

crepe 12 inches AG x 20 inches WG. Fold the crepe in half widthwise to form a piece 10 x 12 inches. The folded edge will be the lower edge of the robe. Don't crease the fold too hard; let it flatten out a little at the bottom so the figure will have more stability. Glue together the open edges opposite the fold, then spread glue along the same edge and wrap it around the neck, forming a fairly tight roll (**Figure R**). Make sure the open 10-inch edge ends up on the back of the figure, and glue it in place.

2. To make the arms, cut a piece of grasscloth crepe 3¼ inches AG x 9½ inches WG. Roll it into a tight tube, 9½ inches long. Set the arm tube aside for the moment.

3. To make the sleeves, cut a piece of brown crepe 3½ inches AG x 8½ inches WG. The sleeves and arms are assembled in the same manner as Mary's, except Joseph's sleeves aren't as wide and don't have cuffs.

4. Center the arm and sleeve assembly across the back, just below the neck, and glue it in place so the arms extend forward and down (**Figure S**). When the glue has dried, trim the ends of the arm roll at an angle, in the same manner as you did Mary's. Place one hand over the other and glue them together.

5. Cut Joseph's cloak from brown crepe, 7 inches AG x 10 inches WG. Spread glue along one 7-inch edge and wrap it around the neck, so it opens at the front. Glue the front edges of the cloak together only

Figure S

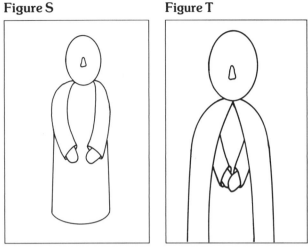

Figure T

Figure U

Figure V

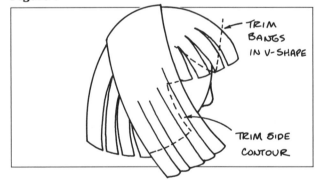

TRIM BANGS IN V-SHAPE

TRIM SIDE CONTOUR

at the neck, and let it hang open over the arms, as shown in **Figure T**.

6. Cut Joseph's beard from brown crepe, using the enlarged pattern. Cut fringe along the lower edge of the beard, as indicated on the pattern. Glue the beard to the face, just below the nose.

7. To make the hair, cut two pieces of brown crepe,

Figure W

each 2 inches AG x 5 inches WG. Cut fringe along both shorter edges of each piece. Glue one piece to the top of the head with the fringed edges at the front and back (**Figure U**). Glue the remaining piece across the first one, with the fringed edges over the ears. Trim the fringe at the sides of the face as shown in **Figure V**.

8. Assemble and attach Joseph's halo in the same manner as you did Mary's.

Baby Jesus

1. To make the head, form one facial tissue into a ball about ¾ inch in diameter, and glue it together. Cut a 6-inch-diameter circle from grasscloth crepe. Glue the crepe piece over the tissue ball, forming it into a head shape, as shown in **Figure W**. Twist the ends together to secure the crepe.

2. To make the nose, cut a piece of grasscloth crepe ⅛ inch AG x 5 inches WG. Make a tiny nose in the same manner as you made the noses for the larger figures, and glue it to the head. Use tiny bits of brown crepe for the eyes and hair, and glue them in place, as shown in **Figure X**.

3. To make the swaddling, cut a piece of gold crepe 4 inches x 4 inches. Fold under a ¼-inch hem to the gold side of the crepe along one edge. Wrap the crepe around the head, white side out, with the hemmed edge around the face (**Figure Y**).

4. To complete the swaddling, cut a piece of gold crepe 10 inches AG x 4½ inches WG. Fold under a ¼-inch hem to the gold side of the crepe, along one long edge. Spread glue along the hemmed edge and wrap it around the neck, white side out (**Figure Z**). Fold the lower end of the swaddling loosely, making sure the edges end up on the back of the figure.

Figure X

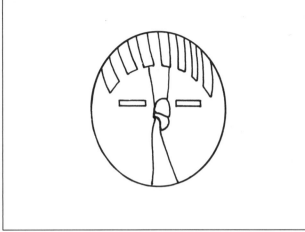

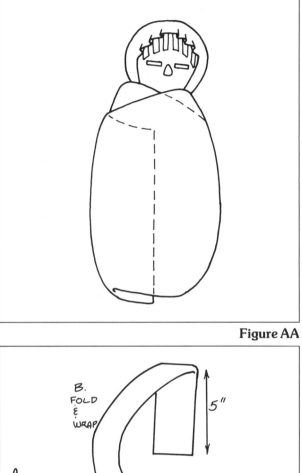

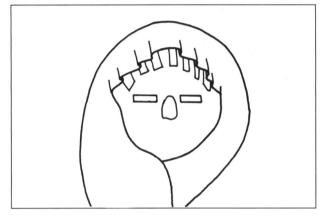

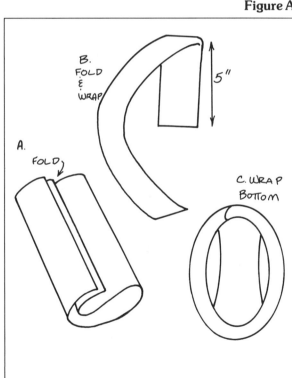

5. Make the halo in the same manner as you did Mary's, using a piece of gold crepe 2¼ inches AG x 4½ inches WG. Glue the halo to the back of the head.

6. To make the manger (**Figure AA**), cut a piece of grasscloth crepe 12 inches AG x 20 inches WG. Loosely fold the crepe in half lengthwise, then fold it again lengthwise, to form a 4-layer piece, 3 x 20 inches (sub-step a). To form the bottom of the manger, fold it 5 inches from one short end (sub-step b). Wrap the remainder of the crepe around the bottom and glue it in place (sub-step c).

7. To make straw for the manger, cut a piece of grasscloth crepe 5 inches AG x 3 inches WG. Cut fringe on all but one 3-inch edge. Glue the straw inside of the manger with the unfringed edge at one end (**Figure**

Figure BB

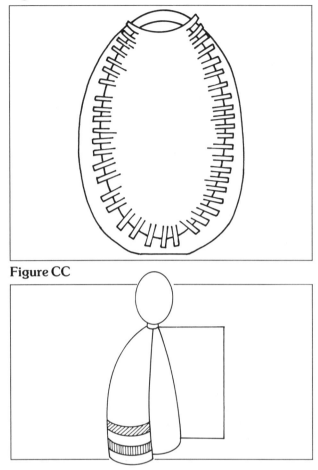

Figure CC

Figure DD

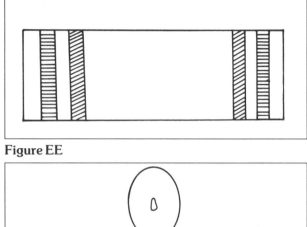

Figure EE

BB). Moisten your fingers and twist the fringed strips to make them look like straw.

8. Glue the Baby Jesus figure into the manger, with his head at the unfringed edge of the straw piece.

The First Wise Man

1. Use the head covered with brown crepe. Cut a grasscloth robe 12 inches AG x 20 inches WG. Fold, glue, and attach it to the head in the same manner as you did Joseph's robe. Spread the robe into a cone shape at the bottom, overlapping the back edge only about an inch, and glue it in place.

2. To make the outer robe, cut a piece of gold crepe 14 inches AG x 10 inches WG. In addition, cut a strip of brown crepe 14 inches AG x ¾ inch WG, and a strip of grasscloth crepe 14 inches AG x ½ inch WG. Place

the gold crepe on a flat surface, gold side up, and glue the brown crepe strip to it near one long edge. Glue the grasscloth crepe strip ⅜ inch from the brown strip. Spread glue along the opposite long edge of the gold crepe piece, and wrap the robe around the neck (**Figure CC**). Make sure the edge ends up at the back of the figure, and glue it in place.

3. To make the arms, cut a piece of brown crepe 3¼ inches AG x 9½ inches WG. Roll it into a tight tube, 9½ inches long, and put the arm tube aside for a moment.

4. To make the sleeves, cut a piece of gold crepe 2½ inches AG x 8½ inches WG. In addition, cut two strips of brown crepe 2½ inches AG x ⅝ inch WG, and two strips of grasscloth crepe the same size. Place the gold crepe piece on a flat surface, gold side up, and glue one brown crepe strip near each short end. Glue one grasscloth crepe strip ¼ inch from each brown strip

(**Figure DD**). Turn the assembled sleeve piece over, and place the arm tube lengthwise along the center. Wrap the sleeve piece around the arm, and glue the two sides together from the arm to the edge, as you did for Mary's sleeves.

5. Attach the arm and sleeve assembly in the same manner as you did Joseph's, but mount it about 1 inch lower on the back of the figure. Trim the arm tubes at the ends in the same manner as the other figures.

6. To make the shawl, cut a piece of brown crepe 3 inches AG x 20 inches WG. Cut fringe 2½ inches deep on each short end. Refer to **Figure EE** as you wrap the shawl around the figure. First, glue the middle of the shawl to the back, just above the arm and sleeve assembly. Drape the shawl over the shoulders and inside the arms, and glue it in place.

7. Cut the beard from brown crepe, using Joseph's beard pattern. Color the beard with a black felt-tip marker. Cut the fringe and attach the beard in the same manner as you did Joseph's.

8. Cut the turban from gold crepe. Fold a ¼-inch hem to the white side of the crepe along the long edge. Refer to **Figure FF** as you wrap the turban around the head. Be sure the gold side of the crepe is facing outward. First, glue the middle of the turban piece to the back of the head, placing the long hemmed edge at about neck level. Fold the top point forward over the head, and glue it to the forehead. Fold the side points around the head as shown, glueing them in loose folds.

9. To make the scroll, cut a 3-inch square of gold crepe. Fold it in half, white sides together, then roll it into a tight tube, glueing the edge in place. Cut another piece of gold crepe, 1½ inches AG x 2½ inches WG. Roll this piece of crepe white side out, around the gold tube, with the smaller tube extending about ¼ inch from one end. Glue the scroll between the hands, bending the arms to get the proper angle (**Figure GG**). Cut four or five ⅛-inch-wide strips of gold crepe and glue them to the top of the scroll, as shown. Twist the free ends slightly.

The Second Wise Man

1. To make the robe, cut a piece of brown crepe 12 inches AG x 18 inches WG. Loosely fold the crepe in half widthwise to form a piece 9 x 12 inches. Assemble and attach the robe to the head in the same manner as you did Joseph's, but spread open the lower ends of the robe.

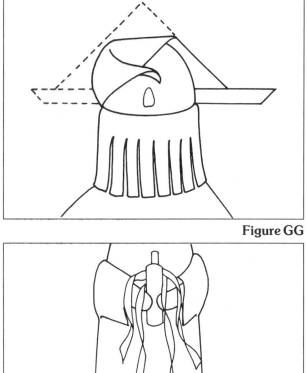

Figure FF

Figure GG

2. To make the cape, cut a piece of grasscloth crepe 9 inches AG x 20 inches WG. In addition, cut three strips of brown crepe ½ inch AG x 20 inches WG, and three strips of gold crepe the same size. Place the grasscloth cape piece on a flat surface. Glue the strips lengthwise to the robe piece about ½ inch apart, alternating colors.

3. To make the arms, cut a piece of grasscloth crepe 3¼ inches AG x 9½ inches WG. Roll it into a tight tube, 9½ inches long.

4. Turn the cape piece over and place the arm tube widthwise across the center. Wrap the cape piece around the arm tube, and glue the two sides together from the arm to the edge, in the same manner as you did Mary's sleeves.

5. Glue the arm and cape assembly to the back of the figure. Bend the arms to form elbows.

Figure HH

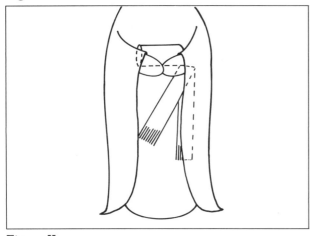

Figure II

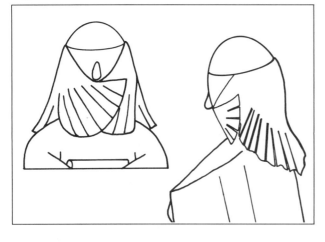

Figure JJ

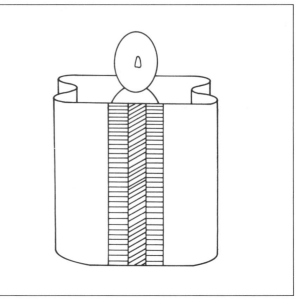

6. To make the gift that this Wise Man holds, cover a 1¼-inch-length of dowel rod with gold crepe. Glue the container in the figure's arms (**Figure HH**).

7. To make the sash, cut two pieces of gold crepe: one 1¼ inches AG x 6 inches WG, and one 1¼ inches AG x 4 inches WG. Cut 1½-inch-long fringe on one short end of each piece. Glue the two sash pieces to the robe, under the cape, as shown in **Figure HH**.

8. Cut four beard pieces from gold crepe. In addition, cut two hair pieces, each 3 inches square, from gold crepe. Glue two of the beard pieces gold sides together, and cut fringe along the long edge. Repeat this procedure, using the remaining beard pieces. Glue the two hair pieces gold sides together, and cut a row of fringe along one edge.

9. Refer to **Figure II** as you glue the beard and hair pieces to the head. First, glue the hair piece across the back of the head, with the fringe at the bottom. The beard pieces overlap the hair at the back of the head. Glue one beard piece across the right side of the face and below the nose. Glue the remaining beard piece to the left side of the face, overlapping the first piece below the nose. To make a bald spot on top, cut a 1¾-inch-diameter circle of grasscloth crepe and glue it on top of the head, over the hair piece.

10. To make the crown, cut a piece of gold crepe 5¼ inches AG x 5 inches WG. Fold the crepe in half widthwise, placing white sides together, to form a 2½ x 5¼-inch strip. Glue the strip into a ring around the top of the head, overlapping the ends at the back.

The Third Wise Man

1. To make the body, cut a piece of grasscloth crepe 9 inches AG x 20 inches WG. Fold the crepe in half widthwise to form a 9 x 10-inch piece. The folded edge will be the lower edge of the body. Glue together the open edges opposite the fold, then spread glue along the same edge and wrap it around the neck. It doesn't matter where the edge winds up, as the body will be covered by the clothing.

2. To make the robe, cut a piece of grasscloth crepe

12 inches AG x 20 inches WG. Fold the crepe in half widthwise to form a 10 x 12-inch piece. To make the decorative strips for the front of the robe, cut a piece of brown crepe 2¼ inches AG x 12 inches WG, and a piece of gold crepe ¾ inch AG x 12 inches WG. Place the folded grasscloth on a flat surface. Glue the brown strip down the center, from the fold to the opposite edge. Center the gold crepe strip along the brown strip and glue it in place. Glue together the open edges opposite the fold.

3. Spread glue along the folded edge. This will be the top of the robe. Refer to **Figure JJ** as you wrap the robe around the neck. First, center the head in the robe so that it faces the stripes in the front. Fold each side of the robe into a pleat, as shown, and press it against the neck at the inner fold of the pleat on each side. To form the shoulders, press the pleated edges of the robe together.

4. Make the arm tube the same size and in the same manner as you did Joseph's (see Joseph, step 2).

5. Use the enlarged pattern to cut the third Wise Man's cape from brown crepe, and the cape decoration from gold crepe.

6. Fold the brown cape piece in half, bringing the curved edges together, but do not glue the halves together. Glue the gold crepe decoration along the center, from the fold to the curved edge (**Figure KK**). Open the cape and place the arm tube widthwise across the center, on the wrong side of the cape. Refold the cape, and glue the halves together from the arm tube to the curved edge. Glue the cape and arm assembly to the figure, so the gold decoration is at the center back. Bend the arms forward.

7. Cut the burnoose from gold crepe. Cut the crepe slightly smaller than the pattern. Spread glue in the circular area on the white side of the crepe, and then glue it to the top of the figure's head. Make folds in the burnoose at the forehead and at the sides and back, as shown in **Figure LL**.

8. To make the headband, cut a piece of brown crepe, 1 inch AG x 20 inches WG. Twist it tightly into a 20-inch-long tube, then glue it around the burnoose at the top of the head (**Figure MM**). Twist the ends of the headband together at the back of the head, and glue them in place. Trim the ends of the headband.

The Shepherd

1. To make the robe, cut a piece of brown crepe 15 inches AG x 16 inches WG. Fold the crepe in half

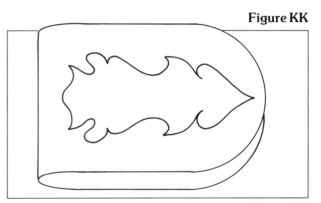

Figure KK

Figure LL

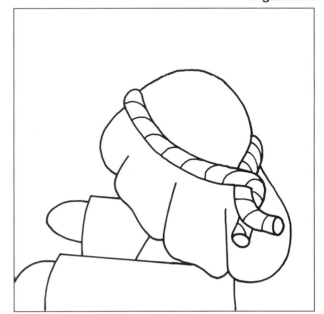

Figure MM

Figure NN

Figure OO

widthwise to form a piece 8 x 15 inches. Assemble and glue the robe to the head in the same manner as you did Joseph's.

2. To make the rope belt, cut a piece of grasscloth crepe 1 inch AG x 20 inches WG. Twist the crepe tightly. Wrap the belt around the waist, tie it in a half-knot at the center front, and glue it in place. Trim the ends so they hang about 1 or 2 inches from the bottom of the robe.

3. To make the arms, cut a piece of grasscloth crepe 3¼ inches AG x 8½ inches WG. Roll it into a tight tube, 8½ inches long.

4. To make the sleeves, cut a piece of brown crepe 2½ inches AG x 7¾ inches WG. Assemble the sleeves and arms in the same manner as you did Mary's. Glue the sleeve and arm assembly to the figure's back, positioning the arms as shown in **Figure NN**. Trim the ends of the arm tube in the same manner as the other figures.

5. To make the staff, cut a piece of grasscloth crepe 3 inches AG x 12 inches WG. Wrap the crepe around a 12-inch length of chenille stem and glue it along the edge. Allow the glue to dry, then bend a crook in one end of the staff, as shown in **Figure NN**. Glue the staff in the shepherd's extended hand.

6. Cut the burnoose from a piece of grasscloth crepe. Glue the burnoose to the top of the shepherd's head, and fold it as shown in **Figure OO**. First, fold one edge of the burnoose down, covering half the face. Further along the same edge, lightly fold the crepe upward, then backward until it is even with the shoulders. Don't make these folds too sharp, so they will produce a wind-blown effect.

7. To make the headband, cut a piece of brown crepe ¼ inch AG x 20 inces WG. Twist the crepe, and glue it to the shepherd's head in the same manner as you did the third Wise Man's headband.

The Sheep

1. To make one sheep's head, bend the stem of a plastic egg into a loop, inserting the end back into the egg. Cut several ¼-inch-wide strips of brown crepe. Wrap and glue one of the strips around the looped stem, as shown in **Figure PP**, beginning at the end closest to the egg. Overlap this strip with another one, covering the end of the loop.

2. The covered loop is the head. To make an ear, cut a ¼-inch wide strip of grasscloth crepe. Make a small

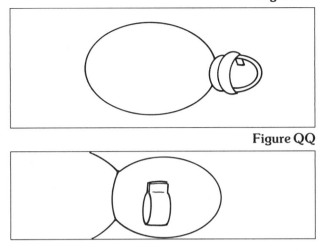

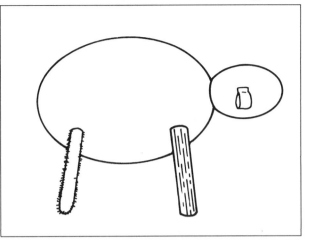

Figure QQ

Figure SS

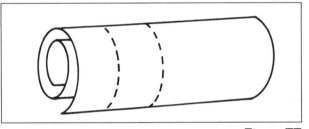

Figure TT

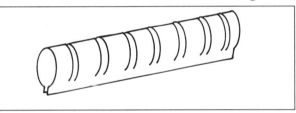

loop, and glue it to one side of the head (**Figure QQ**). Repeat this procedure on the opposite side of the head.

3. To make one leg, cut a 1¼-inch length of chenille stem, and insert it into the underside of the egg (**Figure RR**). Cut a piece of brown crepe 1½ inches AG x 1¼ inches WG. Wrap and glue the crepe around the chenille stem. Attach and cover three more legs in the same manner.

4. To make the sheep's wool, first refold the remaining grasscloth crepe, as shown in **Figure SS**. Cut it AG to form 1-inch-wide strips.

5. Unroll one strip and fold it in half lengthwise, but do not crease. Cut a series of slits across the fold (WG), at approximately ¼-inch intervals. Each time, begin your cut at the fold, and cut to within ¼ inch of the aligned long edges (**Figure TT**). Glue the aligned long edges together, as shown. Fold and cut each strip in the same manner.

6. Wrap and glue one of the cut strips around the egg as shown in **Figure UU**, beginning at the head and overlapping each tier. Do not stretch the paper. Continue to glue the strips in place, until the entire egg is completely covered.

7. To make a tail, cut a strip of grasscloth crepe about the same size as the ear strip, and glue it to the end of the egg opposite the head.

8. Repeat all the steps in this section to make another sheep. For a little variation, try positioning the legs on the opposite side of the egg (in relation to the head loop). The sheep appears to be either grazing or looking up, depending on the leg position.

Figure UU

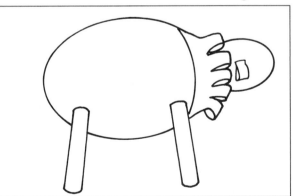

Pollo Piñata

A most unusual piñata! It's made of fabric and has a unique system of releasing the candy. This 24-inch-tall pollo (pronounced pō´yo, Spanish for chicken) piñata will be a real hit when the children pull the correct ribbon and release a shower of Christmas candy.

Materials

1½ yards of 44-inch-wide yellow cotton fabric
Scrap of yellow felt for the beak
Ten skeins of yellow rug yarn
One skein each of red and gold rug yarn
1 yard each of ½-inch ribbon in four different colors for the pull cords
12-inch length of ribbon for the hanging loop
Two ⅝-inch-diameter black buttons for the eyes
One large oblong shank-type button in any color
12-inch length of narrow elastic
Hot-melt glue and a glue gun (or white glue)
Heavy-duty yellow thread, regular yellow thread and a regular sewing needle
8-inch circle of plastic (A large coffee-can lid works well, or you can use heavy cardboard, poster board, or similar material.)
Individually wrapped candy

Figure A

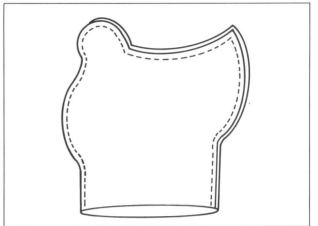

Figure B

LEAVE OPEN

Figure C

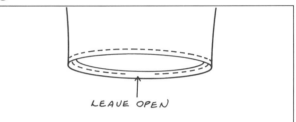

CASING
BASE
GATHER HERE
BODY

Cutting the Pieces

1. Scale drawings are provided on pages 243-244 for the Body, Beak, and Base. Enlarge the drawings to make full-size paper patterns. (See the Tips & Techniques section on enlarging scale drawings.)

2. Cut one Base and two Body pieces from the yellow cotton.

3. Cut two Beak pieces from the yellow felt.

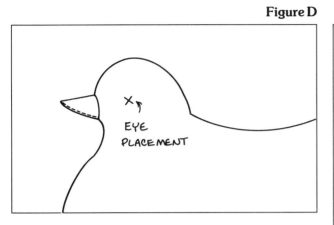

Making the Piñata

1. Place the Body pieces right sides together and stitch the long contoured seam (**Figure A**), leaving the straight lower edge open and unstitched. Clip the curves and turn the body right side out.

2. To make a casing for the elastic, turn under and press a ¼-inch hem along the lower edge, and then turn it under another ½ inch. Stitch the casing (**Figure B**), leaving an opening for the elastic. The elastic will be inserted later.

3. Begin with the head and tail, and stuff the piñata firmly up to about 6 inches from the edge of the casing.

4. For this step, it will be easier to turn the piñata upside down and hold the stuffed section in your lap as you work. Insert the Base piece inside the piñata until it is flush with the fiberfill, as shown in **Figure C**. (If the fiberfill packs down too much, insert enough to give the chicken a well-stuffed body before continuing.) Thread a needle with yellow thread and stitch around the edge of Base, securing it to the body. Gather the excess body fabric as you stitch, as shown.

5. Insert the length of elastic inside the casing. Secure the ends of the elastic, and slip it inside the casing. Whipstitch together the opening in the casing.

6. Fold the Beak piece in half along the fold line marked on the scale drawing. Stitch or glue the slightly rounded edges together, leaving the short straight edge open. Insert a small amount of fiberfill inside the beak. Place the beak on the chicken's head (**Figure D**), placing the glued edge on the bottom. Glue or stitch it in place.

7. Stitch one black button to each side of the head for the eyes.

Figure G

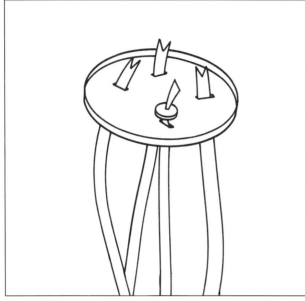

Figure H

PUT CANDY IN HERE

Adding the Feathers

1. Use a long piece of yellow thread, and tack one end of a yarn skein to the top of the head.

2. To make one "feather" (**Figure E**), wrap the yarn about twenty times around, making 3-inch diameter loops. Place the looped yarn on the body close to the tacked yarn end. Tack the loops to the body, as shown.

3. Continue with the same yarn and thread, and repeat the procedures in step 2 until the body is completely covered (**Figure F**). Don't attach feathers below the gathered line of the base. When the thread becomes too short, lock the stitch, and rethread the needle. Use all skeins of yellow yarn, if necessary.

4. For the comb, wattle, and tail, use two strands of the red and gold yarn, and make the loops a bit larger. Place two yarn clusters for the comb along the top ridge of the head. Place one yarn cluster for the wattle just beneath the beak, and the tail cluster right on the tip of the tail.

Finishing

1. To make the hanger, first fold the 12-inch length of ribbon in half, and pin it to the top of the chicken's back. Hold the piñata by the hanger and adjust the placement of the hanger until you find a balance point. It must be balanced so the pinata won't tip forward or backward when suspended. Stitch or glue the hanger in place.

2. Cut four ¼-inch slits in the center of the plastic circle. Tie the shank-type button onto the end of one 1-yard length of ribbon. Thread the ribbon through one slit in the plastic circle, pulling it through until the button is against the inside of the plastic (**Figure G**). Insert the remaining ribbons in the slits in the plastic circle. Tie a knot in the free end only of each ribbon, as shown.

3. Fill the base area with individually wrapped candy. Place the plastic circle inside the base with the ribbons hanging loose (**Figure H**), and let the elastic hold the the plastic in place.

4. Hang the piñata from the ceiling. Let each child choose one ribbon. If they choose the wrong ribbon, it will slip right out of the plastic. But the lucky child who chooses the ribbon with the button on the end of it will be rewarded with a shower of candy!

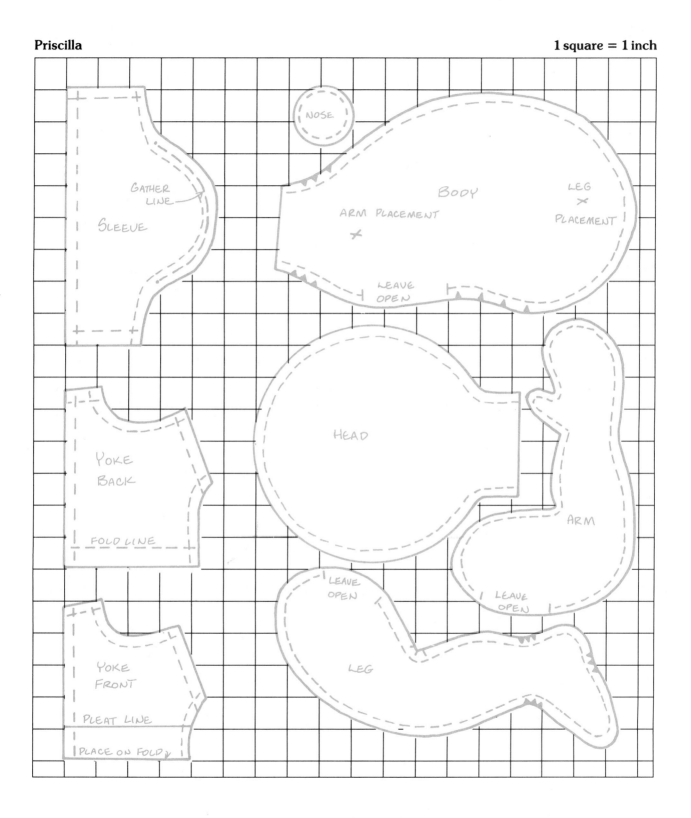

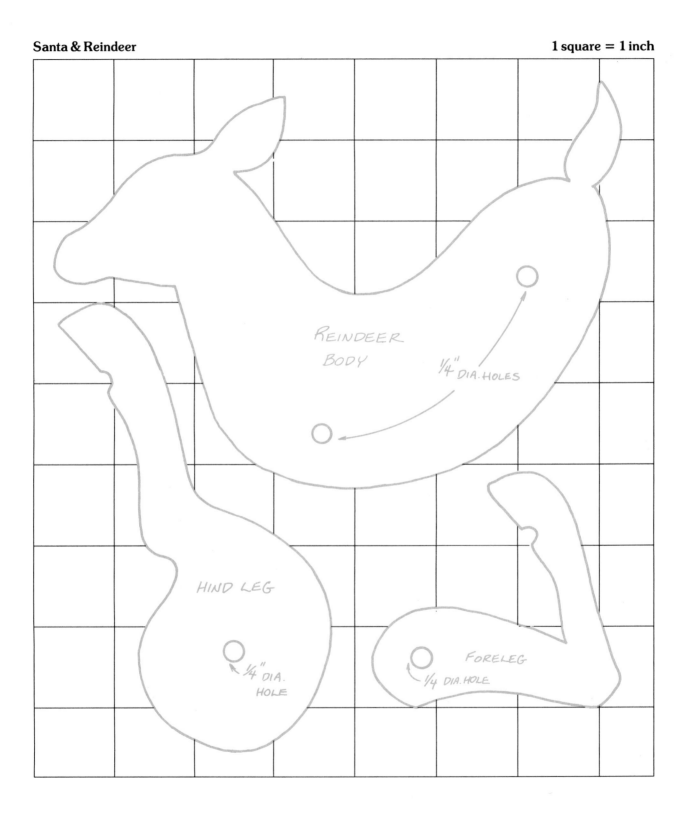

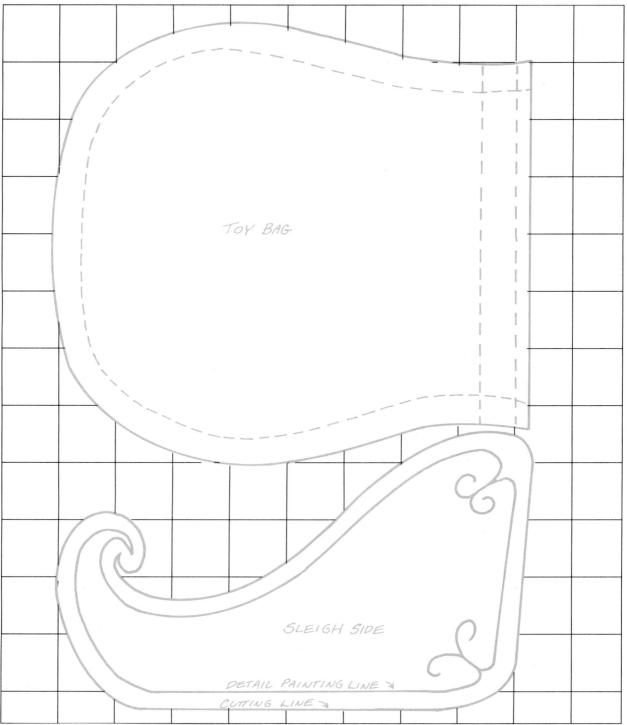

TOY BAG

SLEIGH SIDE

DETAIL PAINTING LINE →

CUTTING LINE →

Santa & Reindeer

FULL-SIZE PATTERNS
FOR SANTA

ARM

¼" DIA.
HOLE

BODY

¼" DIA.
HOLE

¼" DIA.
HOLE

¼" DIA. HOLE

LEG

Ballerina & Clown Draft Stopper

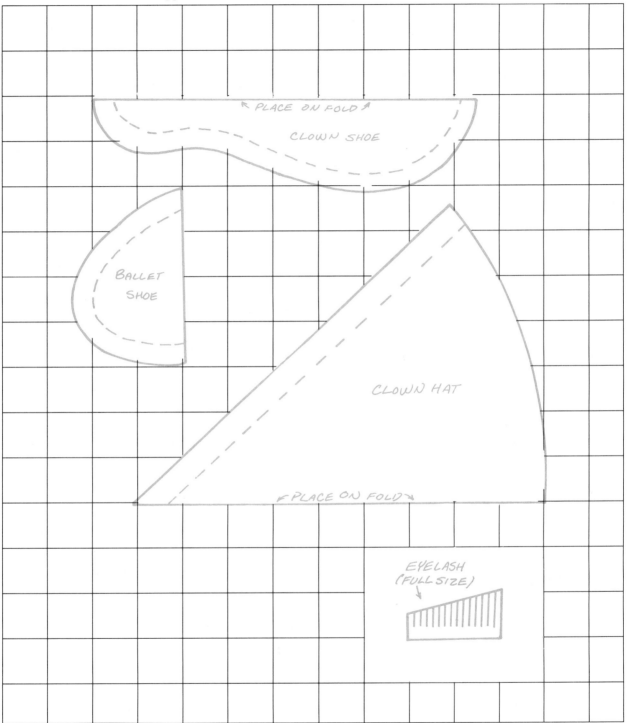

PLACE ON FOLD

CLOWN SHOE

BALLET SHOE

CLOWN HAT

PLACE ON FOLD

EYELASH (FULL SIZE)

Changeable Charlie

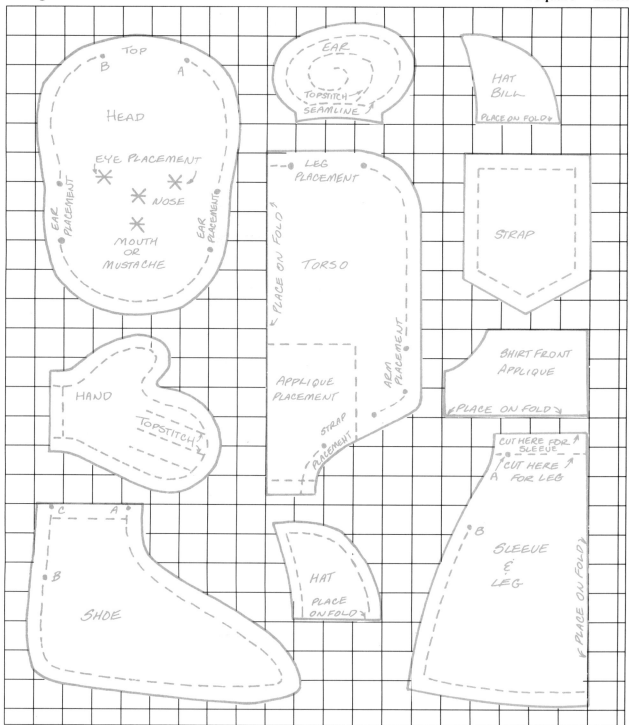

CELEBRATIONS OF CHRISTMAS

Changeable Charlie

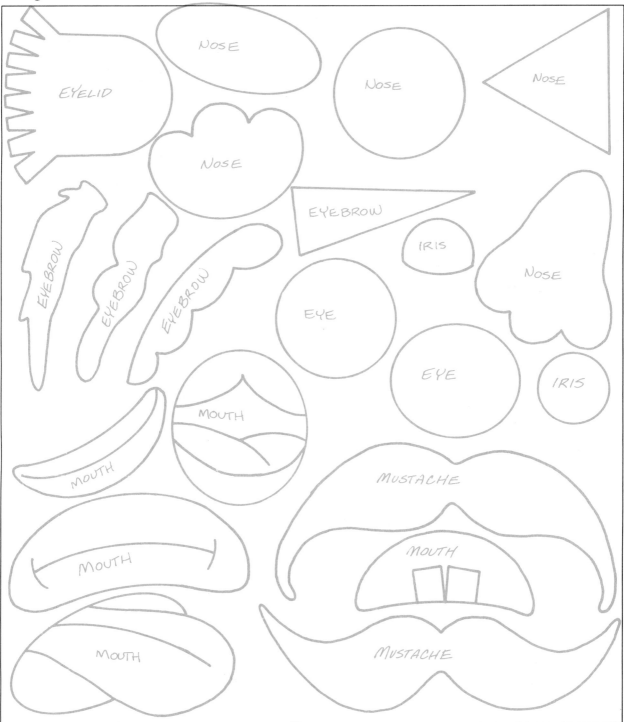

Country Rocking Horse

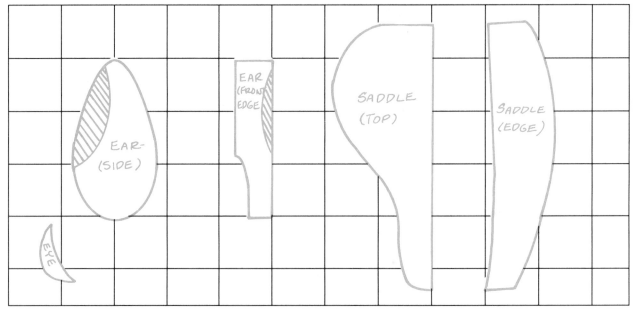

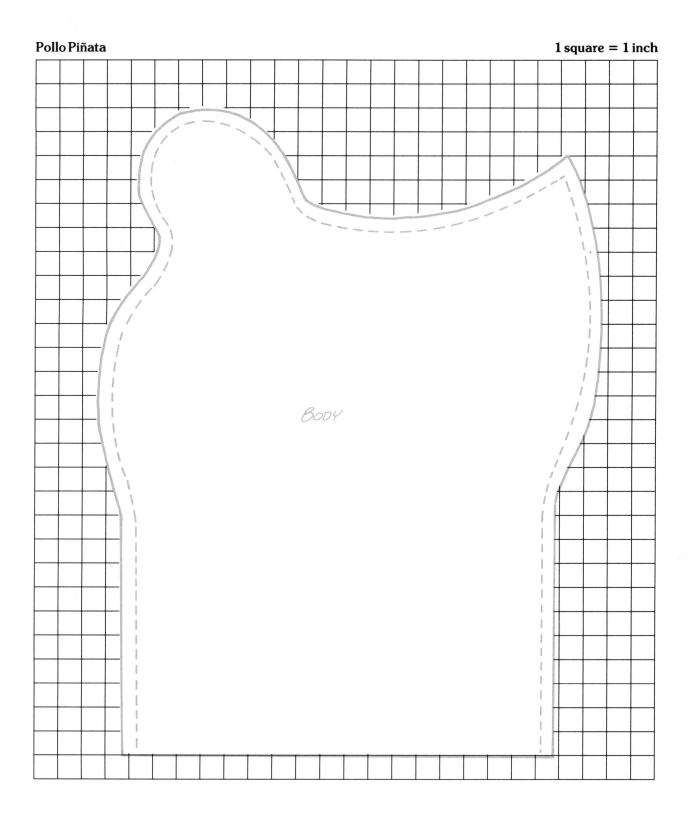

BODY

Pollo Piñata

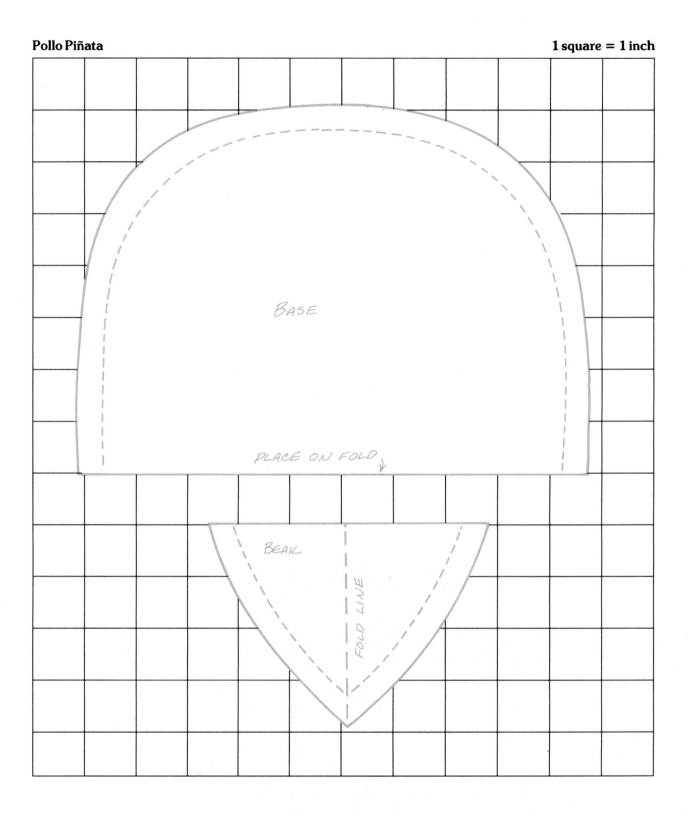

BASE

PLACE ON FOLD

BEAK

FOLD LINE

CELEBRATIONS OF CHRISTMAS

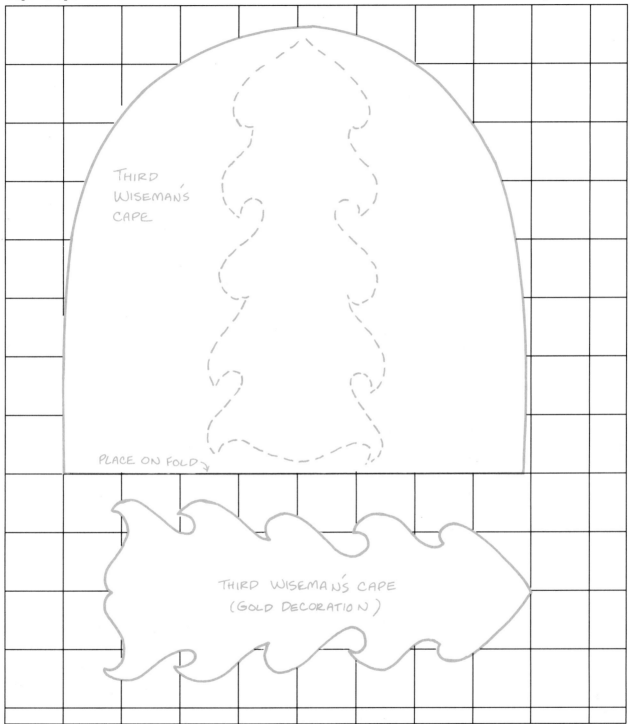

THIRD
WISEMAN'S
CAPE

PLACE ON FOLD

THIRD WISEMAN'S CAPE
(GOLD DECORATION)

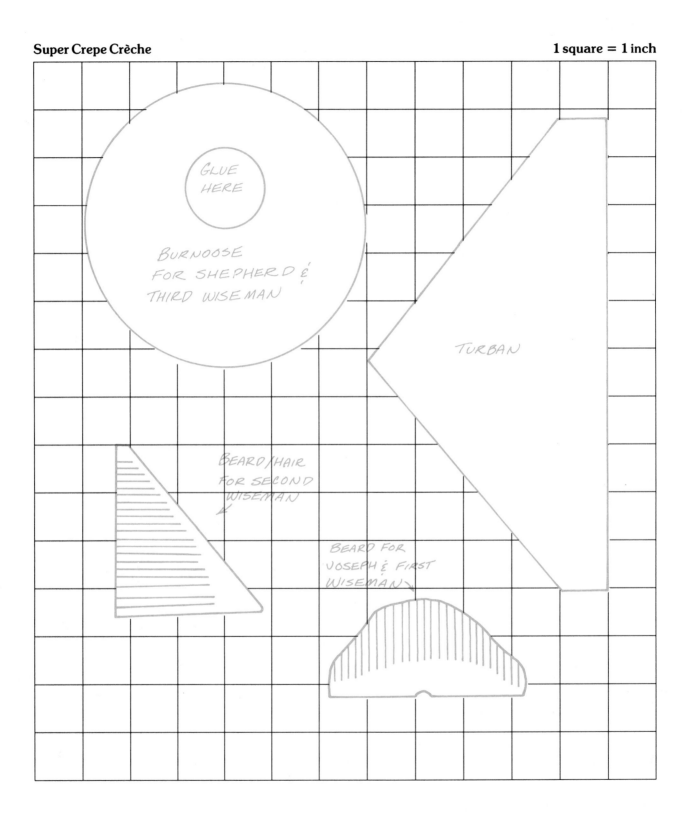

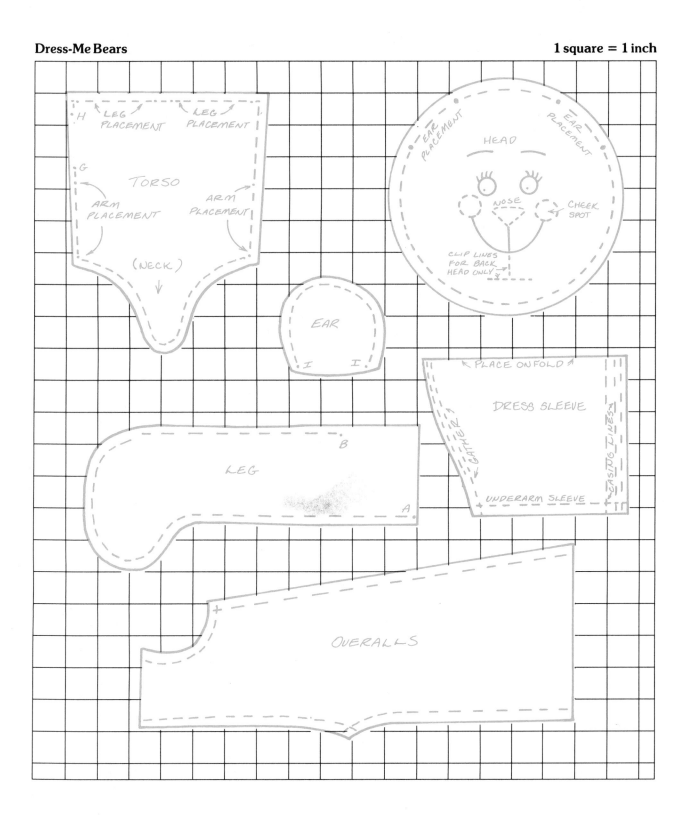

WESTFIELD MEMORIAL LIBRARY
WESTFIELD, NEW JERSEY

Dress-Me Bears

1 square = 1 inch

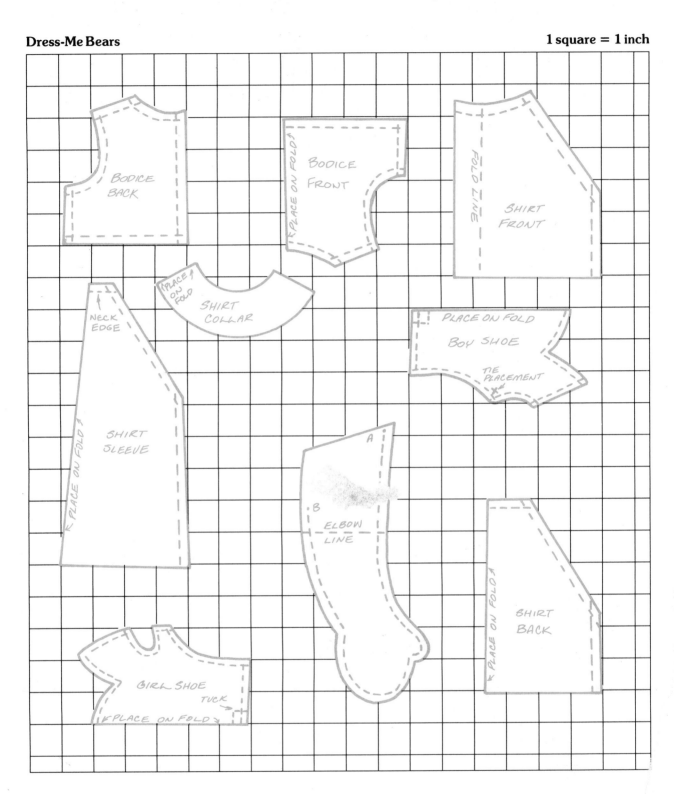

BODICE BACK

BODICE FRONT

PLACE ON FOLD

FOLD LINE

SHIRT FRONT

PLACE ON FOLD

SHIRT COLLAR

NECK EDGE

PLACE ON FOLD

BOY SHOE

TIE PLACEMENT

SHIRT SLEEVE

PLACE ON FOLD

A

B

ELBOW LINE

PLACE ON FOLD

SHIRT BACK

GIRL SHOE

TUCK

PLACE ON FOLD

248

CELEBRATIONS OF CHRISTMAS